Brian Viner grew up in Southport, near Liverpool, where he became a passionate Everton fan, following the Toffees home and away from 1977, the year he turned 16. He was educated at King George V School, Southport and St Andrews University. He has been a television critic, a feature writer, a sports columnist, a prolific interviewer and a film critic during a long and varied career in national newspapers, and is a former winner of a *What The Papers Say* award for excellence in journalism. This is his seventh book. He is married with three children and lives in Herefordshire.

Also by Brian Viner

Ali, Pelé, Lillee and Me: A Personal Odyssey Through the Sporting Seventies

Cream Teas, Traffic Jams and Sunburn: The Great British Holiday

Nice to See It, To See It, Nice: The 1970s in Front of the Telly

Tales of the Country

The Good, the Dad and the Ugly: The Trials of Fatherhood

The Pheasants' Revolt: More Tales of the Country

Praise for *Ali, Pelé, Lillee and Me*:

'[A] beautifully structured journey through a sporting life, constantly enlivened with unexpected detours ... [Viner] has a keen eye and a sharp ear, and skewers contemporary vanities with the same accuracy that he applies to the excruciating lessons of childhood' Andrew Baker, *Daily Telegraph*

'Hilarious' *Independent*

'Wonderfully readable' *Mail on Sunday*

Praise for *Nice to See It, to See It, Nice*:

'Viner's history of this seminal decade is witty, warm and informative' *Daily Mail*

'A wonderful book ... compelling' *Daily Express*

Praise for *Tales of the Country*:

'Brilliant ... Sparkles with anecdotes, good jokes and observations' *Daily Mail*

'Very funny ... You feel you have been royally treated by a self-deprecating, hilarious host, with an eye for the local peculiarities that make England what it is' *Mail on Sunday*

Praise for *The Good, the Dad and the Ugly*:

'This splendid, goodhearted book will strike a chord with many of us' *Mail on Sunday*

'A wonderful book' *Daily Express*

Looking for the Toffees

In Search of the Heroes of Everton

Brian Viner

**SIMON &
SCHUSTER**

London · New York · Sydney · Toronto · New Delhi

A CBS COMPANY

First published in Great Britain by Simon & Schuster UK Ltd, 2014
This paperback edition published by Simon & Schuster UK Ltd, 2015
A CBS COMPANY

Copyright © 2014 by Brian Viner

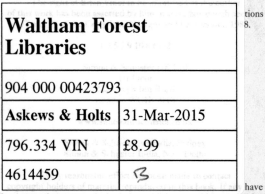

of this work has been asserted by him in accordance with sections
8.

have
inadvertently been overlooked, the publishers would be glad to hear
from them and make good in future editions any errors or
omissions brought to their attention.

A CIP catalogue record for this book
is available from the British Library

ISBN: 978-1-47113-171-4
Ebook ISBN: 978-47113-172-1

Typeset in the UK by M Rules
Printed and bound by CPI Group (UK) Ltd, Croydon, CR0 4YY

For Jez Sykes, Chris Barry and Jimmy Mulville . . .
fellow travellers on the Blue roller coaster

Not forgetting my old Gwladys Street muckers,
Mozzer, Rafe, Briggy, Mugsy and Bean

And in affectionate memory of Christopher James Barry
(1930–2014), a true Evertonian

Chapter One

The only good thing to come out of the Cheshire town of Ellesmere Port, according to a mischievous old saying on the Welsh side of the nearby river Dee, is the road to Wales.

Actually, the jibe doesn't bear much scrutiny. Ellesmere Port is certainly an insalubrious place, dominated by the vast Stanlow oil refinery, but it has spawned some famous sons, including three of the finest footballers to have worn Everton blue in Sam Chedgzoy and Joe Mercer, who plied their trade in the 1920s and 1930s, and Dave Hickson, the wonderful 1950s centre forward, nicknamed the Cannonball Kid.

Moreover, the road to Wales out of Ellesmere Port is a flat and rather featureless thoroughfare. There's nothing remotely noteworthy about it, least of all the Cheshire Yeoman pub, which lives up to its name insofar as a yeoman might be thought of as honest, ruddy and a bit tired. It is not what anyone would call a destination pub, and yet on a Saturday morning in the summer of 2013, I set off on a 100-mile journey with the Cheshire Yeoman's postcode plugged into my car's sat-nav system. It was very much my destination, for it was where I had arranged to meet Bob Latchford on one of his occasional jaunts to England from his home in rural Germany.

That big Bob Latchford now lived in a house at the end of a dirt track in the countryside near Nuremberg, and had a young son devoted to Bayern Munich – who, should he grow up to be an international goalscorer like his old man, will score them for Germany rather than England – seemed odd enough. But it was odder still that a desultory exchange of emails and a couple of fleeting phone calls had yielded a pub car park rendezvous with a fellow whose name I had chanted week after week as an Everton-mad teenager in the late 1970s, bouncing up and down with thousands of sweaty strangers who metamorphosed into cherished extended family when we all sang, over and over and over again: 'Bobby Latchford walks on water, nana nana na, nana na na.'

If I had a personal anthem as a 16-year-old, that was it. Some of my school friends had taken to heart the lyrics of the emerging Elvis Costello; others were wedded to the works of Genesis, Led Zeppelin and Queen. But the only musical refrain I needed to elevate my soul to a higher, happier realm was 'Bobby Latchford walks on water...'

For a brief period in late 1979, when Lena Martell's version of an old Bible Belt country song called 'One Day at a Time' was riding high in the charts, this was supplanted by another hosanna to Latchford's goalscoring prowess. 'One goal at a time, Bob Latchford/That's all we're asking of you/When you hit the bar/We all say "aaah"/One goal at a time.'

As terrace reworkings of popular lyrics go, those are just about the most risible and indeed nonsensical lines that I have ever spouted. How could anyone score more than one goal at a time anyway? And who says 'aaah' when a shot hits the bar? I was aware of that even then, and happy to get back to the far more sensible tribute to Latchford's Messiah-like qualities. Almost the same spiritual result was achieved with 'We all agree, Duncan McKenzie is magic', and 'Andy is our King'.

Those chants bespoke an Everton performance of attacking verve, as Latchford and the gifted maverick McKenzie stormed forward, to the left of them the scintillatingly brilliant winger Dave Thomas, socks round his ankles, and behind them the Luton larrikin, Andy King. To King's left glided the ever-elegant Martin Dobson, so ineffably debonair that he looked as if he should have played football in a velvet smoking jacket.

But when Everton were on the back foot, and became reliant on their handsome Scottish goalkeeper George Wood, another cry rose from the terraces, and where it erred in punctuation, it resounded with demonic conviction: 'Scotland's, Scotland's, number one! Scotland's! Number one!' When we serenaded Latchford and McKenzie, we did so with joy. But when we championed the claims of Georgie Wood to supplant the hapless Alan Rough as Scotland's first-choice goalkeeper, it was with fierce purpose, like lifelong socialists intoning 'The Red Flag', or temperance campaigners singing 'Away with Rum'.

I have carried my passion for Everton into my fifties, but it never burned brighter than it did between the ages of fifteen and eighteen, from 1977 to 1980, when I not only held a season ticket for Goodison Park's Gwladys Street End, but followed the team around the country, making intrepid journeys to such distant footballing outposts as Middlesbrough's Ayresome Park and even, for a fourth-round League Cup tie one rainy Tuesday, Grimsby Town's ramshackle old Blundell Park stadium.

We were only crossing England from west to east that miserable night in October 1979, but it felt like crossing the Russian steppes. I can remember the journey as if it were yesterday, the day before yesterday, and the day before that. It seemed to go on forever, and could not have got substantially wetter had we overshot Grimsby and ended up in the North Sea.

There were four of us squeezed into my friend Rafe Parker's rusty white van, and on the M62 visibility stopped pretty much at the windscreen-wipers, which were wheezing back and forth like two pensioners forced to do step aerobics. I was convinced that we were going to swerve off the road, or aquaplane into the vehicle ahead of us and end up in a coffin of twisted metal. And while there wasn't much I wouldn't do in the Everton cause, which certainly accounted for just about all my earnings (60p an hour plus tips) as a rather cack-handed waiter at an Italian restaurant most Friday and Saturday nights, I didn't fancy laying down my life. On the other hand, it would at least have extracted the pain from the even less pleasurable journey home.

That sodden evening at Blundell Park produced three faint highlights, one of which was the amusing quirk of the ground actually being in Cleethorpes rather than Grimsby. Another was to find ourselves, so rooted was the stadium in the 1970s, bunched in the Osmond End. 'What do they call the other end, the fucking David Cassidy End?' ventured a fat Scouser who smelled, like we all did, of wet wool. The third highlight was the chant we sent up to poke gentle fun at our hosts, 'Sing when you're fishing, you only sing when you're fishing . . .'

In those days there was a much wider repertoire of chants than there is today, and some of them were reserved for particular sets of opposing fans. It was an era of rampant hooliganism, of bottles hurled at supporters' coaches, of pitched battles in narrow terraced streets, yet many of these chants were innocuous to the point of being affectionate. Nobody sang that the manager of the opposing team was a pederast, or that the opposition captain's wife likes to take it up the arse, as they do now. Admittedly, there was nothing especially affectionate about a favourite staple of the time, 'You're going home in a fucking ambulance', but when Ipswich Town or Norwich City or even Bristol City supporters came to Goodison it became, 'You're going home in a combine harvester', which was really rather sweet.

Besides, as a podgy lower-middle-class grammar school boy from the genteel seaside town of Southport, I was never entirely comfortable with telling opposing fans that they were going home in a fucking ambulance. I could have thumped any of them in a test on the function of the Fool in *King Lear*, and pulverised them in a timed paper on the foreign policy of President Woodrow Wilson, but had it been possible for them to single me out in the crowd of angry Everton fans threatening to beat them to a pulp, they would have laughed their way home, rather than got there by ambulance. So I was always much happier with the alternative line about the combine harvester.

As it happens, the Grimsby fans that night didn't only sing when they were fishing. They sang more or less from first whistle to last, and with good reason, because their team, lying thirteenth in Division Three, ended up as convincing 2-1 winners over my team, the First Division aristocrats, who then as now had played more games of top-flight football than anyone else, and whose starting XI included my two great heroes, Wood and Latchford.

As for the scorer of both Grimsby goals as the rain sheeted down, he was a Scotsman who had briefly been on Chelsea's books, called Mike Brolly. This, of course, made matters considerably worse because I knew how gleefully it would be received not only by the back-page headline-writers, but also by the many Liverpool fans at school the following day. On the Wednesday morning, sure enough, decidedly jaded after not getting home until 1.30am, I was asked half a dozen times even before I reached the school gate whether I had my brolly with me. It wasn't funny then, and it isn't funny now.

Quite aside from that defeat by humble Grimsby Town, the 1979-80 football season was dismal for Everton, and for a while even threatened the unthinkable indignity of relegation. While Liverpool strutted to their second successive title, Everton finished just one place above the drop zone. Poor as they were, Bolton Wanderers, Derby County and Bristol City were poorer, thank God.

Yet to put it mildly, the previous ten years had not lived up to the promise of greatness that had shimmered beguilingly over Goodison Park when Harry Catterick's wonderful side clinched the League Championship in 1969-70. Never mind Bill Shankly's Liverpool, Don Revie's Leeds, Bertie Mee's Arsenal and Bill Nicholson's Spurs, it looked as if the new decade was Everton's for the taking. But it wasn't. Or if it was, they didn't.

In a way it was my misfortune not to be either a few years older, or a few years younger. In May 1970 I was eight, not quite old enough to revel in the exhilarating spectacle of that gilded midfield trio of Alan Ball, Colin Harvey and Howard Kendall, the so-called 'holy trinity', propelling Catterick's team to the title. And by the time Kendall, reborn as a manager, steered Everton to new glories in the mid-1980s, I was away at university, first in Scotland, and then for a year in America.

When Everton played Liverpool in the 1986 FA Cup final, I was staying with friends in a log cabin on the Buffalo River in Tennessee. Our host was a Weeble-shaped oil man called 'Chucky' Cameron, and when I managed to explain the colossal significance of the big soccer occasion I was missing by inviting him to imagine the New York Yankees playing the New York Mets in the World Series, old Chucky obliged me by somehow wiring up a small transistor radio so that the tin roof of an outhouse effectively became a powerful aerial.

Astoundingly, after much frantic knob-twiddling and visits to more country music stations that you would think possible, I picked up the unmistakeable voice of Peter Jones in the BBC commentary box at Wembley.

It was still 0-0, but moments later Gary Lineker slotted Everton into a 27th-minute lead. Never has an outhouse in *Deliverance* country seen so much half-crazed euphoria, at least not without a gallon of moonshine and a couple of male hikers to rape. But alas, my delight was short-lived, as Liverpool, damn them, scored three in the second half. Indeed, if my friend Colin Shindler hadn't already done such a memorable number on Manchester United, I might reasonably have called this book *Bloody Liverpool Ruined My Life*.

On the other hand, it is the rampant success of Liverpool at that time which explains why two First Division football matches almost exactly six months apart in 1978 – one on 29 April, which finished Everton 6 Chelsea 0, and another on 28 October, which ended with the even more memorable scoreline of Everton 1 Liverpool 0 – filled me with such all-consuming joy that after more than 35 years it hasn't yet entirely subsided. This book tells the story of those two games, the story of English football in the years leading up to them, and in particular the story of 1978, which as well as being Everton's centenary year was also a landmark year for the game.

It does so partly from my own perspective, which for you means having to share the trauma of my O levels, since I was cruelly expected to grapple with them while the World Cup was unfolding in Argentina. Football lovers of my generation will understand why, in a word association game even now, I might connect 'Teófilo Cubillas' with 'Chemistry' and 'Willie Johnston' with 'Geography'.

But far more significant than me in these pages are the men who featured for Everton in those two memorable league victories.

In telling their stories, the stories of how they had reached a level of success in life which meant their names being chanted by thousands of people week after week, and the sometimes more poignant tales of how life has treated them since, I hope to shed some light on what football was like then, compared with what it has become.

Moreover, in the English game's extraordinary transformation between 1970 and now, the summer of 1978 represents a kind of watershed, for that was when the Argentinian pair Osvaldo Ardiles and Ricardo Villa, in signing for 'Tottingham', first opened our eyes to the remarkable possibility that English teams might recruit top players from beyond the British Isles. Beyond Europe, even. And we all know what an alarming conflagration those innocent early sparks have produced.

In 1977-78, you could bet your house on the virtual certainty that the twenty-two players taking part in any randomly chosen First Division football match would all hail from these islands. Now, in the Premier League, it's just as certain that less than half of them will.

In some ways the coffin lid was shut on English football as a game predominantly for British and Irish players on Boxing Day 1999. It was fitting, perhaps, that the end of a footballing era should come less than a week before the end of a millennium, and striking too that it should come at the Dell, the home of Southampton FC since 1898.

With a stand designed by the great football stadium architect Archibald Leitch, and a penalty area bombed during the Blitz, the Dell was as traditional an English football ground as any. Yet it was there that Boxing Day afternoon that the Chelsea manager Gianluca Vialli fielded a team, for the first time in the 111-year existence of the Football League, comprising precisely no British players. His team was: De Goey, Ferrer, Thome, Leboeuf, Babayaro, Petrescu, Deschamps, Poyet, Di Matteo, Ambrosetti, Flo. Southampton's team, by positively patriotic contrast, featured six Englishmen and a Welshman. But it was Chelsea who won, 2-1.

The trend continued and gathered pace. Of the players participating on the opening day of the 2013-14 Premier League season, roughly two-thirds – two-thirds! – were foreign nationals. But it was in August 1978 that the first stirrings of that trend were felt. So, while not even the Spurs fans who so worshipped Ossie Ardiles would quite lift him to messianic status, he nevertheless does the same job as Christ in dividing epochs. There was English football before Ardiles, and English football after.

And that wasn't all. Something else happened in 1978, something that could no sooner happen now than you or I could buy an ordinary suburban house for £13,820, which back then was the national average. For that was the year not just of Tottingham, but also of Nottingham.

Nottingham Forest, who had begun the season in August 1977 as the third of three clubs promoted from the Second Division, ended it in April 1978 as league champions. The only conceivable way in which a promoted club could do that now would be with the committed support of a glory-hungry billionaire, filling his team with £50 million players on £150,000-a-week wages. In 1978, however, the transmutation from promotion also-rans to First Division champions (and, the following season, to champions of Europe) could be wrought with such quaint old virtues as vision, charisma and motivational genius, albeit that there was only one Brian Clough. He too looms large in this book.

But not as large as another old-school manager, a lugubrious-looking son of Staffordshire called Gordon Lee.

In 2003, as a national newspaper columnist who rarely missed a chance to trumpet my feelings for the Toffees, I was invited by the Everton Supporters' Association to give a speech in a function room at Goodison Park, following a dinner to celebrate the club's 125th anniversary. My speech was well received, not least because I first exhorted the assembled throng of several hundred people to give a proper standing ovation for an overweight man sitting quietly and anonymously at a table near the door. This was Gordon West, the goalkeeping colossus of that championship-winning 1970 team, and when I spotted him and announced that he was one of my earliest footballing pin-ups, I meant it. As dear old Gordon rose a trifle uneasily to his feet, there was thunderous applause, which sustained me through a speech about my own golden age as an Evertonian, the rusty-white-van years between 1977 and 1980.

There was laughter when I relived the journey to Grimsby, and again when I talked about the games against Chelsea and Liverpool in 1978 that had such enduring significance in my life. To a man and a woman, the audience was with me, and I then prepared to finish with a toast, having once been advised by a wise old after-dinner speaker that it is a reasonably sure way of getting an audience to its feet, whether or not they have enjoyed what you had to say.

If I had invited them to raise their glasses to Everton's memorably potent late-1970s forward-line of Latchford, McKenzie and Thomas, every chair in the room would have been scraped back, every glass drained. And if I had asked them to toast Gordon West, they'd be clapping and cheering still.

But I chose a different Gordon. I asked them to drink to the health of Gordon Lee, Everton's manager from January 1977 to May 1981. This had a strange effect. It wasn't quite as if I'd asked them to toast Kenny Dalglish, but I still felt as if I'd blown it right at the end of a rousing piece of oratory, rather as if Churchill had growled 'we shall defend our island whatever the cost may be, we shall fight on the beaches, we shall fight on the landing grounds, we shall fight in the fields and in the streets, we shall fight in the hills, but if there are too many of them, and they're too tough for us, we shall probably surrender.'

Most people stood, echoed 'Gordon Lee', and drank up, but a significant number, about 30 per cent, did not.

It was true that Lee never entirely won over the Everton faithful, and true too that his lugubriousness sometimes seemed to define him. He had a long face, both figuratively and actually, and had he been a bit-part actor rather than a football manager, he would have been typecast as an undertaker or at best a gloomy manservant. Every time he opened his mouth to a reporter, you half-expected him to ask whether the family favoured a burial or a cremation. And even when you'd heard him out, his public utterances did not exactly overflow with exuberance. 'People keep on about stars and flair,' he once grumbled. 'As far as I'm concerned, you find stars in the sky and flair at the bottom of your trousers.'

This was evidently aimed squarely at the uncontainable trickster that was Duncan McKenzie. Where the crowd saw magic, Lee saw self-indulgence. It was his predecessor, Billy Bingham, who had bought McKenzie, and Lee didn't want him. In September 1978 McKenzie was sold to Chelsea, and on 11 November came back to Goodison Park with his new club and, with characteristic effrontery, opened the scoring.

Amazingly, the Everton fans cheered the goal, followed it with a quick salvo of 'We all agree, Duncan McKenzie is magic' and then began furiously berating Lee, who sat scowling in the dugout, for selling their favourite entertainer. That Everton bounced back to win 3-2 that day did not save the manager from the accusation that he had been wrong to move McKenzie on, or from the entirely unreasonable suspicion that it had been the culmination of some kind of misplaced personal vendetta.

Among Everton fans of a certain age that has coloured his reputation ever since, together with the unarguable fact that, on his watch, the team finished in 19th place in 1979-80 (mercifully at a time when there were 22 rather than 20 clubs in the top division), followed by 15th in 1980-81. For a club still considered to be one of English football's big five, along with Liverpool, Manchester United, Arsenal and Spurs, that was plainly not good enough. On 6 May 1981, Lee was even more entitled than usual to look like a man with toothache burying his pet dog. He was sacked, which cleared the way for the prescient appointment of Kendall.

Now, I don't suppose that even Mrs Lee would argue that Everton would have climbed back to the pinnacle of the English game had her Gordon remained as manager and Kendall not taken over, and yet I will always think of him fondly, for it was also on his watch, in 1977-78, that Everton played some of the most swash-buckling attacking football I have ever seen in the English game, winning even away matches by three- and four-goal margins. Yes, Forest won the title in 1978, and yes, Liverpool were runners-up, but in finishing third that season, Everton scored more goals than both of the teams above them. And precisely 30 of those goals were bagged by Bob Latchford, which brings us back to where we started – the Cheshire Yeoman pub on the road to Wales from Ellesmere Port.

Chapter Two

When I arrived at the Cheshire Yeoman for my midday rendezvous with Latchford, the pub was locked and there were no vehicles in the car park, just a strong smell of urine from the night before. It was an inauspicious start to an encounter with a man whose smiling face – first bearded, then clean-shaven, initially with a perm and later without, according to the latest representation in *Shoot!* magazine – had adorned my bedroom wall for most of my teenage years, directly above a picture of the marginally (but only marginally) more appealing Debbie Harry. This book thoroughly undermines the maxim that you should never meet your heroes, but it's true that you should be careful where you meet them. A grubby pub car park stinking of Friday-night piss wasn't the backdrop I would have chosen.

After waiting for about 20 minutes, I was beginning to lose confidence in the plan. Could there possibly be another pub called the Cheshire Yeoman? Or had I got the date wrong? Was Latchford at that moment sitting at home near Nuremberg tucking into a plate of blutwurst and sauerkraut? But just as I was rebuking myself for not phoning or emailing him to double-check the arrangement, a small convoy of cars arrived and a group of men stepped out, one of whom I recognised immediately even though it was more than three decades since I had respectfully removed his image from above my bed, following his transfer to Swansea City.

Bob Latchford, aged sixty-two, looked as if he could still walk on water. He was what my old mother would have called 'a dish', with greying hair but as handsome as a gently ageing movie star. If my three children had been with me, they would have had no trouble understanding why their dad had grown up idolising this bloke. Which isn't always the case. Many are the fat and dissolute-looking ex-sportsmen I have pointed out down the years, and said, 'You won't believe it, kids, but he was once a bit of a hero of mine.' And, of course, they never do believe it. Or if they do, it merely emphasises to them my own slide towards decrepitude.

With Latchford though, their only difficulty would have been in believing that he was born more than eleven years earlier than me. He was in remarkable shape. And let me be even more obsequious. If goalkeepers as a very general rule are considered to be a bit on the nutty side, then centre forwards, according to the same rule, are meant to be innately cocksure. It makes sense. The best of them are propelled by utter self-belief, which is what makes them more likely to score goals than anyone else in the team, and also makes them more likely to be a pain in the arse off the field. Even in retirement there is a swagger about them. I have never caught much of a whiff of self-doubt around Andy Gray, for example. But Latchford does not fit this blueprint at all. I found him softly spoken, courteous to a fault, almost shy, and I liked him instantly, as I had so profoundly hoped I would.

The men with him were not what anyone would call shy. One was Dave Cockram, a fanatical Evertonian who ran a sandwich shop in Ellesmere Port but as a sideline organised 'legends' events, for Liverpool as well as Everton supporters, at which fans could meet their heroes from the 1970s and 1980s and listen to some well-oiled anecdotes. The strange thing was, he told me, that Everton events were always sell-outs, but the Liverpool legends didn't seem to hold the same appeal.

'It's amazing,' he said. 'They've won five European Cups, but I've got a night on next week with Alan Kennedy, Jimmy Case and Joey Jones, and I can't sell the tickets. We've only sold half of them. Maybe it's because they had so much success back then, whereas we were desperate for it and still are. Whatever the reason is, we seem to cherish our old players much more than they do. You should have been there last night. We couldn't stop them singing, eh Bob?'

Sitting at an adjoining table in what passed for the pub's garden, signing a huge stack of shirts and posters, Latchford smiled a little bashfully, while Cockram told me about the function the evening before, at the Naval Club in the Liverpool suburb of Broadgreen. Apparently, the chanting had all but lifted the roof, and had gone on for minutes on end, before the guest of honour could make himself heard. I was half-sorry I hadn't been there, but also half-relieved. It would have been altogether weird, as a man of fifty-one, to join in a thunderous mass chant of 'Bobby Latchford walks on water, nana nana na, nana na na'. Some things, however precious, are best left in the past. But who knows? Maybe my 16-year-old self would have been briefly reincarnated. Maybe, on last orders being called and just for old times' sake, I might even have led a chorus of 'You're going home in a fucking ambulance'.

Which brings me to another of the Evertonians accompanying Bob Latchford to the Cheshire Yeoman, a fast-talking North Walian called Andy Nicholls. I liked him. He was warm and had a quick-fire wit, which was deployed at the expense of an amiable fellow called Steve Zocek who arrived a little later, and, lest there be any doubting his blue credentials, quickly tugged up his shirt to show us the faces of seventeen former Everton players tattooed on his back, with Latchford recognisably prominent among them, gazing out from between the shoulder blades, flanked by Alan Ball and Dixie Dean.

'That's cost me three grand so far,' said Zocek. 'But the money's irrelevant. If you love something, you just do it, don't you?'

Zocek, it turned out, was a regular contributor to the fan website Blue Kipper, posting his own interviews with ex-Everton players. 'I was with Archie Styles last night, Bob,' he said. Latchford expressed polite interest. 'I saw Ken McNaught the other week, Bob,' he said, a few minutes later. Latchford asked after McNaught, and continued signing shirts. Zocek ambled off to get himself a drink, then came back and said: 'Hey Bob, I was chatting to Peter Eastoe a few days back.' Latchford looked up and smiled. Zocek sipped his drink, and then remembered another encounter. 'I met up with Pat Heard a couple of weeks back, Bob,' he chirped. 'He's a driving instructor now, and also a qualified stage hypnotist.'

'Fucking hell,' blurted Nicholls, 'is there anyone you haven't spoken to in the last two weeks, apart from your missus?'

We all laughed, including Zocek. Latchford wanted to finish his marathon signing session before telling me the story of his life before and more significantly after he earned his place between Steve Zocek's shoulder blades, and while he did so Nicholls kept us entertained with a raft of anecdotes about following Everton round England and Europe. He seemed excited to hear that I was writing a book about the 1977-78 season, and I judged that he was about the same age as me, so presumed that his experiences of supporting Everton in those days had been similar to mine. I couldn't have been more wrong.

Nicholls, I later learnt, had been one of English football's most notorious hooligans, a Category-C trouble-maker – the worst kind – whose 2002 book *Scally* I have since read, and which contains the following dubious boast: 'Since the age of 16 I have been arrested over 20 times, spent weeks in court, been jailed, paid thousands of pounds in fines, been battered, cut up, had failed relationships and a broken marriage, and lost well-paid jobs, all because of football violence.'

It transpired that the man I'd met at the Cheshire Yeoman, who'd been bantering away with the charming and mild-mannered Bob Latchford, had at one stage been banned from every football ground in Britain, and had been officially deported from Belgium, Sweden and Iceland.

His book begins with a chapter entitled 'If You Know Your History', a nod to the rousing line in the Everton anthem 'It's A Grand Old Team'. Yet Nicholls was referring not to Everton's proud footballing legacy, but to the club's heyday as a breeding-ground for thugs such as him. In the 1970s, he reflected with wistful pride, Goodison Park and its environs 'was one of the most evil places for a travelling football fan ... You needed safety in numbers, serious numbers, as we would have mobs of over a thousand at every game and one in ten was a blade merchant. There cannot be a ground in the country that has seen as many cuttings as Goodison.'

If this is true, then it surprises as well as horrifies me, although my late father will be looking down from his celestial armchair, saying 'I told you so'.

My dad died in the first week of February in 1976, of a sudden heart attack while on a train only a mile or two out of Lime Street station, on his way from Liverpool to a business meeting in London. He was sixty years old; younger than Bob Latchford was that day at the Cheshire Yeoman. It was a Wednesday, and a particularly rubbish week both to be Allen Viner's son and an Evertonian. A 3-2 home defeat by Burnley on the previous Saturday was followed, a week later, by a dispiriting 0-0 draw at Sheffield United. Everton hadn't won a game since before Christmas, when Latchford bagged the first in a 2-1 win at Coventry City.

It was my father's unexpected death that shook my world, of course, not an indifferent run of results for the Toffees. I was fourteen, and with the turmoil of puberty still to come it was a bad time to become fatherless, the more so as it left just my mother and me. And yet the heavy cloud that settled over me had the slightest glimmer of a silver lining. I had yearned to go to Goodison Park ever since the 1969-70 season, when I started supporting Everton for the solid reason that my friends Jez and Chris Sykes did, but my dad would never allow me to, sternly citing the dangers of hooliganism and the crush of big crowds.

Other boys' dads had no such qualms, to my great frustration. Much later in life I became friendly with a man called Martin Davies, whose great-grandfather's brother was Ted Sagar, the accomplished Everton goalkeeper of the pre-war era, who played 495 games for the club and was the first footballer to wear a number 1 on his back, in the 1933 FA Cup final.

Martin told me that his dad took him to Goodison from the time he was about ten, and would go for a pre-match pint in the Carisbrooke pub while young Martin was safely despatched to the Boys' Pen. Or maybe not so safely.

'The Boys' Pen was where I learnt to fight,' Martin told me. 'My dad would give me money for a pie and a programme, but on my first week in there, I think in the 1969-70 season, I was robbed. The second week, I was robbed again. The third week, I fought back. It was also where I learnt to negotiate. Sometimes they'd agree to leave me my pie money, but take every penny above that.'

If that was where he honed his business skills, those young racketeers did him a favour; Martin is now a millionaire many times over. Moreover, those tough early experiences notwithstanding, he has only fond memories of his Boys' Pen years. 'We had our own songs, and with all those high-pitched voices, we were almost a choir, only with swearing. My mates were all really jealous that my dad took me to the match.'

If I'd known him then, I would have been sick with envy. My own dad had grown up in Liverpool and would have been twelve years old when Dixie Dean scored 60 goals for Everton in the 1927-28 season, so I never understood why he hadn't embraced Everton himself. He just wasn't much of a football fan, preferring horse racing and boxing. That might be why he so demonised football, or at least large football crowds, having never been part of one. He had also heard some horror stories from his business partner Jack Fry, a passionate Liverpool supporter who took his own sons to Anfield and had occasionally been separated from them in the melee. In our house they were legion, those stories about Jack Fry losing his boys at Anfield.

Ordinarily, neither of my parents were what you might call overprotective, in fact my dad's response when I reported, aged eleven, that I was being bullied at school, was not to march in to see the headmaster but to send me for boxing lessons with an amateur heavyweight champion he'd known in Liverpool, called Sam Rose. Unfortunately, almost half a century had passed since Sam's glory days in the ring. My dad was thinking of the alpha male he had been, but by the time I went to see him, he was a feeble and slightly smelly old man, who couldn't have taught me to punch my way out of an empty crisp packet.

So the bullying continued and so did the Goodison Park veto. The only league football matches my dad would let me attend were at Haig Avenue, humble home of Fourth Division Southport FC, and even that was with some reluctance. The stern message was that I would only go to Goodison over his dead body, and that's pretty much what happened.

Within a year of his death, with my mother either too upset to care or taking the view that I probably wouldn't be flirting with death every other weekend, I was a Gwladys Street regular. And one morning in early August 1977, I came downstairs at 58 Lynton Road, our three-bedroomed semi that backed on to the Liverpool-Southport railway line, to find a small package on the carpet just inside the front door which caused me broadly the same excitement that King Arthur might have felt if someone had posted the Holy Grail through his letter box.

The package contained my first season ticket. It had cost me £40, which amounted to a lot of evenings clumsily waiting tables at 60p an hour plus tips.

My friends Rafe Parker, Jeff Brignall and 'Mugsy' Rimmer had acquired season tickets too, and so commenced a Saturday ritual which, every fortnight during the football season, started just before noon at Southport's Ribble bus station, where we were often joined by our other Evertonian mates, 'Bean' Rimmer and 'Mozzer' Richards. Our Ribble bus adventures lasted for two years, until Rafe passed his driving test and bought his knackered old van, which he ill advisedly attempted to glamorise by fixing a dark-green strip across the windscreen bearing the message 'Sex relieves tension'. As an attempt to amuse and attract girls, this was never likely to yield much success, least of all in the car park of Walton Hospital, where we parked before Everton games. Nor did the van afford much more comfort than the rickety old bus, but if nothing else it enabled us to cut down on travelling time.

On the bus we'd had to set off before noon for a three o'clock kick-off – which all Saturday games were in those halcyon days before football was conquered by television – because it took an hour and 25 minutes for the number 28, always the oldest and unhealthiest in the Ribble fleet, to creak and wheeze the 17 miles to Derby Park in Bootle, where we alighted and walked to

Goodison. We never saw any violence on this journey to and from the ground, probably because, unlike Andy Nicholls and his crew, we never went looking for it.

Going to away matches, needless to say, was a different story. Manchester City's Maine Road and Elland Road, home of Leeds United, were the two stadiums I least enjoyed visiting, the two grounds where there was always palpable menace in the air, as well as the odd battery or bottle. But I never saw any pitched battles, and it always seemed to me that Evertonians took in good heart the indignity of being herded away from grounds by mounted police, usually issuing a loud collective moo-ing or baa-ing noise. Judging by the tales Nicholls tells, though, I was lucky not to run in to orchestrated mayhem.

These days, football hooliganism is nothing like the blight on the game, and on England's reputation abroad, that it used to be. But carefully planned violence lives on, especially in the lower leagues. It is not a subject to treat lightly, but a good friend of mine, a policeman in Cheshire, tells a marvellous story about a bunch of teenage ruffians who follow Crewe Alexandra, and who before a pre-season friendly against Aston Villa in July 2013, decided to organise a post-match tear-up with a gang of much older Villa thugs, well-known in hooligan circles, apparently, for being very big and very brutal.

The venue was arranged – a deserted supermarket car park – but the fight didn't happen, for the simple reason that when the Villa gang turned up and saw the Crewe lads, hard but fairly scrawny boys of sixteen and seventeen, they thoughtfully pointed out that it would most likely be a terrible mismatch. 'Listen, son, I think you and your friends should probably all go home,' said the Villa gang leader to his Crewe counterpart, and, slightly sheepishly, they all did. That would be a good story even without my favourite detail, which is that the Crewe gang called themselves the

Crewetons, presumably thinking that it made them sound tough, an uncompromising hybrid of the Teutons and the Kryptons. I can't imagine that they wanted their name to evoke comforting bowls of tomato soup, with small cubes of sautéed bread floating on top.

As for Andy Nicholls, I'm assured that he's a reformed character now, perhaps even happier eating croutons than battering Crewetons. He has served a ten-year ban from Goodison Park and attends matches with his daughter these days, looking like any other doting parent. But it still seems incongruous to have found him in Bob Latchford's entourage, and a story he tells about Everton's last fixture of the 1977-78 season certainly doesn't chime with either Latchford's experience that day, or mine.

Chelsea were the visitors, and according to Nicholls, were followed up to Goodison by one of their most fearsome mobs, led by a ferocious black guy with one arm, known, a trifle improbably, as Babs. It's safe to assume that not many people bothered to point out to Babs that his name was a bit girly, or that he shared it with the most buxom member of the dance troupe Pan's People. In fact, I'm uneasy committing such an observation to print, even now. He might be reading this.

I don't know whether Babs and his gang ruined the day for any Evertonians. It would have been a great shame if they had, because for most of us it was a day that put a swagger in our stride for the rest of that summer and well into the following season, a day when we celebrated as extravagantly as if we had won the league championship, European Cup and FA Cup Treble. And what ignited the near-hysteria was a penalty, 13 minutes from the end of the match, hammered low by Latchford just beyond the right hand of the diving Peter Bonetti.

The 6-0 scoreline was incidental. It wasn't even much of a thrashing, by comparison with a game that took place at exactly the same time in the country that Latchford would much later call home. For that afternoon, in what was also the final game of the 1977-78 season for Borussia Mönchengladbach and Borussia Dortmund, Mönchengladbach coasted to what is still the Bundesliga's record victory, beating Dortmund 12-0. No fewer than five of the goals were scored by one man: Jupp Heynckes, later a hugely successful manager at Real Madrid and Bayern Munich.

At Goodison Park, meanwhile, Latchford scored only two. But two were all he and we needed to send us into a frenzy. The last goal of the afternoon mattered not because it was Everton's sixth, but because it was Latchford's second, and therefore his 30th league goal of the season.

In the 1970s, defence had become more sophisticated than attack and it wasn't easy for strikers to score prolifically. There was nothing especially magical about the 30-mark in the 1960s; it had been matched or exceeded nine times. But in the 1970s only Francis Lee had done it, for Manchester City in 1971-72, and 13 of his 33 goals that season were penalties. That was why, at the start of the 1977-78 season for the second consecutive year, the *Daily Express* – a rather more successful and better-resourced newspaper then than it is now, I might add – had promised a handsome reward for the man who could pull off such a feat again.

'The *Express* shoots ahead this soccer season,' declared the paper on the opening day, 'and for kick-off day we have set that 30-goal target again – worth £10,000 to the first player in the First or Second Division to get that number in league matches.'

Latchford led that exciting quest for most of the season, and yet with less than 20 minutes of the season left, and Everton 3-0 up, he still hadn't found the back of the net. For those of us on the terraces it felt decidedly odd to be cruising towards such an easy victory, and at the same time to feel so cruelly denied.

Even when Latchford rose commandingly above Steve Wicks to

bag a characteristically powerful 72nd-minute header, putting Everton 4-0 up and himself within a single score of the prize, the clock continued to tick rapidly towards an agonising anti-climax. There was actually an audible collective groan when a few minutes later Mike Lyons, our beloved captain and centre half, scored the fifth.

But then Everton were awarded a dubious penalty by the referee, an obliging police road safety officer from County Durham, called Peter Willis.

'We'd just been pounding them,' Everton's first goalscorer that day, Martin Dobson, later told me. 'But we couldn't get Latchy that goal. Then, when we were 5-0 up and Latchy just needed one more, Lyonsy got bundled over in the penalty area. It was a dodgy penalty; I've got to say that. And Latchy hasn't taken too many. I remember him asking me, "Dobbo, what should I do?" And I said, "Just get your head over the ball and smack it."'

Latchford followed those instructions to the letter. If he hadn't kept it down, it might be rising still. But he did. And when it hit the back of Bonetti's net, the 39,504 of us inside Goodison Park – minus Babs and a few thousand Chelsea fans – reacted pretty much as if we had each won £10,000, not just him. After all, and here is the crunch, it was something that an Everton player had done that a Liverpool player hadn't.

We knew, of course, that 30 goals in a season wasn't exactly a European Cup, which Liverpool had won for the first time the previous May and would win again less than a fortnight later, but Latchford's achievement nevertheless had an effect on the Goodison crowd a bit like lifting the heavy lid of a pressure cooker. All the frustration that had been stored up since 1970, as Everton repeatedly failed to fulfil their potential and Liverpool repeatedly realised theirs, erupted in a spectacular whoosh of jubilation. Long after the match had ended, the streets around

Goodison and I dare say elsewhere in the city, echoed with a happy and familiar refrain.

'Bobby Latchford walks on water, nana nana na, nana na na!'

And in the sense that he was our saviour, and had delivered us if not from evil then at least from Liverpool's shadow, we really believed that he did.

Chapter Three

B̶ob Latchford had woken up that morning in his new house in Formby, a small dormitory town between Liverpool and Southport, with the ironclad conviction that by the end of the afternoon he would have scored the two goals he required to win the *Daily Express*'s magnanimous prize. Such utter self-assurance was rare on the morning of a game. Normally he awoke with a flutter of nerves, but on this day – the penultimate day of April 1978 – there were no nerves at all. 'I'm going to do it,' he told his wife Pat. 'I know I am.'

Latchford was twenty-eight and in his formidable prime. He had made his full England debut the previous November in front of more than 92,000 people at Wembley, in a World Cup qualifier against Italy, and at Everton was a fearless centre forward in the club's great tradition of No. 9s.

The first and indisputably the greatest of these – despite the later heroics of Tommy Lawton, Dave Hickson, Alex Young, Joe Royle, Latchford himself and Graeme Sharp – was 71-year-old Bill Dean, who had generously told reporters in the run-up to the Chelsea game that scoring 30 league goals in 1977-78 would be the equivalent of his own tally of 60 that had so regrettably failed to make an Everton fan of my dad exactly fifty years before.

Goals were harder to come by than they had been in his day, said Dixie Dean, and three cheers for his humility, but even if goal-keepers were better protected in 1978 than they had been in 1928, it was still something more like a medicine ball than a modern foot-ball that he'd had to manoeuvre into the back of the net.

That he did so 60 times remains the transcendent goalscoring achievement in English football history, fully worthy of the record books. His 60 goals beat George Camsell's total for Second Division Middlesbrough the season before by just one, but the roundness and neatness of the number gave it a magical quality that will endure for as long as football is played. Very few men have since scored even 40 league goals in the English top division in a single season, and in the Premier League era, not many have exceeded 30. For two consecutive seasons in the late 1990s, nobody even reached 20. It is unimaginable that anyone will ever again score 60 – not even Lionel Messi, should he come to England (though he did bag fifty in La Liga in 2011-12).

Dixie Dean reached the last day of the 1927-28 season needing three rather than two goals to reach his record-breaking target, but like Latchford he scored them with less than 15 minutes of the season remaining, like Latchford with the help of a penalty, and like Latchford he got the exact number he needed in a six-goal thriller against London opposition at Goodison Park. It had been Arsenal rather than Chelsea playing the supporting role on 5 May 1928, and the game had finished as a 3-3 draw rather than a 6-0 win. Nor had there been a one-armed black man called Babs hoping to lead the away fans on a violent rampage, in which respect football's strides forward in those fifty years had led it headlong into a cesspit. All the same, the parallels across half a century were remarkable.

If there were no butterflies in the pit of Latchford's stomach that

Saturday morning, the same was not so of my own as I set off for the Ribble bus station, nor of a boy of about my age called Dave Prentice, who lived a few streets away from Latchford, in a less ritzy part of Formby. Prentice was devoted to all things Everton, and years later would be able to indulge his devotion by not only becoming the Everton correspondent for the *Liverpool Echo*, but also, still more impressively, by marrying Dixie Dean's grand-daughter. At fifteen, however, his troth was plighted only in the direction of Goodison Park.

I didn't know Prentice before I started researching this book, but it was strangely comforting to sit down with him, in a coffee shop in the *Echo* building one afternoon, and hear how an obsession with Everton coloured his youth blue just as it had mine. Like me, he and his fellow Evertonians were greatly outnumbered at school by volubly smug Liverpool fans, who in his case congregated outside his house on the night Liverpool beat Borussia Mönchengladbach, yet to enjoy that 12-goal fiesta, to win the 1977 European Cup. 'Prenny, Prenny, show us your scarf!' sang the Liverpool fans. That, at least, was a form of provocation I didn't have to suffer.

Living in Formby might have had its disadvantages for a school-boy Everton fan, but it also had the incalculable benefit of proximity to Bob Latchford Menswear on Piercefield Road, a bou-tique specialising in tank tops, shirts with collars like sails, and all those other garments that saddle the 1970s with that most unfair label, 'The Decade that Fashion Forgot'.

Bob Latchford Menswear was not a business in which the Everton and England centre forward had merely invested and sanc-tified with his name. No, he actually worked behind the counter, and whether that extended to measuring inside legs I don't know, but if I'd heard that it did, I would have been straight round there feigning interest in a pair of flared fawn slacks. My feelings about England's, England's number nine! England's number nine! didn't quite amount to a schoolboy crush, but at a time when I had next to no experience with the opposite sex, bar one disastrous French kissing experiment with a girl I'd known since I was three, big Bob holding a tape-measure against my thigh would definitely have constituted a thrill.

For 15-year-old Prentice, the thrill was just seeing him in there. 'I can remember hovering outside one day trying to build up the courage to go in,' he told me. 'After a while he spotted me, and told me to come in. He was as personable as anything, and when I asked him to sign a stack of pictures I had of him, he said he'd be happy to. But after he'd got about halfway through, there were a couple of pictures full of dart holes. That was my brother's doing, because he supported Liverpool. I was mortified, but Bob just laughed and signed them anyway.'

The notion of a top Premier League player now working behind a shop counter in his spare time is laughable, of course. Indeed, the whole story of Latchford's 30-goal season underlines L. P. Hartley's famous observation that the past is a foreign country; they do things differently there. Even the £10,000 prize sounds downright quaint now that some footballers earn ten grand in a few hours, and football's calendar that season might as well be tinted in sepia.

If you can cast your mind back to a time when the top division's league campaign finished before April was out, leaving a whole week before the season's blue riband event, the FA Cup final, then you probably also remember Spangles sweets, Chopper bikes and Reggie Bosanquet reading the news. For my money, there is no sadder side effect of the Premier League and Champions League bonanza than the inexorable devaluation of the FA Cup final. Shifting it to a teatime kick-off so that Premier League matches could be accommodated on the same day amounted to an act of desecration, like urinating on a statue. The guardians of the English game should hang their heads in shame. Alas, the only time they do actually hang their heads is when they're counting their TV-generated readies.

But let us get back to April 1978, and an unforgettable match that belongs to a bygone era for so many reasons. Roman Abramovich, for example, was an 11-year-old orphan growing up in humble circumstances in the Arctic Circle. In the highly unlikely event of news reaching the desolate Soviet region of Komi that Everton had thrashed Chelsea 6-0 in a football match far, far away, we can reasonably suppose that young Roman wouldn't have taken much interest. In England, meanwhile, there was not even the faintest shimmer on the most distant horizon of a weird new order that would put some of our most famous football clubs in the soft, manicured hands of foreign billionaires.

The nearest thing the First Division had to oligarchs in 1978 were self-made men such as Louis Edwards, the meat-packaging tycoon who owned a majority shareholding in Manchester United, and Manny Cussins, his counterpart at Leeds United, whose fortune came from selling furniture. At the western end of the M62, Everton's version of Edwards and Cussins was the even richer founder of the Littlewoods empire, John Moores, whose gleaming Rolls-Royce rather uncannily swung on to the Formby bypass just in front of Rafe Parker's rusty van, practically every match day. I can remember getting a kick out of the idea that two such contrasting vehicles, one carrying an octogenarian Croesus and the other four hard-up schoolboys, were both heading to the same place, their occupants all willing the same outcome. Then, as now, football's great like that.

But the past is still a foreign country, and as a further example, there is no surviving televisual record of that Everton v Chelsea game, for the simple reason that the BBC, able to feature the highlights of only two matches and having televised Everton the previous two Saturdays in anticipation of Latchford reaching 30 goals, decided to take their *Match of the Day* cameras elsewhere that afternoon, doubtless to watch the coronation of Clough's Nottingham Forest.

Younger readers used to blanket coverage of football wherever and whenever it is played, will be bemused to learn that no league football matches were covered live on telly then. None! The BBC had a two-match Saturday-night highlights package, and on the Sunday afternoon the ITV regions carried extended highlights of one of the previous day's First Division games, which we watched with breathless excitement even though we'd known the result for the best part of 18 hours, and had already lapped up the reports in the Sunday papers. With extreme willpower it was just about possible to sit down in front of *The Big Match* on a Sunday afternoon having not heard the previous day's score, but that meant living like a hermit, or clapping your hands over your ears and ululating like a madman whenever there was the slightest hint that someone might break the news. I did that quite often.

The dearth of live league football on TV is another reason why the FA Cup final was so venerated in those days, and, of course, both main broadcasters made a sumptuous meal of it. Cup final day on 6 May was the one day in the 1978 calendar that bears some resemblance to the commonplace schedules now on Sky Sports 1, 2 and 3. The BBC's exhaustive coverage began at 11.30am, with 'Cup Final Mastermind' at 12.12pm the day's first unmissable treat, even though it clashed with well-known football enthusiasts Eric Morecambe and Elton John over on ITV giving their views on the finalists, Arsenal and Ipswich Town.

Even in the 1960s, before the advent of colour, Cup final day had been a TV institution. I happen to have the issue of *Radio Times* for the week of 14–20 May 1966, detailing the BBC's coverage of Everton v Sheffield Wednesday at 'the Empire Stadium, Wembley', and that began even earlier, at 11.15am, leading up to the thrilling moment that would hold a nation in thrall, by which I don't mean kick-off but the 2.50pm 'Presentation of the Teams to HRH The Princess Margaret, Countess of Snowdon'.

As a small aside, in March 2010 I went to Buckingham Palace to interview the late Princess Margaret's brother-in-law, the 89-year-old Duke of Edinburgh. I felt then, and still feel now, that it was something of a coup to secure a rare interview with Prince Philip, not that my then-employers, the *Independent*, who liked to treat the royal family with a self-conscious and rather posturing indifference, gave me much credit.

Anyway, I conducted a big sports interview every week for 13 years for the *Indy*, and felt that the elderly duke might be a left-field candidate for that slot on the basis that he had occupied a unique place in the sporting life of the nation since 1947. He had twice served as president of Marylebone Cricket Club, had been president of the Football Association, patron or president of countless other sporting organisations, and in 1971 and 2006 had even seen his daughter and then his granddaughter crowned – which admittedly wouldn't have been the verb they used at the Palace – BBC Sports Personality of the Year.

I also wanted to hear about all those big Wembley occasions he'd been to, and to find out which of them stuck out in his memory. Regrettably, none did. In fact, he admitted that he'd attempted to make the FA Cup final a less regular royal treat.

'In the King's day we used to go every year to the Cup final,' he told me, in that wonderfully fruity voice, so posh that it sounded almost as if he were being strangled, 'but I thought soccer was rather hogging it, so I tried to suggest we went alternately to the soccer final, the rugby union final and the rugby league final.' I asked whether his suggestion was rejected. 'No, but the collective memory in a place like this is very short. They didn't reject it, they just didn't remember it.'

Surely, then, he'd been at the famous 1953 FA Cup final, the so-called 'Matthews final' between Bolton Wanderers and Blackpool, exactly a month before the coronation? 'I think we must have been,' he said, an answer which slightly broke my heart. Imagine not knowing for sure whether you were at the Matthews Cup final. But he had a solid excuse. 'Presumably the games all merge into one after a while?' I ventured.

'They do, rather,' he replied, and said he felt similarly hazy about the celebrated 1956 final between Manchester City and Newcastle United, in which City's German goalkeeper Bert Trautmann so famously soldiered on with a broken neck. I was able to assure Prince Philip that he had in fact been there, because I'd read a biography of Trautmann which described how, on being introduced to the players before the game, the duke (born, as you will know, into the House of Schleswig-Holstein-Sonderburg-Glücksburg) reached him and said a stiff '*Sehr gut*'. Whereupon Trautmann instinctively bowed, equally stiffly, from the waist in the Teutonic style, much to the amusement of his City teammates.

All of which has led me well away from the limited coverage of football on television in the 1970s, which for ten weeks between August and October 1979 became even more limited, as ITV dropped off the air completely, on account of a strike called by the broadcasting union ACTT.

This too will cause younger readers some bemusement. Blank screens on ITV? For ten weeks? It's nigh on unthinkable now. But in the benighted 1970s, hardly a month went by without one union or another calling a strike, and by August 1979 Britain had waded through the political, social and economic quagmire known to posterity as the Winter of Discontent.

Nowhere was that discontent more acute than in the city of Liverpool, where in January 1979 even gravediggers went on strike, creating a problem so grievous that Cabinet papers released in 2009 revealed that the city council were on the verge of allowing the bereaved into municipal cemeteries to 'make their own arrangements'.

That was a measure of how bad life sometimes got in the 1970s, and why on blighted Merseyside, success on the football field was seized on as a blessed distraction from the unremitting gloom of it all. Who knows how many of the 38,504 people at Goodison Park on the final day of the 1977-78 season were out of work? A very sizeable chunk, certainly. And so the sheer escapism afforded by football in those terribly troubled times – as during Dixie Dean's pomp in the 1920s and depressed 1930s – made the occasion even more special for low-earning dockers and factory workers, and the long-term unemployed, than it was for school kids like Dave Prentice and me.

'Now that I look back on it,' Prentice told me thirty-five years later, 'it was actually quite embarrassing how we celebrated. There was a pitch invasion when he scored the goal, and another one at the end of the match. By the time I got on the hallowed turf, someone had already pinched the penalty spot. So I tore up another bit of the pitch and stuffed it under my denim jacket. For a while I had it in a plastic container next to my bed, until my dad cottoned on to what I'd done and made me transplant it in the back garden. My sister had a swing with a scuffed bit of ground underneath, so that's where it went. We've long since moved out of that house, but number 6 Byland Close in Formby still has a piece of Goodison Park in the garden. Whoever lives there now, I hope they're Evertonians.'

Amen to that.

Chapter Four

Unlike Dave Prentice, I wasn't part of the two Goodison pitch invasions that day. But I was caught in a dramatic surge on the Gwladys Street terracing, a tidal swell behind the goal in which Latchford had stuck his penalty past Bonetti, which carried me off my feet and deposited me at least 20 yards further forward from where I usually stood.

Utter euphoria flavoured with underlying terror was the bizarre cocktail of emotions during those tsunamis of jubilant supporters, and again my old departed dad, looking down, would have felt that his Goodison Park veto was entirely vindicated. I only really experienced two major surges, once when Latchford reached 30 goals, and again six months later when Andy King scored the only goal of the game against Liverpool. But that was enough. They were far more scarily exhilarating than even the whitest white-knuckle ride at Blackpool Pleasure Beach, and 11 years later we found out what could happen when too many football fans were herded into one place. The tragedy of Hillsborough shocked everyone who stood on football terraces in the 1970s and 1980s, but it probably shouldn't have surprised us.

*

My own spot on the Gwladys Street's concrete steps was just behind and to the left of an iron stanchion from which a frizzy-haired character we all knew as Fozzie Bear used to hang, leading us in song. Fozzie was a kind of self-designated cheerleader, and when he went too long without striking up a chant, he would become the subject of one himself: 'Fozzie, Fozzie, give us a song!' On the very rare occasions that he was absent from his stanchion, it was rumoured that he was spending a couple of days residing at Her Majesty's pleasure. Which, of course, just added to his considerable aura, at least as far as a relatively law-abiding grammar school boy from Southport was concerned.

There were a few other blokes in our section of the Street End with the presence and authority to start songs, but a clear hierarchy prevailed. You knew who they were, and equally you knew who they weren't. Once, during a dreary second-half against Aston Villa, with the Goodison crowd silenced by boredom, my mate Rafe boldly decided to bellow: 'Give us an E!' But nobody did give him an E, not even me, let alone a V-E-R-T-O-N. He never did it again.

Like most of those who came of age as football fans on the terraces, I regret the demise of standing support, while of course understanding why, at least at that level of the game, it had to happen. But I loved the strange familiarity of standing cheek by jowl with the same strangers every other Saturday, and, better still, under floodlights in midweek. Or if not cheek by jowl, nose by neck. I knew the backs of some necks – one horribly pimply, one as scrawny as a chicken's, one as rough and thick as a tree trunk – as well as I knew my own house, and yet I would have been hard-pressed to identify those blokes from the front, and certainly never knew their names.

I loved the wit, too, which rose from the terraces like the smell of Bovril and cigarette smoke and sweat, and if the men standing at Goodison – and nearby Anfield, it must be conceded – were not the drollest football supporters in the land, then I'd like to know who were. Regrettably, my favourite example of terrace wit comes from the Kop, where one Saturday afternoon in the 1970s a bloke grew agitated at the reluctance of the Liverpool midfield to spread the ball wide to Stevie Heighway.

'Wing!' he screamed. 'Wing! Wing! Wing! Wing!'

There was a brief silence, and then came another Scouse voice, flat and slightly long-suffering. 'Will somebody please answer that fucking phone!'

I don't know how that razor-sharp, bone-dry Scouse wit developed. Perhaps it is peculiar to big multicultural ports, those racial melting pots honed and shaped by decades, if not centuries, of economic boom and bust. After all, Glaswegians have it too, and I dare say there was always a vibrant wit on the terraces at Ibrox and Parkhead. But at Goodison Park and Anfield it lives and thrives as surely as the grass, and always has. Another Evertonian of my generation, Eugene Ruane, tells a lovely story about talking to his father, not long before the old man died, and relating a funny comment he'd overheard at Goodison. His father responded with his own favourite shaft of terraces wit, dating back to the 1960s, when the racing tipster for the *Daily Express* went by the pen name The Scout.

It was a day that Lord Montagu of Beaulieu popped up in the news. The same Lord Montagu who in 1953 had notoriously been charged with taking sexual advantage of a 14-year-old Boy Scout in a beach hut on the Solent (though he was subsequently cleared). And as Eugene's father told the story, one flat-capped old Evertonian was reading a newspaper shortly before kick-off, and muttered something about a 'dirty bastard'.

'Who is?' asked his flat-capped mate.

'Lord Montagu.'

'Lord who?'

'You know, that fella who was accused of fucking the Scout.'

The riposte was immediate.

'That twat wants fucking, the tips he's been giving recently.'

Returning to that seismic afternoon of Saturday 29 April 1978, I can't remember how long it took for the police to clear the pitch so that Peter Willis could restart the match, but when eventually they did, and the 22 players were in position ready to play, an elderly man clambered out of the stands and shuffled purposefully over to Latchford on the edge of the centre-circle to shake his hand. Goodness knows how long it had taken the old boy to get down to the pitch from where he was sitting, or standing, but he wasn't going to be denied, and neither the police, nor Mr Willis, nor any of the players, tried. They all waited politely for him to offer Latchford his congratulations, and then for him to make his way off the pitch, before kicking off again.

At the final whistle just over ten minutes later, of course, pandemonium broke out all over again. And when eventually we did set off for the interminable bus journey home, it was with the quasi-religious certainty that we were properly blessed to be Evertonians – even though, in the eight years since our team had last won a trophy, the other lot had won the European Cup once (and were about to win it again, damn them), as well as three championships, the FA Cup and the UEFA Cup twice.

But for my friends and me, big Bob Latchford scoring 30 goals made up for all that. Liverpool's gilded players might have had medals coming out of their ears but none of them had ever won ten grand from the *Daily Express*.

Latchford too floated home that evening, aptly enough on the cloud that carried his shirt number. He stopped for a few celebratory beers at the Pheasant pub in Ince Blundell and then drove on home to Formby, doubtless in breach of drink-driving laws but then, to our collective shame, nobody paid much heed to them in 1978. The party continued with friends and family back at his house, or so he was later told. It was such an unforgettable knees-up that he has never been able to remember it. Most appropriately, number one in the charts that week was 'Saturday Night Fever', by the Bee Gees.

Latchford, occasionally looking rather like a Bee Gee himself, had been an Everton player since February 1974, and had scored during the epic saga that was the 1977 League Cup final against Aston Villa, which went to two replays before Brian Little's heart-breaking last-minute winner for Villa. So he knew what it meant for the fans to have something to celebrate at last.

I don't suppose he felt the crushing inferiority complex instilled by Liverpool's success as viscerally as we did – you had to be a life-long Evertonian for that to seep from every pore of your being – but then he had his own reasons to toast his 30 goals, which con-firmed him as English football's pre-eminent striker. And, of course, there was the golden egg, a cheque for £10,000. Although the golden egg, alas, turned out to hatch an albatross.

Once he'd finished signing the huge piles of merchandise and memorabilia at the Cheshire Yeoman, Bob Latchford told me his story, starting with the £10,000 prize. 'I didn't keep it,' he said. 'I gave £5000 to be divided between the Football League Jubilee Provident Fund and the PFA Benefit Fund, and put £4000 into the players' pool to be split between my teammates. I kept back £1000 for myself, which was nice enough – my basic weekly wage at the time was £400 – but not exactly a fortune.

'Then I got a letter from the taxman demanding his cut of the £10,000, and I had to get my accountant involved, and solicitors, to prove that I wasn't liable. It literally went on for seven or eight years, and even when he accepted that I'd given £5000 to charity, he still wanted to tax me on the other £5000. When I proved that

I'd given four-fifths of that away, the taxman took me to court for the £1000. And the court ruled in his favour, so I had to pay him, as well as all the legal and accountancy fees, which cost more than I'd kept. The moral of the story . . .'

'. . . is that you should have missed the fucking penalty,' said Andy Nicholls, with a guffaw.

'No, I should have given it all to charity,' said Latchford, equably. 'Mind you, a few years later, the Liverpool players won some money for scoring 100 goals in a season, and that was tax-free. I suppose there was some sort of anomaly in the system, in that mine was an individual prize and therefore taxable, whereas theirs was a group effort.'

'Either that or the taxman was a Liverpool fan,' I said bitterly, the inferiority complex having mutated, down the years, into a persecution complex.

I don't mind owning up to that feeling of persecution, or being what Liverpool fans routinely call a 'bitter Blue'. After all, there is absolutely no doubt that Everton have been dealt more than their fair share of footballing ill fortune over the years, particularly at the hands of their neighbours from the other side of Stanley Park.

The episode most often cited in this bitterly blue regard is the European ban on English clubs instituted in the wake of the Heysel stadium disaster, which denied Howard Kendall's wonderful side of the mid-1980s the chance to compete in the European Cup.

I know that Evertonian indignation should hardly register on a scale of emotions when compared with the grief still felt by the families of the 39 Juventus fans killed at Heysel, but football fans have never been very good at perspective. I was once with a fellow Toffeeman who was sounding off about the unfairness to Everton of the Heysel ban when another guy, a West Ham fan as it happens, stopped him, telling him firmly to stop feeling sorry for himself and his team, and to imagine himself in the place of those men whose fathers and sons and brothers went to a football match in Belgium and never came home.

My mate listened gravely, and slowly nodded his head. 'Yeah, you're right,' he said. 'It's wrong to think of the football consequences when people died, of course it is.' There was a long, solemn pause. 'But I still think we would have won the fucking European Cup.'

For Evertonians of my generation, bred on underachievement, the bitterness towards Liverpool had all started with referee Clive Thomas disallowing a perfectly fair Bryan Hamilton goal at Maine Road, on St George's Day 1977. Bundled home with seconds to go and the score at 2-2, it would without doubt have propelled Everton into the FA Cup final, at Liverpool's expense. Instead, the game went to a replay, which Liverpool, inevitably, won at a canter, 3-0.

Now St George's Day, 23 April, is also William Shakespeare's birthday, and there is indeed something Shakespearian about the way in which Evertonians over the age of fifty still consider Clive Thomas to be an artfully fiendish villain, Iago with a whistle. We all know that a burning grievance against a referee should probably have been extinguished after more than three-and-a-half decades. And yet it flickers away still. That's what football does to you. No matter what your club, it is always difficult to adjust the mindset established during your formative years.

Take Manchester United. Fans in their teens and twenties, too young to remember a time when United were a mid-table outfit labouring in the long shadow of the Busby Babes and the brilliance of Best, Law and Charlton, now consider trophies to be their birthright. Yet contemporaries of mine, who came of age in what I always think of as the Arthur Albiston years and even saw United relegated in 1973-74, know in their hearts that success is transient.

The equation applies even more to those Manchester City fans who still remember all too vividly league fixtures away at Colchester United and Macclesfield Town, and who ingested that brand of gloomy fatalism so unique to City fans that I think it must have been served up in the pies at Maine Road, probably disguised as gristle. As far as those men and women are concerned, the Abu Dhabi oil wells are about to run dry, if not next week or next month, then next year. Or, if they don't, then the rule of the sugar-daddy sheikhs will turn out to be a hallucination. Those older City fans simply cannot believe what has happened to their relegation-prone club, and assume they will snap awake one day just in time for a bottom-of-the-table six-pointer at Chesterfield.

So it is with Evertonians raised in the 1970s. If we count the league title at the very start of the decade as having belonged spiritually to the 1960s, which it did, then the 1970s was a moribund era, trophy-wise. The mentality we have carried into middle age was therefore fixed in the Billy Bingham and Gordon Lee years, not the Catterick or the Kendall years, which psychologically is rather helpful.

Everton were by no means cannon fodder in those years. Under Bingham they finished in the top four in 1974-75, and did so again under Lee in 1977-78 and 1978-79. These days that would mean the Champions League and count as a lucrative success story, but in those days it counted for precisely nothing, not even bragging rights over Liverpool, who always finished higher. So we continue to celebrate our sporadic triumphs, such as the 1995 FA Cup win for Joe Royle's 'Dogs of War', or fourth place under David Moyes in 2004-05, much as we celebrated Latchford's 30 goals. Like a parched man unexpectedly being handed a small bottle of chilled Evian, we know that the pleasure won't last, so while it does we must make damn sure we relish every drop.

That is why Bob Latchford, who got his big hands on precisely no silverware during his seven years at Goodison Park, remains such an Everton icon. And why I was so interested to hear how life has turned out for him. Whether, indeed, he is still selling tank tops.

Unusually for a footballer born in 1951, or really in any era, he came from a middle-class background. 'My father was assistant director of a mental hospital in south Birmingham,' he told me. 'Our house backed on to it, so my brothers and I used to go into the grounds to play football. It was very *One Flew Over the Cuckoo's Nest*, dear me.'

If I had not already so warmed to Latchford, then the 'dear me' would have won me over. Would any modern-day footballer say 'dear me' when describing the landscape of his childhood? Almost certainly not. 'Fuck me', possibly.

'My mother died of cancer aged fifty-one, when I was eighteen,' he continued, 'I was the youngest of four boys, and my eldest brother, John, is ten years older than me. He was a bloody good footballer, actually, but for some reason it just didn't happen for him as it did for the rest of us. My other brothers, David and Peter, became professional footballers, both goalkeepers, and my dad had been a goalkeeper, too, in the army. I joined Birmingham City as an outside left, and Denis Law had been my hero growing up, but I'd actually played in goal for Warwickshire Boys one year. In fact, I have league experience in goal. David broke his finger [playing for Birmingham] against Wolves, just before half-time, and I took over for the remaining 56 minutes. We won 2-1, and they'd already scored their goal. So I kept a clean sheet.'

It would make a good trivia question: which future England centre forward once replaced his injured brother as goalkeeper in a League match, and then kept a clean sheet for almost an hour?

By the time Latchford left Birmingham for Everton in February 1974, his England prospects looked pretty decent. It was an English record transfer, too, valued at a jaw-dropping £350,000, with Howard Kendall and Archie Styles going the other way in part-exchange. His Everton debut was a lively 4-3 defeat at West Ham, but he didn't score, not a particularly momentous beginning to what would be the most important relationship of his football life.

'I'm a Birmingham boy,' he told me, 'but when you play for Everton it gets into your blood, and stays in your blood. I'm not just saying this because I have these boys around me, but the fans of this club are different to other clubs' fans, in the way they cherish their players. I'm always amazed when I go to functions like the one last night. The enthusiasm is incredible.'

Andy Nicholls, Dave Cockram and Steve Zocek all nodded in earnest agreement.

'Hey Bob,' said Zocek, after a suitably respectful pause. 'I saw Mickey Pejic the other day. He's got his own taekwondo academy now. You wouldn't want to argue with him.'

'I wouldn't want to argue with Pej anyway,' replied Latchford, with a smile.

Pejic was a hard-tackling but skilfully adventurous left back who had played four times for England by the time he joined Everton from Stoke City, his boyhood club, in 1976. Together with Martin Dobson and Dave Thomas, he made Everton's left flank much stronger and more productive than the right, rather as it became for a few seasons after 2008, thanks to the Leighton Baines/Steven Pienaar double act.

'Dave Thomas was the best winger I ever played with, with the two best feet,' Latchford added. 'Glenn Hoddle had two great feet, but "Ticer" could do what Glenn did, except at speed. I played with some good wingers over the years, like Gordon Taylor, who became the PFA chief, in the early days at Birmingham. And for England, Stevie Coppell and Peter Barnes, although with Barnes you never knew when he was going to deliver. He'd jink one way and then the other. And then do it again.'

Latchford played 12 times for England and scored five goals, a highly respectable return, although he felt that the call-up should have come earlier. 'When Don Revie took over as manager, he invited eighty of us to Manchester to go through his ideas, and he must have played seventy-nine of us, but he never played me. I don't know why to this day. I felt ready back in 1974, actually. There were other centre forwards about, like big Chiv [Martin Chivers], "Sniffer" Clarke, Micky Channon, but I'd played in the under-23s under Alf [Ramsey] and I thought I deserved a chance.'

His greatest footballing regret, though, was not winning anything with Everton. 'We should have won the league in 1974-75 and I think we would have done if we'd signed Peter Shilton, which was a possibility. Other than that, we were unlucky. In the League Cup final [the second replay, v Aston Villa, in 1977] Chris Nicholl scored from 40 yards, which he'd only ever done in his dreams. And we should have won both those FA Cup semi-finals, in 1977 and 1980. I was in the stands, injured, when Clive Thomas robbed us of the Cup in 1977, and I'm convinced he did rob us because we'd beaten Man United in the April and I think we would have beaten them at Wembley.'

It was pleasing to hear a distinguished ex-player indulge in the 'if only' rewriting of history that sustains supporters years after disappointing events, and pleasing too, I said, to know that Latchford's resentment towards a referee had endured as long and as bitterly as mine. 'Yes, well, I remember a plan to start having two refs on the pitch, but Clive Thomas didn't like the idea because he thought there was nobody good enough to referee with him. He would never admit to any mistakes. But he certainly made a mistake against us. And then against West Ham in 1980 we lost to a Frank Lampard header. When did he ever score headers?'

Again for the benefit of younger readers, the Frank Lampard in question is not the future Chelsea legend, who has scored a lot of headers but not in April 1980, being not quite two years old at the time. This was Frank Senior, his father, a rugged, right-footed left back, whose headed goal against Everton was such a rarity that it inspired a famous West Ham song to the tune of 'White Christmas': 'I'm dreaming of a Frank Lampard/Just like the ones I used to know/When the ball came over/And Frank fell over/And scored the fucking winning goal . . .'

That song lived on at Upton Park for years, and any light rain that fell during a rendition can only have been Irving Berlin's tears.

Lampard's goal was the second for Second Division West Ham, in a replay at Elland Road four days after a 1-1 draw at Villa Park. It had been 0-0 at full-time, with a second replay on the cards, but Alan Devonshire opened the scoring in extra-time and then Latchford equalised with a dramatic diving header at the near post that he celebrated as excitedly as he had his 30th of the season two years earlier, leaping on to the railings in front of his ecstatic worshippers. They included my friends Rafe, Briggy, Mozzer, Bean and me, happy to have made it safely to the home of Leeds United without receiving the traditional Elland Road welcome involving a mob of angry-looking tykes literally screaming blue murder.

A roar of 'Bobby Latchford walks on water' raised the Elland Road roof, followed by the even more heartfelt chant of 'You only sing when you're winning', in strident reply to the West Ham masses who had been loudly revelling in Devonshire's opener, and were now as silent as the grave. Commentating for *Sportsnight*, the splendid Barry Davies (whom I would later get to know, and who

for my money was the best football commentator of his generation), slightly missed the point, venturing that it was most odd to
be chanting 'You only sing when you're winning' when nobody
actually was winning.

With just two minutes of extra-time remaining, Lampard fell
over and scored the fucking winning goal, reversing the crowd's
emotions again (and sending Davies in the commentary box crazy
with excitement), leaving me and my friends with yet another miserable journey home across the Pennines in Rafe's rusty yet
improbably trusty white van.

That journey west was even gloomier than the one from
Grimsby six months earlier. Although this beating by lower-league
opposition wasn't quite as humiliating as that had been, for the
second time in three years we'd had our dream of a day out at
Wembley cruelly punctured. And it was a much more stirring
dream then than it is now, now that semi-finals, absurdly, are held
at the national stadium too. I watched the subsequent final, a
pretty tepid affair between West Ham and Arsenal, with a heavy
heart.

'I'll tell you a funny story about the day of that final,' said Andy
Nicholls. 'A load of us hired an old furniture van and went to the
Scottish Cup final instead, at Hampden Park, and as we were
coming out of Liverpool there was a Liverpool fan hitching. We
stopped and said, "Where are you going, mate?"'

'He said, "I'm going to the Cup final."'

'We said, "So are we, mate, jump on."'

'He had a ticket but he wasn't going to the match, he was going
down to sell his ticket outside Wembley. Anyway, he couldn't see
out of the back of the van because we had mattresses in there,
barrels of ale, you name it, and when we stopped at Carlisle he
thought it must be Watford Gap. Then he realised that it wasn't.
He said, "Where's this?" We said, "It's Carlisle, mate. Didn't we

tell you? We're going to the Scottish Cup final, Celtic v Rangers."
He said, "You fucking blue bastards."'

The car park of the Cheshire Yeoman reverberated with laughter. 'It was Brian Kidd who cost us that semi by getting sent off in the first game,' said Dave Cockram.

'Yeah, I'll tell you about Brian Kidd,' said Nicholls. 'To cut a long story short . . .'

'When have you ever cut a long story short?' said Latchford, with a grin.

'Oh, here we go,' said Nicholls. 'Wait till Bob starts telling us about his penalty against Chelsea. There'll be four skeletons sat here by the time he finishes.'

His Brian Kidd story, he said, dated from the period when Kidd, who played forty times for Everton in the Gordon Lee era, was Sir Alex Ferguson's assistant at Manchester United. He and some friends boarded a plane at Manchester Airport one day, and as they made their way down the aisle, passed Ferguson and Kidd sitting in the business-class seats. It was a few days prior to a big European game involving United.

'So we go . . . "Best of luck, Alex lad," and he says, "I can't believe I'm getting good wishes off Scousers."

'We said, "Look, we're Everton. For what you've done to Liverpool, we fucking adore you."

'So he laughs and as we walk on, Brian Kidd goes, "All the best, lads."

'And we stop and say, "You, you can fuck off!"

'He looks all hurt and goes, "Why, what have I done?" And we say, "You cost us that semi-final against West Ham, you prick, by getting sent off for fighting." And to be fair to him, a bit later he sent us a drink up the plane, with a serviette saying "Sorry".'

Latchford and I chortled, although later I was faintly troubled by the ease and affection of the banter between the former England centre forward, who gave so much pleasure to so many, and the former Category-C hooligan, who gave nothing to anyone except some serious hidings. But in a way it exemplifies the remarkable solidarity that football engenders. Latchford's experiences in those stadiums all those years ago were decidedly different from Nicholls's, but they were both there, as I was, and I suppose there comes a time when that's what matters most.

Chapter Five

Bob Latchford left Everton in 1981, deciding that with Gordon Lee gone and Howard Kendall about to take the managerial reins, he needed a fresh challenge. There was a certain symmetry in him leaving as Kendall arrived, having arrived seven years earlier as Kendall left, but he later came to regret his departure, wishing he'd stayed a few more years to play some sort of part in the mid-1980s revolution that Kendall oversaw. The Gwladys Street faithful, by contrast, regretted his departure instantly.

Latchford joined Swansea, where his old Liverpool adversary John Toshack had been manager since 1978, pulling off the remarkable achievement of three successive promotions. Back to back to back, in the modern parlance. So when Latchford signed that summer, Swansea were facing their inaugural First Division campaign, and were widely tipped to return straight to the Second Division. In fact, they would confound expectations by finishing sixth in that 1981-82 season, and in their first game in top-flight football served spectacular notice of their ambitious intent, with a 5-1 win over still-mighty Leeds United. Latchford scored a second-half hat-trick. The Swansea fans had a new hero. I was heartbroken.

A strikingly similar scenario unfolded twenty-three years later, when Wayne Rooney, wearing a Manchester United shirt for the first time after leaving Everton, bagged a hat-trick against Fenerbahce. In the sports column I then wrote in the *Independent* I compared my feelings about Rooney's departure for Old Trafford with the turmoil I'd felt some fifteen years earlier, on breaking up with a long-term girlfriend.

'It was at my instigation,' I wrote. 'She wanted to get married after six years together and I didn't, a familiar enough tale of couples in their late twenties. But she then coped with the situation much better than I did. Within a month she was going out with someone else, while I moped around in a fug of self-pity. When I saw her with her new boyfriend at a pub one night, my insides did a kind of Fosbury flop, a sensation I experienced again on Tuesday night, as I watched Wayne Rooney score a remarkable Champions League hat-trick on his Manchester United debut.

'I think my fellow Evertonians will understand this broken-relationship analogy, even if nobody else does. Fans of other clubs must think, "Stop the bleating, the kid made you 27 million quid." Yet my feeling on Tuesday, truly, was exactly the same as the one I had in that pub in north London circa 1989; a cocktail of self-pity, regret and yearning.'

And I'd had it before, in 1981. True, a seasoned centre forward leaving at the age of thirty, with 236 appearances and over 100 goals behind him, wasn't quite the same as 18-year-old Rooney heading down the East Lancs Road to fulfil his colossal promise elsewhere. But it was still painful to think of Bobby Latchford walking across Swansea Bay rather than the mouth of the Mersey.

He stayed at Swansea for a second season, in which Toshack and everyone else ran out of steam and the journey back down through the divisions began. Then he joined NAC Breda, in the Netherlands. 'And after that I was with Coventry for a short while, then Newport County, then in 1986 I joined Merthyr Tydfil, who actually had a bit of money at the time, in fact we got into Europe by winning the Welsh Cup.'

That was 1987, and it was Latchford's first and only trophy. In the same season, Kendall's Everton won the championship for the second time in three years, which must have rather underlined the irony that after all those years at Goodison big Bob had to wait until he joined (no disrespect) Merthyr bloody Tydfil to win some silverware.

'Then I drifted out of the game and concentrated on a business we had, a small childrenswear business in Swansea,' he recalled.

So what had become of Bob Latchford Menswear on Piercefield Road, Formby? He laughed. 'It lasted no time at all. It was in the wrong place, and it was obvious after two or three months that it wasn't going to work, so we cut our losses. Kevin Sheedy took it over, funnily enough.'

By the mid-1990s Bob and Pat Latchford were living in Birmingham again, where he worked for Ladbrokes, in a promotional role, for a couple of years leading up to Euro 96. Then Trevor Francis, who'd been at Birmingham with Latchford as a player and was now back as manager, invited him to rejoin the club to work with the youngsters, as assistant director of the academy.

'I spent four or five years there,' he recalled, 'but during that time my wife died, of cancer.'

He said it matter-of-factly, but Pat's death must have turned his life inside out. I doubted whether he'd want to talk about it even if I asked, but in any case the Cheshire Yeoman car park was no place to go into the emotional tumult unleashed by her illness and death.

'That was in 2000,' he continued, 'and 18 months later I went on holiday to Spain for a couple of weeks, on my own. I'd done a coaching badge, I was working hard at the Birmingham academy, and I felt I needed a bit of rest and relaxation. That's where I met

Andrea, a young German lady, who was there with a girlfriend. We got together, but she was working in Salzburg, so I moved to be with her there for two or three years. Then she got pregnant and wanted to move back to Germany to be nearer her parents, so that's what we did. And now we have two young kids, and my job is looking after them. Andrea and I share the housework; share the cooking. We live a very sedate, quiet life, 40 minutes from Nuremberg, in the sticks, at the edge of nature.'

He also has two grown-up children by Pat, Richard and Isobel, and indeed is a grandfather to Marley. 'As in Bob Marley,' he said, a little apologetically. I don't suppose either of his older offspring expected their father to wind up living at the end of a dirt track near Nuremberg, but then life has a habit of nutmegging all of us. I asked whether he had become fluent in German? 'Oh, I can get by, but I can't really get to grips with it,' he told me. 'I've been seven years in Germany and I was in Austria for three years before that, but I still can't master the grammar. Most of the words I understand, but I can't convert it in my head quick enough, and by the time I've done it they've moved on . . .'

'They're on the pudding and you're still having your soup,' said Andy Nicholls with a guffaw.

'Yeah, pretty much.'

There clearly wasn't much chance of Latchford inviting me to see his home in Germany. Approachable and amiable as he was, he seemed slightly coy – or perhaps just private – about his circumstances there. But when I pressed him on whether a glittering career in the upper tiers of football in the 1970s had given him a strong financial foundation on which to build the rest of his life, he smiled – a little sadly, I thought – and shook his head.

'I wouldn't say it gave me any foundation, but between the two of us we're OK. I have my pension, and other bits and pieces. I come across here sometimes to do this sort of thing. Things could be worse, though they could be better too. Football never made me wealthy. The most I ever earned in one season, the year of the League Cup final and the semi-final with Liverpool, was just over £54,000. Which was quite a bit in those days, of course, and we lived comfortably. But it certainly didn't set me up for life like football salaries do now.'

Like just about all the men I've met who plied their trade as footballers before television rights propelled salaries into the stratosphere, Latchford was perfectly content to have played when he did. I have interviewed dozens of men who played in the 1980s and before, some of them so talented that had they been playing today, they would be in the £250,000-a-week wage bracket. But I don't think any of them would have accepted a lift in Dr Who's Tardis, and started their careers twenty, thirty, fifty years later.

In 1999 I had the huge privilege of interviewing the 'Preston Plumber', Tom Finney, whose career didn't even stretch into the £100-a-week era. Yet if he'd played fifty years later, with his astonishing talent, he might have had as many Ballons d'Or as Lionel Messi, and as much money in the bank. Financially, he was comfortable enough when he died at the grand age of 91 on Valentine's Day 2014. But at the height of his wonderful ability in 1950 he was on just £12 a week, although that was still enough to upset one of his teammates, a certain Tommy Docherty, according to an old story. I asked Finney whether that oft-told tale was apocryphal or true.

He chuckled. 'Yes, that one's quite true,' he said. 'Tommy came down from Celtic, and had a fairly good season with us. In those days we used to line up in the corridor before going in to the manager to find out our terms for the following year. I went in to see Bill Scott, the manager, and he said I'd be on the same terms as the year before, £12 a week during the season, and £10 a week in the summer, which was known as 12-and-10. Tommy went in after me, and was told he'd be on 12-and-eight.

'"I'm not signing," he said. "I've just found out that Finney's on 12-and-10." The manager couldn't believe it. "But Finney's a far better player than you," he said. "Not in the bloody summer he's not," Tommy said.'

Finney also told me that in April 1952, shortly after he had sparkled in a 1-1 draw between England and Italy in Florence, he received a message that the president of the Sicilian club Palermo wanted to see him. 'He offered me a £10,000 signing-on fee, £120 a week, a house and a car. I was on £14 a week at the time, and I must say I was very tempted. My room-mate Ivor Broadis couldn't believe his ears. I came home and told the chairman of Preston, a man called Nat Buck, who was in the building trade and had a broad Lancashire accent. He said, "I'll tell thee now, if tha doesn't play for us, tha doesn't play for anyone." And that was the end of it.'

Nobody would wish a return to the days when footballers were treated like chattels by men like Nat Buck, but the pendulum has swung so far the other way, and with such force, that it has broken clean out of its mahogany casing. And that pendulum was beginning to swing in the 1970s. The game was still run on feudal lines, despite the abolition in 1961 of the egregious maximum wage, but players were starting to flex their muscles. The serfs were stirring.

In February 1979, five years almost to the day after Birmingham City had sold Latchford to Everton in a deal worth a record £350,000, Birmingham were again the vendors in an even more historic sale, as Latchford's old striking partner Trevor Francis became Britain's first million-pound player. Nottingham Forest paid £1,180,000 for Francis, in fact, so the record had more than trebled in five years, which was quite a percentage leap even by current profligate standards. Not, of course, that Forest manager Brian Clough dealt with the razzmatazz surrounding the landmark seven-figure transaction in any way predictably.

As Francis himself remembers it, Clough arrived late at the press conference because he'd been playing squash. As others recall, he was impatient throughout because he was due to play squash. Either way, squash played a part, with the old fox doubtless trying to play down the significance of the deal, probably because he didn't want Francis to get too big for his Umbros. There was room for only one big 'ead at the City Ground.

At Birmingham, Francis had been cock of the walk. A friend of mine, John, was an apprentice there in the mid-1970s, and remembers Francis refusing to do a series of exercises the physio demanded of him, lying on a bed in the treatment room saying: 'I run this club.' Perhaps it was so. I know that at Queens Park Rangers, Stan Bowles was such a favourite of the chairman, Jim Gregory, that a word from him was sufficient to have an unpopular coach sacked. That wasn't quite player power of the kind wielded in September 2013 by a disgruntled posse at Sunderland, who rose up so effectively against Paolo di Canio that he was sacked, but it was an early manifestation of the same thing.

If I might just quote myself here, I wrote in my memoir about growing up as a sports nut, *Ali, Pelé, Lillee and Me*, that 1970s football seemed to specialise in those gifted but unpredictable mavericks such as Bowles, Frank Worthington, Rodney Marsh, Alan Hudson and Tony Currie, none of whom ever seemed to quite fulfil their scintillating potential, and all of whom were entirely lacking in deference. It was Marsh who supposedly came out with a chirpy and immortal rejoinder, when Alf Ramsey told him prior to an England game that if he didn't put in a proper shift in the first 45 minutes then he could certainly expect to be pulled off at half-time. 'That's nice,' he said. 'At Man City we just get a cup of tea and an orange.'

Everton's version of those cheeky chappies was Duncan McKenzie, who supposedly got on about as well with Gordon Lee, given that they were meant to be pushing in the same direction, as Margaret Thatcher did around the same time with Ted Heath, her predecessor as leader of the Conservative Party.

Latchford, though, thinks that the differences between Lee and McKenzie have been overstated, not least by the irrepressible McKenzie himself, in hundreds of entertaining after-dinner speeches.

'Gordon was a lovely man,' Latchford assured me. 'He had a bad public image and was unfairly labelled as dour, but that wasn't the man. He was actually very passionate about football. He lived and breathed it. It was all he could talk or even think about. I liked him a lot.'

And the feeling was plainly mutual, when in Lee's first full season of 1977-78 Latchford scored four away at QPR, followed six weeks later by a hat-trick at home in a 6-0 drubbing of Coventry City.

'I remember that game well,' Dave Prentice told me. 'The two teams were quite well matched actually; in fact I think Coventry might have been third at the time and we were fourth. And in the first half they were well in it, but then we went on the rampage, and I can still remember Gerald Sinstadt's commentary for *The Big Match* the next afternoon, when Latchford got his first – "What a goal!"

'I also remember Latchford running to the dugout when he scored his third, which he didn't normally do, but maybe it was to thank Gordon Lee for buying Dave Thomas that summer. Everton paid £200,000 for Thomas and after he came, big Bob was a man transformed. He'd been a regular scorer before, but now he had a winger feeding him. He scored so many from corners that whenever we even got a corner a chant would go up: "It's a goal, it's a goal, it's a go-go-goal!"'

By Christmas, Latchford was well on track to reach 30 goals

before the end of April, but the first ten weeks or so from the start of 1978 produced a pretty meagre return. He scored seven goals in the next seven games, however, taking him to 28. And the 28th was a penalty, his first for Everton, against Ipswich at Goodison Park in an encounter unequivocally described in the *Daily Express* as 'a clash of monumental boredom'.

That monumentally boring game still merits a small footnote in football history, as the debut of a 19-year-old Ipswich defender destined for great things, Terry Butcher. But more significant than young Butcher's debut that afternoon was not so much the win, for the league title was now out of reach, as the identity of the scorer. That goal left Latchford with only two more to get in three games. Moreover, he was now, with the blessing of Lee and his teammates, Everton's official penalty-taker.

In ordinary circumstances, he would have been one of the last choices to take penalties. Striking a dead ball was not one of his strengths, oddly enough, and outside the penalty area he didn't strike many moving balls either. Latchford was brilliant in the box, a formidably fearless header of the ball, and wonderfully adept for a big man at making a yard of space for himself. But he was no Cristiano Ronaldo. I used to watch him play for England with as much pride as if he were a close relative, but I recall him playing keepy-uppy by himself in a lull just before kick-off in a match at Wembley, and, a bit like me on the local recreation ground, he had to run around kicking the ball higher and higher to keep it airborne.

Even if he had been a Ronaldo with a dead ball, or a Leighton Baines, in those days there was almost an unwritten law that centre forwards didn't take penalties. Phil Neal, a full back, was Liverpool's penalty specialist, and for Everton newcomer Trevor Ross had taken over from his fellow midfielder Andy King. But Ross, a hard but obliging Lancastrian who'd arrived from Arsenal, was happy to hand over the spot-kick duties. The players decided before the Ipswich game that if any penalties were awarded in what remained of the season, Latchford would take them. So when Russell Osman clumsily bundled over Martin Dobson while defending a cross and a penalty was awarded, the big man stepped up.

'The Ipswich keeper was Paul Cooper, who had an incredible reputation for saving penalties, but Bob just blasted it into the roof of the net,' recalled Prentice.

In fact, Cooper got a hand to it, but was lucky it didn't break his wrist. There was never likely to be much in the way of guile about that penalty, and nor would there be the next time, in Latchford's 12-yard showdown with the ageing Bonetti. But before then there were two away games to come, at Middlesbrough and West Bromwich Albion. Evertonians prayed that Latchford would at least score once in those games, leaving him with just a single goal to get against Chelsea. But the Middlesbrough game finished goalless and at the Hawthorns Ron Atkinson's West Brom won 3-1, with Latchford's strike partner George Telfer claiming Everton's only goal.

And so to an anxiously expectant Goodison Park, where the first against Chelsea was bagged by Martin Dobson, a regular scorer from midfield, and the second by a central defender, Billy Wright, the nephew of Tommy Wright, who'd played right back in the Catterick era and indeed for England, alongside his Everton skipper Brian Labone, in the famous match against Brazil in the 1970 World Cup.

Incidentally, I wonder how many people other than Everton fans could now name Tommy Wright as England's right back that day in the Mexican city of Guadalajara? He is the forgotten member of that fine team, and yet George Best once described him as the trickiest opponent he ever faced.

While nobody was ever likely to say that about young Billy, who

had only turned twenty the day before, he was already an authorita-
tive defender who read the game well, and was good enough to win
six under-21 caps for England. He also scored ten goals for Everton
in 166 appearances, not a bad ratio for a centre half (the great Labone
only bagged two in 451, and Kevin Ratcliffe, to whom Wright would
eventually lose his place, two in 348), so it wasn't a huge surprise
when he popped up to net the second against Chelsea.

That was not so of the next scorer, however. This was Neil
Robinson, a 21-year-old novice at right back and a boyhood
Evertonian whose first and only Everton goal that was. In a way it
was his misfortune to score it at that particular stage in that particular game, yielding the peculiar spectacle of him celebrating wildly
on his own, with the crowd only moderately chuffed and his teammates beseeching the referee to give a penalty for an earlier
infringement, rather than a goal.

At 3-0, with Dobson, Wright and now, of all people, young
Robinson on the score sheet, it seemed as though the football gods
were malevolently toying with us. But if they were, they relented.
'I got on the end of a Mick Buckley cross to get our fourth, my 29th
of the season,' recalled Latchford, at the Cheshire Yeoman. 'Then
there was a corner, and I was about to get on the end of that one as
well when Lyonsy gets in front of me and heads it in. I remember
a half-roar, half-moan from the Gwladys Street, and Lyonsy being
Lyonsy, apologises to me. "Sorry Latch," he says. It was the only
time I ever heard a player apologise for scoring a goal.

'I said, "Get back and stay back", but he took no notice. A few
minutes later, in the box, big Micky Droy puts his arms round him,
and Lyonsy falls over like the proverbial sack of potatoes. Peter
Willis gives the penalty, and the Chelsea players argue the toss for
two or three minutes, which I find odd even now, considering they
were 5-0 down at the time, and there was nothing hanging on that
game except me scoring 30 goals.

'Anyway, I put the ball on the spot. Peter Bonetti was coming to the end of his career at Chelsea, but even though he'd just had five scored past him, there was no way he wanted to let in that penalty, and, of course, he was still a good keeper. I wasn't nervous at all, though. I still felt that I'd do it, just as I had when I'd woken up that morning. I hit it low, to Bonetti's right, and then, as you know ... Goodison exploded.'

Chapter Six

I knew. How I knew, for I was part of the explosion. But nobody had known eight months earlier, when a season that would end with an eruption of joy began with a whimper of disappointment, in the form of a 1-3 first-day defeat at Goodison at the hands of newly promoted Nottingham Forest.

Latchford was out, suspended after the only sending-off of his career, during a pre-season friendly against his old club Birmingham City in which he got two yellow cards. His first booking was for a thumping challenge on his brother, Dave. So much for 'friendly'.

A few years later, by the way, while at university, I would play football myself with a post-graduate from Iran called Araz Ali, whose halting English memorably led him to confuse 'friendly' with 'lovely'. 'Excuse me, Chris, is Saturday's match a lovely?', he would enquire solemnly of the university football captain, my good friend and fellow Evertonian Chris Barry. We never corrected him, just rejoiced in the mistake. Anyway, the word 'friendly' was never likely to apply to a match with highly competitive brothers on opposing sides, let alone the word 'lovely'.

Even without Latchford – and the influential Martin Dobson,

who was injured – my friends and I set off from the Ribble bus station as certain as we could be that the season would get off to a winning start. Everton had only finished ninths the season before, but Lee had since acquired an exciting England international in Dave Thomas, as well as Second Division Blackpool's big goalkeeper, George Wood, who was rumoured to have been coveted by several other top First Division clubs.

A word here about football rumours in the 1970s. With no Twitter to stoke them, no Sky Sports News, no blogs or websites, they were ignited mainly by word-of-mouth. True, there were some football writers who might drop a speculative line into print here or there, and when they did they could usually be trusted, because journalists and players in those halcyon years were often as thick as thieves.

I could offer any number of examples of how that has changed, but let me venture just one. From 1999 to 2012 I had a weekly interview slot in the sports pages of the *Independent*. I interviewed hundreds of the best-known sportsmen in the world, proper sporting giants such as Shane Warne, John McEnroe, Jonah Lomu, Sachin Tendulkar, Seve Ballesteros, Lester Piggott, Sugar Ray Leonard ... the list goes on and on. I bagged some great football names too, among them Zinedine Zidane. But Premiership footballers were so cocooned by their clubs, their agents, and their own sense of self-importance that getting any decent time with them, enough to merit a 2000-word double-page spread, was almost impossible.

Nonetheless, I managed to arrange to meet Robert Earnshaw one week, when he was playing for West Bromwich Albion. His wasn't exactly a name to compare with many of the others I was able to drop, but I thought he might have an interesting story to tell (and by the by, he remains the only footballer to score a hat-trick in the Premier League, the Championship, Divisions One and Two, the FA Cup, League Cup and at full international level, too, for Wales).

The arrangement with the club's press officer was that I would turn up at the West Brom training ground for midday, and then get some proper time with Earnshaw. But the player decided he needed some extra training that day, so it wasn't until after 1pm that I got to meet him. Of course, that was an occupational hazard. I was quite used to hanging around. But then I was told that in fact he could only spare me fifteen minutes, and that I ought to feel privileged, because the boys from the local press, who'd also been waiting for over an hour, would only be getting five minutes.

I recall reflecting how far the game had travelled, in almost exactly the wrong direction, since my predecessors in the media had hobnobbed with players day in, day out, drinking, gossiping and even travelling to games with them. Moreover, it was the local hacks to whom players were closest back in the 1970s and earlier, and rightly so. What kind of closeted world was the game inhabiting when a footballer of the calibre of Robert Earnshaw – perfectly good, but some way short of being a superstar – was offered to the media for interviews, on condition that a national newspaper journalist could speak to him for a maximum of quarter of an hour, and the local boys for no longer than five minutes?

Now that I think about it, maybe it's this distance that encourages the endless speculation these days. In the 1970s, rumour and counter-rumour about this or that player possibly moving to club A, B or C were nothing like the journalistic currency they have become. So secrets were much easier to keep, and when rumours did fly, it was usually as a consequence of your cousin's best friend's mother talking to someone in the launderette.

As I recall, we had no proof in the late summer of 1977 that Wood had been coveted elsewhere, but that was the word on the terraces, doubtless by way of a launderette, and we certainly needed a reliable new goalie. With due respect to Dai Davies and David Lawson, the main incumbents since the retirement of Gordon West in 1973, neither of them had been exactly impenetrable as a last line of defence.

In fact, as far as impenetrability went, they both had a tendency to evoke the Maginot Line *circa* June 1940. And at the worst possible times, too. Just to add insult to the grievous pain of the Clive Thomas affair a few months earlier, not only was Bryan Hamilton's perfectly legitimate winning goal disallowed in that FA Cup semi-final against Liverpool, but Terry McDermott's strike in the same game ended up not merely in the back of David Lawson's net, but as the BBC's Goal of the Season.

It was a decent enough goal, a left-footed chip from just outside the area sending John Motson in the commentary box into raptures, but it had to be said that Lawson was so far off his line that Motty, then a fresh-faced football zealot of 31, could probably have scored it himself ... from the commentary box. At the time I fancied myself as a cartoonist, and consoled myself in the ensuing days by drawing a picture of Lawson on a bike, pedalling merrily towards Ray Clemence at the other end of the pitch, while McDermott insouciantly lobbed the ball into an open goal. This George Wood fellow had to be a better bet, a worthier successor to West, and Ted Sagar, and other great reliables who had worn Everton's green jersey (with the greatest of them all, Neville Southall, yet to come).

As the bone-shaking double-decker rattled along the Formby bypass, there were plenty of other reasons for optimism, about the season in its entirety and this match in particular. This would be Gordon Lee's first full season in charge, and since replacing Billy Bingham in January he had steered us, if you counted the replays, to three League Cup finals and two FA Cup semi-finals. He might have looked like a pall-bearer but he seemed to have breathed animated life back into a sleeping giant.

It was also Duncan McKenzie's first full campaign, and we on the Gwladys Street were already in agreement that he was magic. Moreover, the opening day's opposition, McKenzie's former club Forest, had only just snuck promotion, in third place behind Wolves and Chelsea, and a single point ahead of Bolton and Blackpool. Two points (football fans had to wait four more years for the wholly sensible adoption of three points for a win) were surely already ours.

If there had been anything clouding my excitement about the forthcoming football season that week it was the mild feeling, recorded in minuscule writing in my 1978 Letts Schoolboy Diary on Tuesday, 16 August, that the football season was starting too early, and really should not be overlapping with a Test cricket series, especially one against Australia (even an Australia grievously depleted by desertions to Kerry Packer's breakaway World Series). For I was a cricket nut too, and had just spent four days in front of our spindly-legged Radio Rentals television set, gripped by the spectacle of England winning the Fourth Test at Headingley by an innings and 85 runs, and with it, for the first time in five years, the Ashes.

It continues to be a source of rather fuddy-duddy disappointment to me that my own children have not grown up, as I did, in thrall to Test match cricket on the telly. After all, had the Ashes series of 1977 come even close to the 2005 version for edge-of-the-seat tension, I would have hyperventilated with excitement.

Instead, by stark contrast, I watched Headingley's favourite son Geoffrey Boycott grind his way to 191 in more than ten hours over two days, securing his hundredth first-class hundred along the way but not even then throwing caution to the winds. As for the TV coverage, the BBC's only technical wizardry was a wonky Letraset graphic occasionally updating Boycott's glacially advancing score. That was a somewhat different proposition to Sky deploying all their bells and whistles in accompaniment to Kevin Pietersen ripping the Aussie bowling apart in 2005, and yet I could not have been more captivated.

For me, in that long summer holiday of 1977, there was no Facebook to help mornings meld into afternoons into evenings; no DVDs or Sky Plus, no texting or tweeting, no Xbox or PlayStation, no iPads or iPods, or paintballing or go-karting trips, and certainly no sleepovers. Television was all there was and only three channels of it, so on the rare occasions that the BBC1, BBC2 or ITV schedules were dominated by sport, I hardly missed a minute. Already that summer had been blessed by one of the most thrilling Open championships that anyone could remember, as Jack Nicklaus and Tom Watson waged their own private battle over the sun-baked Turnberry turf. And now an emphatic Ashes win – secured with a Test match still to play, for the first time in England since 1905 – compounded the notion that summer was for sports other than football.

But I was nothing if not fickle. By Saturday morning, I had suffocated that notion almost to death. After all, it was my first Everton game with a season ticket, a little blue booklet that fitted perfectly into the top pocket of my denim jacket. There weren't many football fans of my age who didn't own denim jackets. Not if they stood on the terraces, anyway. It was a garment that we all fancied made us look hard – although in my case it manifestly didn't – and mine bore a dozen or so cloth badges, obligingly sewn on by my mother. These proclaimed my team's greatness, Liverpool's inadequacies (which they kept irritatingly well hidden) and, of course, Bobby Latchford's messianic abilities.

But let me, by way of placing that week in the context of the times, both those times and these times, go three days further back, to 17 August 1977. My father's newspaper of choice had been the *Daily Telegraph*, for no reason other than that it had, in his opinion, the best horse racing coverage. He'd been dead for 16 months, but it would still have seemed faintly sacrilegious to cancel our 9p daily order, so the *Telegraph* continued to thump on to the doormat every morning, and on that particular morning, a Wednesday, I picked it up to read that Elvis Presley was dead.

This news had a profound effect on me, although I'm still not entirely sure why. I wasn't a huge Elvis fan, and yet he was somehow a cultural presence in my life, I suppose because like everyone else I watched the occasional TV special featuring what we now think of as late-period, fat, spangly jumpsuited Elvis. It was our occasional sightings of Elvis at that time, and the even more flamboyant Liberace, and more frequently a bejewelled Huggy Bear on *Starsky & Hutch*, that kept a strike-ridden, half-broke Britain in wide-eyed touch with American excess.

So I was shocked to find that he had dropped dead, and my gasp at the news represented a small rite of passage in that it was the first time that I had been brought up short by anything on the front page of what I still considered to be my dad's newspaper.

The usual fare of news – walkouts at British Leyland and Cammell Laird, paramilitaries murdering British soldiers in Northern Ireland, erupting volcanoes and *coups d'état* in far-off places – didn't interest me, greatly. But this seemed like proper news, however pompously it was reported by the dear old *Telegraph*, which allowed that Presley, 'the hip-gyrating singer', had 'literally hundreds of thousands of fans around the world.' Perhaps unsurprisingly, Elvis's death was relegated to third lead on the front page, behind 'Two-Strike Threat to Heathrow', and a warning from Michael Foot, the Leader of the House of Commons, that the already beleaguered Labour government might have to ban political demonstrations likely to provoke violence.

Unfortunately, my mother had left for work, so I was alone in the house with nobody to tell that Elvis had died. Standing in our little porch I read the front-page account of his death, and then a supplementary story on page 15, which began: 'Elvis Presley, who has died aged 42 and who used to perform with slicked-back black hair, sideburns and a perpetual sneer when singing songs like "You Ain't Nothing But a Hound Dog" and "Blue Suede Shoes", was the son of ardently religious parents.'

Naturally, I then practised a perpetual sneer in the hallway mirror for a few moments, before turning to the sports pages, the only reliably interesting part of any daily paper it seemed to me then. There it was reported that Ron Greenwood, 'generally regarded as British soccer's foremost thinker', was on the verge of being appointed caretaker England manager following the sudden resignation of Don Revie five weeks earlier to take up a hugely lucrative position (yielding an other-worldly £85,000 a year) managing the United Arab Emirates.

Astonishing as it seems, now that England managers are rewarded with great sackfuls of money above rather than below the counter, Revie had rather grubbily sold the story of his abrupt and hugely controversial departure to the *Daily Mail* (for a whopping £20,000), even before the FA had received his formal letter of resignation. It was true that he was merely jumping before being pushed, having failed to steer England to the 1976 European Championships, and with qualification for the 1978 World Cup very much in the balance. But he won no new friends, and lost more than a few old ones, by decamping for the UAE in the manner he did.

In 2002, the fascinating memoirs of former *Daily Mirror* editor Richard Stott shed significant new light, or at least old light, somewhat forgotten, on this episode. Revie was long dead by then – he died in 1989, and dead men can't sue – so Stott recounted in detail the discoveries he had made as an investigative reporter in 1977, an investigation which won him the Reporter of the Year gong in that year's prestigious British Press Awards and yet which did not seem to have damned Revie's name as it really should have done. Even now, the most committed football fans seem only vaguely aware that Revie was corrupt and that the main reason for his sudden resignation as England manager – at least according to Stott, who had plenty of reliable evidence – was that he thought his former protégé Gary Sprake, the Leeds United goalkeeper for most of Revie's glory years, was about to blow the whistle on him as a match-fixer.

Sprake did assure Stott that Revie had repeatedly attempted to fix results, but couldn't remember the particular games. In the event, it was Bob Stokoe – another man who looms large in the memories of all those who came of age as football fans in the 1970s – who gave Stott what he really needed to know. Stokoe, who had so unforgettably got the better of Revie when his Second Division Sunderland team beat Leeds in the 1973 FA Cup final, remembered vividly an exchange in 1962 when he was manager of humble Bury, and Revie was just starting out at Leeds, who were themselves in the Second Division and in danger of relegation to the Third.

Apparently, Revie offered Stokoe £500 if he would 'take it easy today'. When Stokoe rejected the idea out of hand, Revie asked if he could at least talk to the Bury players. For Stokoe, the 1973 FA Cup final had been his revenge, because the attempt to bribe him, even though he turned it down flat, had left him feeling sullied. 'It always riled me when I see the career Revie had,' he later said. 'At the back of my mind, the bribe is always there. He was always an evil man to me.' Evil might have been pitching it a bit strong. Nevertheless, the brief conversation clearly had a lasting effect on Stokoe. 'As he eventually told me the details in a room at Newcastle's Royal Station hotel, tears rolled down his face,' wrote Stott.

With Stokoe's testimony under his belt, the four-month investigation gathered momentum. The *Mirror* eventually identified five games that Revie tried to fix, and also found that he had bribed Alan Ball, in the early August of 1966 when Ball was a World Cupwinner but still at Blackpool, to encourage the player to whip up a contractual dispute with his club so that he, Revie, could pounce and whisk him back across the Pennines to Leeds.

Ball himself told Stott that he used to drive to Saddleworth Moor on the other side of Manchester, coincidentally made infamous just four months previously in the trial at Chester Assizes of the Moors murderers Ian Brady and Myra Hindley. There, Revie would meet him and on each occasion give him £100 in cash, to keep him in funds while he played the rebel. One can only guess what Revie's response was when he heard a week or two later that Ball had chosen Everton ahead of Leeds, which gives me my very own very tangential role in the story, because the Sykes brothers at 66 Lynton Road later started supporting Everton after John Williams at number 54 told Chris that he looked like a young Alan Ball. And, as I have already disclosed, it was because my good friends Chris and Jez were Blues that aged eight I joined the fold myself.

Ball was subsequently fined £3000 for taking those illegal payments, but did not hesitate to finger Revie, who had made him England captain in 1975 but then after six games relieved him of the captaincy without so much as a thank-you, and never picked him again. As Stott wrote, a little melodramatically: 'The Boss had forgotten the first rule of a criminal conspiracy; know those you look after, and look after those you know.'

Whatever, in 1977, the *Mirror* handed a 315-page dossier to the FA, with masses of incriminating detail of Revie's misdeeds. This was a shade ironic, as Revie was himself a great lover of the dossier: his insistence on handing to every England player a detailed written analysis of the opposition has, bizarrely, besmirched his name more than the allegations of corruption.

And strictly speaking, they do remain mere allegations, even though Stott, a highly reputable and talented journalist, felt that he had cast-iron evidence. He was disgusted with the FA for not launching its own full investigation, suspecting that 'the old men of Lancaster Gate' were alarmed by what they might find. Doubtless there were other managers prepared to pay the opposition to 'take it easy'. Other managers who, like Revie, had played themselves in the era of the maximum wage, had made little money out of the game, and were determined to milk it of what they could, while they could. So, although the FA did eventually ban Revie from English football for ten years, that wasn't for corruption, but for breach of contract. And in any case, the ban was later overturned after Revie appealed to the High Court.

Reading the sports pages of the *Daily Telegraph* on 16 August 1977, I was blithely unaware of any of this.

In other news that day, 20-year-old Nick Faldo led the £20,000 Skol Lager Individual Tournament at Gleneagles, Bishen Bedi had taken a match-winning 6 for 83 for Northants against Middlesex, and the British Lions, in the last match of their Southern Hemisphere tour, had just been defeated 25-21 by Fiji. According to the *Telegraph*'s respected rugby correspondent John Reason, the 'biggest crowd that has ever watched a game of rugby football in Fiji was augmented by hundreds more waving about perilously in the palm trees surrounding the ground and they fell out of trees like coconuts whenever Fiji scored.' Overexcited natives of the South Pacific, blithely described in the *Daily Telegraph* as falling out of trees like coconuts? It was truly another age.

The reason I can quote so precisely from that issue of the *Telegraph*, incidentally, is because I kept it, and have it still. I'm not sure why, given the constipated way Presley's death was covered for all those *Telegraph*-reading lieutenant-colonels in Tunbridge Wells, but something told me that it was worth holding on to a newspaper recording such an event. Subsequently, I have built up quite a collection of newspapers from really seismic news days – Diana's death, 9/11, Everton winning the European Cup-Winners' Cup, that sort of thing – but that was the day I started. Which might be why I remember that week so well, and the almost grudging way in which I counted down the days to the start of the new football season.

Once the season began, of course, I was entirely captive to it, all qualms buried as surely as Elvis would be, or possibly wouldn't be, if you believe that he's still alive and living in an old folks' home in Sweet Lips, Tennessee. And it began not at three o'clock that Saturday afternoon, but at the moment I left the house for the Ribble bus station, patting the pocket of my denim jacket every 30 seconds thereafter to make sure that a Liverpool-supporting genie hadn't spirited away my precious new season ticket.

Walking back up Lynton Road early that evening I checked the presence of that blessed little booklet less neurotically, perhaps only every minute or so, its preciousness microscopically eroded by the entirely unexpected home defeat. Who could have known that victory away at Goodison Park was merely the opening salvo in one of the most remarkable campaigns English football has ever seen? Brian Clough, possibly, but nobody else.

On the morning of Saturday, 20 August 1977, Nottingham Forest were 30-1 long shots to win the title, and for all the interest they attracted, they might as well have been 300-1. But as Clough later recalled it, with possibly just a dash of poetic licence, he had known earlier in the summer, on the day the league fixtures were published, that it would be Forest's championship.

This was not because Forest were playing Everton on the opening day, or facing an East Midlands derby against his former charges Derby County a week later, or visiting Highbury the week after that. Rather, it was because newly relegated Stoke City were opening their Second Division campaign at ramshackle Field Mill, insalubrious home of Mansfield Town. And Clough knew that the man he considered the best goalkeeper in Britain, the player he coveted most for his team, Stoke's Peter Shilton, would step out at Field Mill and wonder what the hell he was doing there.

Shilton was well aware of how good he was, and thoroughly disgruntled to have been overlooked by Don Revie at international level. For most of Revie's tenure he was deputy to Liverpool's Ray Clemence, and yearned to re-establish himself as first-choice England goalkeeper. Beginning a season at Field Mill would ripen him perfectly for a transfer bid. Clough didn't need to do what Revie himself had done with Alan Ball and bribe Shilton to fall out with his club. He let the fixture list and Shilton's healthy appreciation of his own prodigious talent do the job for him.

The story is related in Duncan Hamilton's wonderful book, *Provided You Don't Kiss Me – 20 Years with Brian Clough*. Hamilton covered Forest for the *Nottingham Evening Post*, bringing him into almost daily contact with Clough, who in 1987 told him: 'When I looked at that fixture list, I nearly choked myself laughing. Peter Shilton at Mansfield? Fuck me! It was like asking Richard Burton if he'd mind doing a few episodes of *Coronation Street*.'

The Stoke-Mansfield result was the first one Clough looked for after his team had despatched my team so convincingly that Saturday afternoon. And it was just what he had hoped for; Stoke had lost 2-1 in front of less than 15,000 people, the perfect recipe for dissatisfaction on Shilton's part.

Clough then set about making the offer as attractive to Stoke as it was to Shilton, offering an eye-watering £270,000. It was easily the most money Forest had ever paid for anyone. Indeed, before

Shilton, only Kenny Burns had commanded a fee in six figures – £150,000 to Birmingham City (where he had been converted from a defender into a striker following Latchford's departure three years earlier; Clough's masterstroke was to convert him back).

Clough had tried to sign Shilton twice before, once at Derby and again at Leeds. He was determined not to miss out a third time, and far from being disconcerted by the widespread abuse he got for spending so much money on a mere goalkeeper, it galvanised him. After all, this was Clough, professor of bloody-mindedness. So when a club director asked him to justify such expenditure on a bloke who might not be involved in the game for 85 minutes, his disdainful response was that he was actually getting Shilton on the cheap. He insisted to Hamilton that if Trevor Francis was worth a million, then so was Shilton.

Clough and his influential right-hand man Peter Taylor, a former goalkeeper himself, both felt that Forest's best chance of winning the title rested not in how many goals they scored, but how few they conceded. 'We preached clean sheets morning, noon and night,' Clough told Hamilton. 'We preached them until our throats were dry.'

Before Shilton's arrival at the City Ground after five games of the season, his predecessor John Middleton had let in six goals, the first of them at Goodison to Latchford's understudy Jim Pearson. But Forest had still won four of those five games, and with the formidable Shilton between the sticks it took another 14 to concede the next six goals. By the time Shilton kept one of Clough's beloved clean sheets at Coventry to secure the title – a game in which he characteristically played a blinder, and made one especially miraculous save from Mick Ferguson – he had let in fewer than one goal every two games. Forest finished the season with a smaller number in the goals-against column – 24 – than any title-winning team before them. We'll gloss over the fact that the very next season, with Shilton's rival Clemence in goal, Liverpool reduced even that low number by a third, to a jaw-dropping 16.

I don't know whether Shilton read Hamilton's book, but if he did it must have been nice to be reminded of Clough's enormous regard for him, such regard that the incorrigible old egotist deemed him even more influential than himself and Taylor in pursuit of the title. 'He made the fewest mistakes of anyone, including the management,' said Clough.

I never met Brian Clough myself, alas, but in 2004 I did interview Shilton, whose memories of the great man were predictably colourful yet tainted by Clough's strenuous efforts to keep his best players feeling humble.

This he sometimes did by bluntly humiliating them. For example, before the 1980 European Cup final against Hamburg, which took place at Real Madrid's Bernabéu stadium, the team stayed in an out-of-town hotel, which to Shilton's consternation lacked anywhere grassy for him to get some shot-stopping practice. When he raised this with Clough, the manager told him that he knew of an ideal stretch of grass, then left it to Taylor to take Shilton to a large traffic island, where his preparation for the biggest match in European club football was accompanied by a cacophony of passing cars tooting their horns, with two tracksuit tops serving as goalposts.

Clough's determination not to pamper his players went way too far, Shilton told me, recalling that he was once ordered to attend a press conference, but when he got there found that he was not fielding questions from journalists as he had been led to expect, but serving them with drinks. 'Come on, get on with it, Peter,' Clough shouted, noting his reluctance. 'You're not too big to serve drinks at this club.'

Even in 2004 Shilton still winced at the memory. 'I knew he had some totally bizarre methods of making us know that he was in charge, but I didn't like the way that was done,' he told me, shaking his head. I understood, though it was presumably a price worth paying by a man who had begun that championship season at Field Mill, Mansfield, letting in two goals for Stoke, while 120 miles away, in what must have seemed an irrelevance to him, Peter Withe, John Robertson and Martin O'Neill were all scoring past Everton's new goalkeeper, George Wood.

It was not a promising start to Wood's love affair with the Gwladys Street End, and yet a love affair is what it became. 'We all agree, Shilton is better than Clemence,' went the cry, at least once every home game. And then the rousing, heartfelt follow-up, 'We all agree, Georgie is better than Shilton.'

Chapter Seven

He wasn't, of course. Nobody was. Shilton was peerless, and the move to Nottingham Forest reignited an England career that endured, on and off, from a victory over East Germany in November 1970 to a defeat by Italy in the third-place play-off in the 1990 World Cup.

When the Polish goalkeeper Jan Tomaszewski, famously dismissed by Brian Clough as a clown, denied England the victory they so desperately needed in a World Cup qualifier in 1973, Shilton was at the other end. When Andreas Brehme scored the opening goal in the 1990 World Cup semi-final, it was Shilton's head over which the ball was so jammily deflected. Even in Britain there is a tendency to think of Italy's Dino Zoff and West Germany's Sepp Maier as the two longest-lasting goalkeepers in post-war international football, yet Shilton made them both look like dilettantes.

But he didn't play once for England under Revie. Coincidentally, his first international appearance for four years was in the 3-1 victory over Wales, on 13 May 1978 in Cardiff, in which Bob Latchford scored his first England goal. For a while after that, the England manager Ron Greenwood chose to rotate Shilton with

Clemence, not the greatest idea ever put into practice by British soccer's foremost thinker.

Wood might not have been a goalkeeper of Shilton's stature, but I'm quite sure that Shilton never had the kind of relationship with the City Ground faithful that Wood enjoyed with the Street End masses at Goodison, as he became a crowd favourite almost on a par with Latchford and Duncan McKenzie. In quiet periods during games, of which there seemed to be many more in the 1970s than there are now, not least because defenders could kill large chunks of time passing back to the goalkeeper, Fozzie Bear used to lead us in a chant of 'Georgie, put the kettle on'. And in response, the ever-obliging Wood would mime putting a kettle on. I laughed along with everyone else, but really I wanted to hug myself with delight.

It would be too fancifully Freudian to suggest that following my father's death this 25-year-old flaxen-haired Scot was in any way fulfilling a need for an older man in my life, because it wasn't as if we had an actual relationship, but it sort of felt like one. I asked him to put a kettle on, and he did so. What was that if not a rapport? The fact that there were several thousand others involved in the exchange seemed neither here nor there.

And around the beginning of March 1978, much to my astonishment, the relationship did become personal. I told the story in my book *Ali, Pelé, Lillee and Me*, but it belongs here too. At school in Southport one morning, another boy, Mark Salthouse, sought me out. He knew that I was an Everton devotee, as most of my schoolmates did, and he had something properly weird to tell me, namely that George Wood appeared to be outside mowing the school lawn.

I reacted with predictable derision, to which Salthouse said that if it wasn't George Wood, it could only be his identical twin brother. So I went to look for myself, and sure enough the man pushing a lawnmower up and down outside the maths block was, unmistakably, Scotland's, Scotland's, number one! Scotland's! Number one! It was as if my year's biggest Queen fan had been shown Freddie Mercury repairing the cricket pavilion roof, a spectacle no less incongruous and unexpected than that.

Word quickly spread, somehow even infiltrating classrooms where teachers were attempting, with rapidly diminishing success, to interest boys in coefficients and gerunds. Then, in front of about fifty boys watching out of various classroom windows, self-conscious and a little nervous but propelled by overpowering curiosity, I made a beeline for the school's improbable new garden maintenance man, introduced myself as a diehard Evertonian, and asked what the hell he was doing there. He told me that he was a neighbour and friend of a man called Tom Pope, who had the contract to look after the school grounds.

'It's my day off, so I thought I'd come to help Tom,' he said.

We had a chat about Everton's patchy form, which had included League Cup and FA Cup defeats at Leeds and Middlesbrough but solid league wins at home to Leicester and West Ham, and then I popped the question. 'We always play football at dinnertimes. I don't suppose you'd like to join us, would you?'

He smiled and said Gordon Lee wouldn't want him to, in case he picked up an injury. 'But I'll come and watch, if that's OK?'

It was a great deal more than OK. It was as if Debbie Harry and the blonde one from Abba had invited me to make up a threesome. And he was as good as his word.

Fortuitously, I was usually stuck in goal in those dinnertime games of football, happy to leave the outfield action to boys with smaller girths. At university a few years later, having shed most of my teenage blubber, I reinvented myself as a right back, less Tommy Wright than Tommy Cooper and less overlapping than overfed, but just about capable of holding down a place in the St Andrews second XI.

But at school, goalkeeping was my thing, and I wasn't bad, as long as I was never required to dive to my right. For some strange reason I could move with something approaching athleticism to my left, but only to my left, so if ever a penalty was awarded – by lively schoolboy consensus rather than a referee – I would have to stand practically on the right-hand post, which usually took the form of three blazers and a jumper.

Removing a blazer and sometimes a jumper was the nearest we ever got to donning an actual football kit. Other than that, none of us ever changed out of our school uniform, nor even changed our shoes, which in those days of platform heels was practically asking for sprained and splintered ankles.

However, I don't recall any injuries, ever. And one of the best dinnertime players was a lad called Tony Rodwell, who wore the highest platforms and the flappiest parallel trousers, yet never seemed remotely encumbered by dubious 1970s fashion choices as he bore down on goal. It came as no great surprise when he later turned pro, playing more than 100 times on the wing for Blackpool, although it would be his kinsman Jack Rodwell who really put the family name in lights, following Wayne Rooney's example, after being weaned and nurtured by Everton, by setting off down the East Lancs Road to embrace the riches of Manchester.

Of course, in Georgie Wood's day, and for some years thereafter, Manchester was a rather less beguiling place than Merseyside as somewhere for a footballer to ply his trade. Which might have had more to do with Liverpool's maddening pre-eminence than anything happening at Everton, but financially my club was at least as strong as United and City were, and no less glamorous.

Wood, tall, blond and handsome, fitted right in. And it was hugely heartening to find that the man who obliged the Street End with his kettle mimes was just as obliging in person. At dinnertime (in the north, in the 1970s, it was always dinnertime, never lunchtime, which would have sounded suspiciously effete) he ambled over to our makeshift pitch on the school playing fields, and stood directly behind me, actually applauding when I parried a shot, mercifully aimed to my left, on to the pile of blazers serving as a post. For the rest of his Everton career, which lasted until he rather heartbreakingly signed for Arsenal in August 1980, nobody on the terraces chanted his name more loudly than I did.

'I never really had the same feel for Arsenal,' said George Wood, as obliging as ever if with significantly less hair, thirty-five years almost to the day after he watched me keep goal. My heart sang.

The media liaison man at Crystal Palace had put me in touch with him, after I learnt that Wood was now a goalkeeping coach at Selhurst Park. So looking for that particular Toffee proved entirely straightforward. Moreover, it turned out that he was aware of me, having come across some extracts from *Ali, Pelé, Lillee and Me* on the internet one day, in which I mentioned him and his grounds maintenance work that long-ago day at King George V Grammar School for Boys. 'Aye, how're you doing,' he said, when I phoned him, in March 2013. 'It's good to hear from you.'

His Scottish accent was undiminished even though he had lived south of the border ever since leaving for Blackpool in 1971. We arranged that I would interview him at his house just outside Pontypridd, and that he would pick me up at Cardiff railway station, across the road from the Millennium Stadium.

I arrived at the station at just after 6pm, on a day of unlikely events. Not as unlikely as seeing Everton's goalkeeper pushing a lawnmower across our school lawns in 1978, because nothing ever would be, but unlikely nevertheless.

I had started the day at a pub in Cumbria, whence the *Sunday Telegraph* had despatched me to follow Prince Charles around a

320-acre hill farm. They wanted me to write a story about the crisis bedevilling farmers, and how Charles had set up the Prince's Countryside Fund in an effort to help, so for most of the morning I trudged up hill and down dale in his shivering entourage as HRH met young farm workers who'd been beneficiaries of the fund. Even in the merciless grip of a raw easterly wind whipping in off the fells, it was an interesting assignment. But a prince of the realm was no match for a lord of the six-yard box, and a childhood hero. Really, I just wanted to get to Oxenholme station and start the long journey down to Cardiff.

I hadn't set eyes on George Wood for more than thirty years, but as I walked on to the concourse there was no mistaking him. For one thing, he had come straight to Cardiff from the Palace training ground, and was still in his tracksuit. And despite having put on a fair bit of weight in thirty years, and lost all that golden hair, he was still entirely recognisable. I even recognised the stance – legs apart and arms dangling, as if waiting for an opposing striker to put a ball on the penalty spot.

We shook hands warmly, and on the twenty-minute drive back to his house, I told him about my morning in Cumbria. It struck a chord, he said, as his father had been a farm worker, his mum had 'worked with the cows', and he'd grown up in a tied cottage on an estate belonging to the 14th Earl of Home, at least until Lord Home renounced his title and became plain, or plain-ish, Sir Alec Douglas-Home.

As a teenage Everton supporter, all I'd known of George Wood's background was that he was born in a place called Douglas, and had played 22 times for East Stirlingshire before joining Blackpool, information I got from the wholly indispensable *Rothmans Football Yearbook*. The same invaluable source also told me that he was 6ft 3ins and weighed 14st. I invited him to fill in the remaining gaps in my knowledge.

'As a kid I used to go around with the estate gamekeeper, on a place called Culter Fell. The Clyde starts on one side and the Tweed is on the other side, so I knew how to fish from a very young age. But my dad couldn't afford fly-fishing stuff, so we went guddling. Youse all call it tickling trout. My older brother would hold my legs and I'd go over the bank, and we'd sell anything we'd caught to the fishermen who hadn't caught anything. We'd sell trout to the lady in the post office too. Some days we'd make quite a few shillings. I was born in 1952, so that would be in the late 1950s.'

By now we had arrived at Wood's house on a nondescript executive housing estate full of the kind of homes that appear to have Ford Mondeos in their drives as part of the planning regulations, but in more ways than one a long, long way from a tied farm cottage in South Lanarkshire. A lifetime in football had not yielded riches, or anything like riches, but he was much more comfortably off than his parents had ever been. He greeted his wife, Gail, put on a pair of slippers bearing the Glasgow Rangers crest – for which he very sweetly and quite unnecessarily apologised to me – then sank back into a capacious, gold-patterned black sofa.

'My dad was football mad,' he said. 'He was a big Motherwell supporter, and I can remember the first game I went to, against Aberdeen. That was 1957, and Motherwell won 4-1, under floodlights. I was hooked on football from then on, but Rangers was my team, not Motherwell. My dad wouldn't let me go to Ibrox, so I'd get on the Motherwell supporters' bus, then jump off and get the train into Glasgow to watch Rangers.

'I loved playing too, like. The nearest village had a church, a school and a little football pitch, and in the summer we'd play until eleven o'clock at night, then walk the two or three miles back home. I never really had any toys as a kid, but I always had balls, and I'd always kid on that I was playing for Scotland, not as a goalkeeper but as a striker. My big hero was Denis Law. I idolised Denis Law. And I was lucky enough to play against him at the end of his career.

'My first goalkeeping hero, believe it or not, was Gordon Banks. I used to save up and do the Wembley pilgrimage [for the England v Scotland Home International] every two years, and that was the only time I saw him play live. My goalkeeping philosophy now all relates back to Banks. You don't have to dive all over the place if you read the game, understand the game. If Banks had to dive, you knew it was a world-class save because he read the game so well. And he had great calmness under pressure, and great distribution too, for those days. It wasn't easy with those balls, on those pitches.'

Wood failed his 11-plus dismally, but still went to Lanark Grammar School, on account of being good at sport, not because he had any academic prowess. 'I was dyslexic,' he said, tripping over the word itself and pronouncing it 'dyxlectic', 'so they all thought I was thick. I spent half my schooldays putting out the chairs for assembly, and then putting them back afterwards. That was all they thought I was good for, and actually I was happy with that. I was good at history, because like lots of dyslexics [dyxlectics] I had a good memory, but I couldn't spell. So when I had some success and people started asking for autographs it was quite embarrassing. I'd ask for their names and then couldn't spell them. That was how I learnt to spell, from memory. And that's why Gail calls me a football anorak, because I remember games and goals from years ago.'

Wood wasn't a bad striker as a schoolboy footballer, but he was a better goalkeeper. At fifteen, he played for Motherwell reserves. 'But then I broke my arm, and they didn't look after me. My dad was really unhappy about that, because it was his team, his club. Then East Stirlingshire came in for me. They were the worst team in Scotland then, and they still are. They gave me a trial, and put me in against Raith Rovers on my sixteenth birthday, playing me as A. N. Other because I wasn't registered. But I played well, in a 1-1 draw in Kirkcaldy. They signed me straight after the game, and I played the whole of that year. I did well, too. There was interest from West Brom I remember, but then Blackpool, who had just been relegated, came in with a £15,000 offer, so I went there.'

Occasionally at Blackpool, Wood got a chance to release his inner Denis Law. He once played centre forward for the reserves at Burnley and scored twice. But his real baptism of fire came in goal, also for the reserves, in the Lancashire Senior Cup at Oldham.

'I came out and caught a cross, and somehow landed on all fours. Oldham's centre forward was Andy Lochhead, a real animal, and he's on all fours too. And he looks at me and then gives me a Sauchiehall kiss. My nose exploded. "Welcome to the game, son," he said. In the second half I took my chance and punched him. "Learn fast, don't I," I said. He just laughed.'

I love that story, and what I love about it most is the lack of any reference to officialdom. There was a referee, of course, but the fact that a violent head butt could be avenged with a punch, without any red or even yellow cards being dished out, bespeaks an entirely different era of football. Not that I'm advocating a return to such lawless behaviour, but at least it was a time when no player would have dared to feign life-threatening pain after a gentle nudge from behind. Didier Drogba, for instance, would have been a fine player in any era, but it would have been more rewarding to see him at a time when he didn't feel the need to writhe around at least once every game as if he'd been bitten by a rabid dog.

In 2008 I aroused the abusive ire of Chelsea fans when, in my newspaper column, I took Drogba to task for the way he tumbled to the turf in the Carling Cup final, seemingly in mortal pain, only to jump up following the award of a free-kick, which he promptly took and scored. Just the day before, the Arsenal player Eduardo da Silva had suffered a badly broken leg in a dreadful tackle by Birmingham City's Martin Taylor and had been carried off with an oxygen mask clamped over his face. That, to my mind, made Drogba's theatrics even more worthy than usual of excoriation. As so often, he went down with his back dramatically arched, like an Apache brave copping a cavalry bullet in a 1950s B-Western, as if being a target man meant literally that, a human target.

So it is interesting to play the time-travel game and wonder how Drogba might have got on thirty years earlier, and similarly inter-esting to imagine how Andrew Lorimar Lochhead might have fared thirty years later. I don't recall ever watching him play myself – his heyday had been for Burnley in the 1960s – but over the years I have interviewed lots of footballers who played in those unreconstructed times, and more than a few of them, when asked who had been their hardest opponent, cited Lochhead. There is no better example of how uncompromisingly brutal football could be in those days. Even towards the end of his career he put the willies up Mark Lawrenson. Yet looking him up on the internet now, he looks like a pleasant, amiable old cove, and I'm sure he is. He is also – God bless Wikipedia – a member of the Dave Clark Five fan club.

If there had been a George Wood fan club in 1978, I would defi-nitely have been its secretary. Yet, as we sat in his front room, two middle-aged blokes sipping coffee and chewing the fat, I had to keep reminding myself that he'd been one of my teenage heroes, on a par with Robert Redford as the Sundance Kid. And when I got back from my strange circuitous journey to see both Prince Charles and George Wood in one day I tried to convey to my two sons, both raised in the Everton faith even though neither of them had ever lived anywhere near Goodison Park, just how impossible it would have been to predict such a situation when I was their age.

'Imagine if thirty-five years from now Tim Howard, or Phil Jagielka, or Leon Osman picks you up from the station and takes you to his house, and his wife makes you a coffee, and you sit there chatting for a couple of hours,' I said. They agreed that it would feel pretty odd. But really it was an inadequate parallel. Those guys didn't loom nearly as large in their lives, and on their bedroom walls, as Georgie Wood had in mine.

Chapter Eight

George Wood nearly played no part at all in my teenage life. In 1976 he met the Manchester United manager Tommy Docherty – by then on the other side of the fence, after his grumpy negotiations as a Preston North End player all those years before – and agreed terms. A fee was settled on, £100,000, and Blackpool said that they would let him go as soon as they could sign a replacement, with David Stewart from Leeds their preferred option. But they couldn't get Stewart and Wood stayed put until the following summer, when he was selected to play in a Bobby Charlton invitation XI touring Australia and Hong Kong.

'I went as back-up to Alex Stepney but I ended up playing all the games,' he told me. He assumed that, under the watchful eye of Charlton, whose foray into management at Preston had been short and not particularly sweet, his performances on that tour increased the likelihood of him heading for Old Trafford.

'Then I came back and started pre-season training, and two days before the season began, Allan Brown, the Blackpool manager [who had previously managed Nottingham Forest, before making way for Clough], phoned me and told me to get myself to the ground. He said, "A club's come in for you". I thought it had to be United.

But when I got to the boardroom at Bloomfield Road, it was Gordon Lee who was there. I knew about Everton, knew what a great club they were, knew of some of the Scottish players who'd been there, like Alex Young and Sandy Brown. So I thought, "That'll do me". But when he talked to me about terms, £150 a week, I said, "No disrespect Mr Lee, but that's what I'm on at Blackpool."

'It was, too. I'd been on £80 a week at Blackpool until the week before, when they suddenly upped it to £150. The reason for that was simple: the more I was on, the more they could get for me. Anyway, Everton paid £150,000, although they stuck to a salary of £150 a week. Later I found what everyone else was on and it was a lot more in some cases, but I didn't mind. I just wanted to play for a big club, and in those days there were only a handful of them, like there are now, but it was a different handful: United, Everton, Liverpool, Arsenal, Spurs.'

Like my friends and me rattling to the ground on the 28 bus, Wood approached the first game of the 1977-78 season, his Everton debut, with confidence. Promoted Nottingham Forest surely wouldn't be too hard to beat. And yet for Everton that day, as for most other teams that season, they proved a nearly impossible nut to crack – macadamias with only your teeth to get through the shell.

Moreover, Wood conceded three goals. The second poked in by John Robertson after Wood had spilled a Tony Woodcock cross, and the third put through the keeper's legs by the irrepressible Martin O'Neill from just a yard or two out. Even I knew, from my stints between the blazers on the school fields, that there was no worse way for a goalie to be beaten. It was an inauspicious debut.

'That hurt, that did,' he told me, looking genuinely pained even after so many years. 'Forest had just pipped Blackpool to promotion, so I was really hoping we'd beat them. And then they went and pipped Everton to the league.'

Actually, it was more than a pipping. There was a nine-point difference with Liverpool in between, but I didn't want to split hairs. I nodded in sympathy. 'And then we went to Highbury on the Tuesday night and lost 1-0,' he continued. 'Trevor Ross, who joined Everton later that season, scored a scuffy one for Arsenal. But apart from that I had one of those games that keepers love. I saved everything else, and won back a bit of faith from the fans after the 3-1.'

That might have been so, but losing the first games of the season wasn't exactly the bright new dawn that we'd hoped for in Gordon Lee's first full season in charge. It was more of a familiar, murky dawn, and the 1-0 defeat at Highbury left Everton in 21st place in the First Division, in the bottom three with Chelsea and Birmingham City, yet those two teams had the advantage of having played one game rather than two. Meanwhile, another win, against Bristol City, had sent Forest top. Liverpool, with a win and a draw, were third.

Everton surely couldn't stay in the basement of the division, and nor did we. Wood remembered the spectacular subsequent run of form as vividly as I did. 'We went to Villa on the Saturday and beat them 2-1,' he said, 'and after those two defeats we went 22 games unbeaten, until Boxing Day.'

Ah yes, Boxing Day. There is in the formative life of every football fan, whether you support Barnsley or Barcelona, a beating so unexpected and so merciless that your entire world feels torn apart, all its certainties cruelly ripped into shreds. The feeling of disorientation can take weeks, months or sometimes years to subside. Even if your team wins the next game and the next one and the one after that, the shock is not exorcised.

I felt something of that shock on Boxing Day 2013 when Roberto Martinez's Everton, protecting a year-long unbeaten home record in the league, went and surrendered it to the bottom club,

Sunderland. But that was nothing compared with that Boxing Day afternoon exactly thirty-six years earlier: Everton v Manchester United. The only merciful dimension to a 6-2 thrashing at Goodison Park that day was that it fell in the middle of the Christmas holidays, so we didn't have to face the United fans at school, of whom even in those Arthur Albiston years, there were a goodly number.

Again for the benefit of younger readers, it's worth re-emphasising that United were nothing like the force at the start of the 1977-78 season either that they had been in the Busby era, or would later be under Alex Ferguson. True, they'd reached the FA Cup final two years in succession, and yet there had been an abrupt and unhelpful change of manager. The colourful Tommy Docherty, who master-minded the famous Cup final victory over Liverpool that May, and had also signed a new four-year contract worth a mighty £25,000 per annum, was sensationally sacked less than two months later.

It was sex that did for him, specifically, revelations of an affair with Mary Brown, the 31-year-old wife of the club's physiothera-pist, Laurie Brown. When Docherty, who was then almost fifty, announced that he was leaving Agnes, his wife of twenty-seven years, and moving in with young Mrs Brown, the United directors decided that his position at the club was, in that perennially dreaded phrase, 'no longer tenable'.

Fortunately, Docherty wasn't jobless for long. He was snapped up by Derby County, who had never adequately replaced Brian Clough, and whose directors saw in the Doc another charismatic schemer who might revive their flagging fortunes.

Why 'fortunately'? Well, for the fun it afforded us on the terraces, of course. I have already asserted in this book that for all the head-cracking that went on at football matches in those days, the chants directed at opposition players and managers were never as obscenely personal as they sometimes are now. But that doesn't mean that we were going to let a good old-fashioned extramarital affair pass us by. When Derby came to Goodison on the morning of 1 April 1978, the Gwladys Street rocked to the taunt, to the tune of 'Knees Up Mother Brown': 'Who's up Mary Brown/Who's up Mary Brown/Tommy Tommy Docherty/Tommy Tommy Docherty . . .' It was followed by huge communal laughter. For poor Agnes, we gave no thought at all.

At United, Docherty's successor was the less exciting but much steadier and more reliably uxorious Dave Sexton. His tenure had started promisingly. On the opening day of the season, as Everton were losing at home to Nottingham Forest, United were winning away at Birmingham City, 4-1. Another good win followed, at home to Coventry, and then, following a goalless draw with Bobby Robson's Ipswich, Sexton had the satisfaction of taking United to the Baseball Ground and beating the Doc's new charges, 1-0.

I expect that the cuckolded Laurie Brown, who had already taken out his anger more directly, by socking the Doc in the eye, enjoyed that one. But to United's fans, beating Derby was much less important than winning the derby. And they didn't. A disastrous run ensued, which began with defeat at Manchester City and, a week before Christmas, reached a nadir with a 4-0 walloping, at Old Trafford, by Brian Clough's irrepressible Forest.

For Clough and his sidekick Peter Taylor, it was a seismic victory. Just a week before that, Clough had been passed over for the permanent job as England manager. Instead, Ron Greenwood was confirmed in the post he had occupied as caretaker since August. Yet Clough had given the best interview of the five candidates, and for further details of that episode, see Chapter Eighteen. For now, we can only imagine how much satisfaction it gave him to mastermind the destruction of United.

Old Trafford back then might have been rather less than a fortress, but even so, visiting teams didn't usually come and stick four past United. Yet Forest did so with ominous ease. And the third of their four goals that afternoon showcased their extraordinary speed and ruthlessness on the counter-attack. Following a blocked Jimmy Greenhoff free-kick, a defensive header was picked up by Archie Gemmill, who burst forward, rode Jimmy Nicholl's attempted tackle as though he were a primary school kid, and then, insouciantly, with the outside of his left foot, released John Robertson, who practically waltzed the ball past the hapless Paddy Roche. Alex Stepney, still United's first-choice goalkeeper, must have sat on the sidelines that day offering a silent prayer of thanks for the injury that had kept him out. In *The Times*, Tom German wrote that United's central defenders finished the game 'as bemused as the man in the middle in some particularly impish game of blind man's buff'.

Nobody tormented them more than John Robertson. There are plenty of 1970s footballers in this book who illuminate the differences between then and now, the fearsome Andy Lochhead – nutting opposition centre halves and goalkeepers – was just one of them. But no example is more striking than that of Robertson, the right-footed left winger from the football breeding fields of South Lanarkshire, which had also produced Georgie Wood. Even in 1977, Robertson didn't fit the template of how a top footballer should look and behave. If the modern-day British player with his six-pack and his diamond earring is an Aston Martin Vanquish, and his lavishly sideburned 1970s counterpart a Ford Capri, then Robertson, even back then, was a Hillman Minx. An anachronism. A throwback.

He didn't look like a footballer even as he shuffled on to the field of play, let alone as he shuffled around off it. As Clough, never one to mince his words, later recalled, 'John Robertson was a very unattractive young man. If one day I felt a bit off colour, I would sit next to him. I was bloody Errol Flynn in comparison. But give him a ball and a yard of grass, and he was an artist, the Picasso of our game.'

Duncan Hamilton, in *Provided You Don't Kiss Me*, was marginally more polite. 'Robertson,' he wrote, 'didn't look like an athlete. He had a slight pot belly ... his skin was the colour of alabaster.' He lacked pace, too. And yet, recalled Hamilton, to watch Robertson 'was a privilege. He would cling to the touchline, his shoulders hunched like a man huddling in a doorway against the rain. But as soon as the ball was fed to him, he set off with it welded to his left foot. He somehow managed to drag the ball back and then around defenders, a trick he performed with such mesmeric skill that it seemed as if everything else around him – the crowd and the players – had been momentarily frozen, and only he and the ball were moving in exaggerated slow motion.'

As Hamilton also put it in his book, 'Whipping United 4-0 was a declaration of intent so exquisite, so emblematic of the side's graceful and imaginative form, that those who still harboured doubts about Forest had to put them aside.' Clough never forgot that game. 'We showed all the clever clogs in the media that we were good enough to win the title,' he said. 'I enjoyed that.'

The clever clogs in the media certainly realised what they'd seen. 'Observers with long memories of Old Trafford football would say they were the best side seen on the ground for many a long year,' wrote Paul Fitzpatrick in the *Guardian*. 'They will not be surprised if Forest win the championship, rather if they don't.'

As for United, it was on the back of that almighty thrashing in front of the Stretford End that they arrived at Goodison Park on Boxing Day, already 12 points behind second-placed Everton in the First Division table. Everton hadn't lost since the second game of the season. They had already, in 24 league and cup matches, scored 51 goals, including 16 in just three games – away at Leicester and QPR, and at home to Coventry. Forest were similarly rampant, but

Everton had title-winning pedigree. They might have laboured in Liverpool's shadow for much of the 1970s, but it was still only seven years since they'd won the title, beating every other team at least once during the glorious course of that 1969-70 season.

Was Gordon Lee in the process of recapturing the glories of the Harry Catterick years? That undertaker's countenance didn't give him the look of a man capable of spreading joy, but then Catterick hadn't looked like one, either. I'd spotted him a few times walking his dog in Ainsdale, where a friend of mine lived. He looked like the grumpy retired manager of a small branch of the Midland Bank, not of one of England's greatest football clubs.

So looks were certainly no impediment to an Everton manager's bid for glory, and it didn't look as if United were going to be much of an impediment either. Lee and his team were on a roll. And as Rafe, Briggy, Mugsy, Mozzer, Bean and I took our usual places on the terracing, Fozzie Bear started up a rousing seasonal chant to the tune of 'Silent Night'. 'Go-or-don Lee, Go-or-don Lee, Goooordon Lee, Goooordon Lee, Gordon, Go-or-don, Go-or-don Lee, Gordon, Go-or-don Go-or-don Lee, Gooordon, Goooordon Leee-ee, Go-or-don Go-or-don Lee.'

Even more than most of our chants, these lyrics did not exactly ring with originality and wit, and yet there was something stirring, even moving, about tens of thousands of people belting out a Christmas carol, albeit with the words so imaginatively amended, and albeit with the object of our always-fickle adoration taking his place in the dugout with his trademark lugubriousness.

I loved those matches just before and after Christmas, not least because the attendances were so reliably huge and the atmosphere so vibrant. In the four league games Everton played between 26 December and 2 January that season, two of which were at home and two away, the smallest crowd was 44,030, at the City Ground, Nottingham.

But it is the other statistic in that sentence, the number of games, that is even more arresting now. Four league games in a week? Faced with such a schedule, modern-day footballers would be appealing to Amnesty International on the grounds of cruelty and torture. Yet Everton played Manchester United on Boxing Day, Leeds United a day later, Arsenal at home on New Year's Eve and Forest on 2 January. And consider the Easter schedule three months later: Newcastle away on Good Friday, Leeds at home on Easter Saturday, then Manchester United away on Easter Monday. Three games in four days. When managers today complain about crowded fixture lists, as some of them so vehemently do, someone should remind them that their predecessors had to cope with much worse. And at a time when treatment for everything from a sprained ankle to a broken neck seemed to be a couple of dabs with a wet sponge.

One of the few mercies, for managers and players in 1977, was that there were no longer fixtures on Christmas Day itself. There hadn't been a top-division Christmas Day game in England since Blackburn beat Blackpool 1-0 in 1959 (another fine trivia question), two years before I was born. Mind you, in Scotland, it was only twelve months since the tradition had expired. As it turned out, atrocious weather decimated the programme, but Saturday, 25 December 1976, remains the last time that top-tier British football matches were scheduled for Christmas Day.

As for Boxing Day football, the only drawback for me was that it meant missing the old films on telly that were a festive tradition as enshrined in my family as mince pies. It was *Jailhouse Rock* starring the late, lamented Elvis Presley, that I'd forsaken by setting off for Goodison Park that Monday morning – the Boxing Day bus service to Liverpool being even slower than usual – and then, even worse, *The Guns of Navarone*. It didn't matter that I'd seen *The Guns of Navarone* at least five times already over previous yuletides. The

big TV films on Christmas Day itself had been decidedly feeble –
National bloody *Velvet* and *The Wizard of* blinking *Oz*, both of which
I felt I'd long outgrown – and so I yearned for some spectacular
shooting, featuring Gregory Peck and David Niven. Just not as
much as I yearned for some spectacular shooting, featuring Bob
Latchford and Martin Dobson.

Dobson and Latchford did both score, as it turned out, and big
Bob's 18th goal in 21 games kept the *Daily Express* prize in everyone's minds. But that was scant consolation in a 6-2 mauling. By
half-time, with Everton 2-0 down, Gordon Lee was no longer getting the 'Silent Night' treatment from the Gwladys Street, just the
silent treatment. But as the game wore on, with Lou Macari scoring twice, and Steve Coppell, Jimmy Greenhoff, Gordon Hill and
Sammy McIlroy also finding the back of Wood's net, a more vocal
disgruntlement set in.

Charlie Chaplin had died the day before and was cited in some
characteristic gallows humour from a shrivelled Scouser in a quilted
blue anorak who stood just in front of me for three years, without
my ever knowing his name or either of us ever even saying hello.
And certainly without ever not wearing that anorak, which clung to
him come rain, hail or shine like a second skin. 'If they want a fucking clown in goal they should fucking dig up Charlie fucking
Chaplin and put him in fucking goal,' he ventured splenetically, to
nobody in particular. I winced, but I understood.

In *30*, Latchford's book about his '*Daily Express*' season, which
he wrote in 2006 with the journalist Martin O'Boyle, the recollection of that game seemed still to cause him pain. 'We got absolutely
turned over – probably a case of too much Christmas pudding,' he
wrote. 'We appeared to be leaden-footed and just couldn't get
started. They just hammered us. Our 18-match unbeaten run in the
league was over and it hurt. When we came into the dressing room
after that game we felt that a little part of our identity was gone and

we were never going to get it back. We couldn't believe that we'd lost and in such a humiliating fashion.'

My friends and I couldn't believe it either, and our misery was compounded the following day at Elland Road, when the only advantage of another comprehensive defeat – 3-1 – was that it drew some of the usual menace from the home support.

In the meantime, Forest were enjoying a bountiful festive period. The thrashing of United had been their fourth successive win, and a 1-1 draw with Liverpool at the City Ground on Boxing Day was followed by two wins away, at Newcastle and Bristol City.

Clough was probably right to say that it was the 4-0 victory at Old Trafford which finally silenced those who believed that such an unfashionable club, newly promoted, could not possibly win the title. In *The Times*, Tom German had written as much. 'Nottingham Forest are equipped to win the championship and assuredly will if the exciting style which demolished and demoralised Manchester United sets their standards for the second half of the season,' he predicted. If there were still some lingering sceptics, then by New Year's Eve they too were keeping their doubts to themselves. Into the new year of 1978, Forest took a five-point lead, and a wholly unfamiliar status as even-money favourites for the First Division title.

Chapter Nine

It was also a World Cup year, 1978, with Argentina due to host a tournament that I already knew would clash with my O levels. That at least had been the cause of some solace when England failed to qualify, for the second of these global football extravaganzas in succession. Without the thrilling distraction of Latchford strutting his stuff on a world stage, I supposed I might get better grades. But it wasn't especially comforting. I'd been eight years old when England last played in a World Cup, and even if they made it in 1982, I would be twenty then. So for the entire duration of my formative years as a football fan, I was denied the spectacle of England competing for the ultimate footballing crown.

England's abject failure to qualify was confirmed in the November 1977 match against Italy, in which Latchford made his debut. A solid 2-0 win for Ron Greenwood's team salvaged some pride that night, but England paid a heavy price for failing to capitalise against the weaker teams in Group 2, and lost out to Italy on goal difference. The real damage had been done the previous month when they mustered only two goals against the part-timers of Luxembourg, and it was nearly only one measly goal, until Ipswich Town's Paul Mariner pinched a second in the dying moments.

Naturally, the watching English fans showed their disappointment by beating up locals and wrecking cafes and bars. And six years later it was worse, I might add. On a November afternoon in 1983, Denmark's victory over Greece meant that even if England beat Luxembourg handsomely later that evening, they could not qualify for the following year's European Championships. Local police and even the Luxembourg army were out in force, mindful of what had happened in 1977, but still the fans ran riot, overturning cars and smashing shop windows. Riot police from across the border in Germany had to be bussed in, and no fewer than thirteen English hooligans received lengthy prison sentences.

It's best not to forget that the soundtrack to all those happy images of 1970s and 1980s football – all the daft haircuts, and dear old Bob Stokoe running across the Wembley pitch to embrace Jim Montgomery, all that lovely stuff – is the shattering of glass, the overturning of tables, the protests of bar owners, the wailing of sirens.

So the football world in general certainly did not mourn Luxembourg 0 England 2. And for warped parochial reasons, nor did some Evertonians, since Greenwood had stuffed his team with no fewer than five Liverpool players that night. We'd had to get used to that in the 1970s, in fact Greenwood in his first match in charge, a scoreless draw against Switzerland a month earlier, had started with six Liverpool players. Six! Even in Liverpool's pomp, it seemed a bit much for their players – Ray Clemence, Phil Neal, Terry McDermott, Emlyn Hughes, Ray Kennedy and Ian Callaghan – to form more than half the England team. And it would have been seven if Kevin Keegan hadn't just joined Hamburg.

That's largely why we Evertonians clamoured so loudly for Latchford to get into the England team and for Wood to be picked for Scotland, desperate to redress the balance even a tiny bit. International recognition was important to fans in those days, much more than it is now that caps are strewn around like confetti, with so many substitutes allowed, and youngsters fielded even before they are regulars for their club sides. It devalues what in the 1970s, England's World Cup disasters notwithstanding, was still a deeply respected currency. And in 1977-78 there was even more kudos in a Scottish cap, with Scotland having qualified for Argentina. So it did Wood no favours, no favours àt all, to concede six goals at home against United.

Splendidly, in his front room on the outskirts of Pontypridd thirty-five years later, he declined to take responsibility for any of them. 'There was not a lot I could have done with them, to be fair,' he said, defiantly.

But the Scotland manager Ally MacLeod – of whom more later in this book – had taken note, and worse still, had already been to Goodison to run an eye over Wood, on 29 October. Everton were playing Newcastle United that day, and Greenwood was also there, mainly to look at Latchford. Both international managers were rewarded with a spectacularly thrilling game, in which Everton equalised three times in 28 minutes. It finished 4-4, which was good news for big Bob, who scored twice, but grim news indeed for big George.

'Ally MacLeod came into the dressing room afterwards and told me to get my head up, but it wasn't the best of times to meet the bloke,' recalled Wood, still rendered disconsolate by the memory. 'He said he'd come and watch me again. But he didn't. I still think I should have gone to Argentina.'

I still think so, too. MacLeod's preferred goalkeeper, Alan Rough, might not have been quite as hopeless as he was habitually made out to be by Englishmen spoilt for choice between Shilton and Clemence, but nor was it for nothing that David Coleman, during the 1978 World Cup, memorably referred to him as 'inelastic'.

The ease with which he was beaten from outside the penalty

area in Scotland's disastrous defeat by Peru became a stick with which the Scots, who I find are peculiarly given to self-flagellation, liked to beat themselves for years afterwards. A Scottish journalist who went to interview Rough in 2010 even referred to the painting he (the journalist, not Rough) had hanging in his hall, depicting the third goal in that fateful Group D game against Peru, the brilliant free-kick by Teófilo Cubillas that flew past a goalkeeper as stationary as the Cenotaph in Glasgow. The title of the work was *Rough Wisnae Ready*. Well, Wood would've been.

He had only been Everton's goalkeeper since August and yet by December I, unlike the little bloke in the quilted anorak just in front of me on the terraces, could forgive him for conceding six at home. After all, he'd already had many more good games than bad, not least a blinder at Anfield two days before my sixteenth birthday. Which was significant, because it was bad enough anyway when your birthday fell on a Monday – which was not only the start of the school week, but also kicked off with double maths, in the not entirely reliable hands of E. T. Johnson.

Bizarrely, E. T. Johnson combined teaching maths at a boys' grammar school with running a pub. I don't suppose that could happen now, either. He was a much better publican than he was a maths teacher, but he was a genial, likeable sort. Rather unimaginatively, we all knew him as 'Etty'. Five years later, a certain Steven Spielberg film would have provided us with lots more ammunition. At the time, a goalless draw at Anfield made double maths with Etty Johnson on my birthday just a little more bearable.

Had we lost the derby, the misery would have been intense and my birthday properly blighted. There were only so many times, as yet another sodding trophy was held aloft by Emlyn Hughes, that you could say to smug Liverpool fans that supporting Everton showed much more character, was a much greater test of a chap's mettle, than cheering for Liverpool.

I had been at the game that Saturday. But it was hard going to Anfield as an Evertonian, because the Kop in full cry, in those days long before all-seater stadiums, was a genuinely intimidating sight. I know we gave a pretty good account of ourselves in the Anfield Road End, but very grudgingly I have to admit that the hairs stood up on the back of my neck when the swaying Koppites, their scarves fully stretched, gave full throttle to 'You'll Never Walk Alone'.

I might as well confess here that I have always rather envied them that anthem. I know that many Everton supporters write it off as a dreary dirge, but it certainly helped to give the Kop a collective personality in the way that only a very few assemblies of fans can claim. I do love the way we Evertonians have made the *Z-Cars* theme our own, and I always feel cheated when I watch Everton home games on TV and the broadcaster cuts to a commercial break just as Fritz Spiegl's famous arrangement starts up. But it's not quite the same as tens of thousands of people declaring hope in their hearts, and the *Z-Cars* music does still tend to make me think of Bert Lynch behind the desk at Newtown police station.

Incidentally, if one small irony of following football in the great city of Liverpool is that Everton actually used to play at Anfield, another is that Spiegl, the Austrian-born polymath who adapted the *Z-Cars* theme from the old folk song 'Johnny Todd', was an avid Liverpool fan, while Gerry Marsden of Gerry and the Pacemakers, whose celebrated version of 'You'll Never Walk Alone' was so wholeheartedly adopted by the Kop, grew up as an Everton supporter. Apparently he changed allegiance when he was 13, on the basis that all his family were ardent Evertonians too, and, contrary little bugger that he clearly was, he wanted to introduce a bit of tension into the family home.

Anyway, let me go out on a limb and assert that 'You'll Never Walk Alone', heretical as it is for an Everton fan to say, surely has to be English club football's most stirring anthem. I've never understood why in recent years it has been rather eclipsed by 'The Fields of Athenry', which the Anfield faithful shamelessly pinched from their Celtic counterparts, following a few clashes between the two clubs in the Champions League. Why be so unoriginal, when they can lay claim to such originality?

Whatever, I mustn't go on about it, or my fellow Evertonians will be throwing this book down in disgust. And I should swiftly and sincerely add that I really don't envy Liverpool fans anything else, not even all the league titles and European Cups, because I still think it's a more special thing to be an Evertonian, and am convinced that Everton is the greater, more characterful club, more viscerally connected with the city. In their Evertonian boyhoods, Ian Rush, Robbie Fowler, Steve McManaman, Michael Owen and Jamie Carragher all knew that too. And, of course, David Moyes swiftly recognised it when he arrived from Preston North End in 2002, probably not expecting his casual epithet, the 'People's Club', to be picked up and amplified for years afterwards.

But despite all that, in the 1960s and 1970s, the Kop singing 'You'll Never Walk Alone' was unarguably one of football's great sights and sounds. It was tough being at the other end.

Moreover, exciting as Everton often were to watch in those first couple of seasons under Gordon Lee, I certainly wasn't alone in being unable to quash that inferiority complex at derbies. Whether on my way to Anfield or Goodison, I went expecting to lose or maybe draw, which is not surprising, as that's all we had done since David Johnson scored the only goal (for the Blues, although he would later be reborn as a Red) on 13 November 1971. It was therefore with the usual pessimism, leavened with hopes and prayers, that I went to Anfield for that derby in October 1977, and it was Wood, more than anyone else, who sent me home happy with a 0-0 scoreline.

'That's the game that still stands out for me from that season,' he told me from the cosy embrace of his sofa. 'Partly because my dad came down from Scotland in a minibus with all his mates. There were six or seven of them in the front half of the bus, and the back half was full of beer. When they got to Anfield they all just fell out.' We both chuckled at the image. 'And I was just so wound up for that game. I can remember that we were supposed to meet at Goodison at 11am, to get the team bus across to Anfield, but I was at Anfield at 9am, psyching myself up. And yeah, I made a couple of good saves towards the end.'

Unsurprisingly, his memories of his rapport with the crowd were as affectionate as mine. 'Aye, if they were quiet I'd get them singing. Gordon got the hump with that. He told me I had to stop it, but I said that it helped me concentrate. I loved Gordon. He was a lovely man, although if anything not as strict as he should have been. There was a wild bunch of lads at Everton, myself included. I was right up there with the daftest ones. We worked hard and socialled hard, and he could have maybe controlled us a bit better. We went away on one break … well, I still can't tell you, but if it happened today it would be front-page news. They talk about the Crazy Gang at Wimbledon. Well, we had that long before. Me, Lyonsy, Kingy, a few others. We were known as the F Troop after that American sitcom. I won't tell you what we used to get up to, but Gordon used to tell me I'd be dead by the time I was thirty. Gail still says I've never grown up. But I've been in football all my life and you don't grow up. It's just an extension of your schooldays. I've never really left school.'

Like every other footballer I've ever interviewed who played in an era before the Premier League conferred instant millionaire status, Wood insisted that he wouldn't change a thing, even if he was offered a ride in that time machine. 'I always thought that if my house was paid for when I finished playing football then I would have had a good career,' he said. 'No, I wouldn't change anything. I don't think players love the game now, not like we did. In my day we'd come back on the coach and we'd all be talking about the game. Now they're on iPods, iPads, whatever. And I might go into training at Palace and say to the lads there, "Did you see that goal last night?" Because I've watched a game the night before, on Sky, maybe from a lower division or the Spanish league or something. But they've never seen it. They're a different breed today. Mind you, it's no wonder there's not the same camaraderie. We play five-a-sides in training at Palace and can't field two teams of British lads. We've got Argentinians, Australians, South Africans, Congolese, you name it.'

I shared with Wood my theory about Ossie Ardiles as a kind of Christ figure in terms of the two football epochs pre- and post-1978, one with foreign players and one without: Before Ardiles and After Ardiles. 'Aye,' he said, looking slightly bewildered.

There was a brief, rather awkward silence. I asked him to give me some idea of the difference the move to Everton made to him financially. 'Well, it wasn't like it made me rich,' he said. 'But when I started at Blackpool I'd only been on £20 a week, which wasn't great even then. I'd been an apprentice bricklayer as a kiddie so in the summer I helped build garages for Wimpy, to make up my money and raise my first deposit on a house. I never had a car. If I couldn't afford it, I'd save for it. That's the way I was brought up and the way I am now. Gail will tell you. No, I used to get the bus to games, with the fans. I'd get the bus from St Annes at 11.45 on a Saturday, have a couple of pints after the game in the supporters' club, and get the bus back. When I went to Everton I was able to buy a four-bedroom detached house in Parbold for £75,000, though, of course, I had a mortgage on it. And for my first year at Everton I drove a bashed-up Morris Marina.' A chortle. 'Bit different now, isn't it?'

Still, in his second year he got a club car, a Volvo estate. 'And on match days, coming in from Parbold along the East Lancs Road, there'd be all these scallies thumbing lifts. I used to pick them up, five or six of them at a time, and, of course, when they recognised who I was they'd be singing away, but I had to keep them quiet to get them in past the gateman. We always tried, but he always spotted them.'

It's another irresistible image, another story with which to measure the chasm between then and now. But there were only a handful of players even in those days who would have picked up lads thumbing lifts to the ground. That Wood did so typified his easy relationship with the fans, and most of us were as jubilant when he did finally make his full Scotland debut, against Northern Ireland in May 1979, as we were aghast to see him leave Goodison for Highbury, for £140,000, in August 1980.

It is one of the curiosities of football that a boy can idolise a man for an ability to make him happier than any man ever has, up to and possibly including his own father and Father Christmas, and then, abruptly, it all ends with his departure to another club. It doesn't really happen in other sports, or at least, it doesn't feel such a seismic letdown when a cricketer moves counties, or a rugby player switches from Saracens to Harlequins. And it's not quite the same in other forms of entertainment, either. The Beatles might have broken up, but John Lennon didn't promptly sign for the Rolling Stones.

No, football is unique as a crusher of devotion, and it happens now as much as it ever did – think of the broken hearts Robin van Persie left behind when he departed Arsenal for Manchester United, or Fernando Torres when he left Liverpool for Chelsea, and indeed Wayne Rooney when he moved from Everton. But in the 1970s and 1980s, as we have established, there wasn't the endless gossip and speculation beforehand, to prepare you for the possibility that your hero might be about to pack his bags. He was there, and then he wasn't.

Evertonians older than me had suffered the pain of Alan Ball leaving a few years earlier when he still, manifestly, had so much to offer. Just like Wood he'd come from Blackpool, become a Goodison hero, and then left for Arsenal. Wood's departure was not nearly as symbolic as Ball's had been, of course. It didn't represent the premature break-up of a great side and the beginning of a slide into mediocrity, like Ball's had. No, Woody leaving didn't break hearts like Bally leaving. But it broke mine.

Chapter Ten

'Gordon had signed Jim McDonagh from Bolton, and I felt like it was time to move on,' Wood told me, by way, even now, of slightly apologetic explanation.

'Ipswich wanted me as well, but Arsenal gave me treble the wages I was on at Everton. I was on £400 a week at Highbury, which was pretty good money. Mind you, I used to drink with a few bricklayer pals and they could make £400 a week, too, if they put in a few extra shifts. Funny how it's all changed. But what I was able to do was put my signing-on fees and quite a bit of my earnings into my pension. That's been my lifeblood ever since. I'm happy with what I've got out of the game. I don't owe anyone anything, I own this house, and we've got the money to buy somewhere in France. We're looking at the moment. The plan is to live out there full-time, when this job goes. Which it will, and that will be it for me. My legs have gone now; my hips have gone. But I've had ten years in coaching that I didn't think I'd get.'

It was wonderful to find one of my childhood heroes so contented with his lot. His only regret was that his international career was restricted to four caps, but he did at least get to go to the 1982 World Cup, as reserve to Alan Rough. Otherwise, at sixty-one,

George Wood felt blessed. He might not have impressed his schoolteachers but somewhere along the line he had acquired the wisdom to look back at his life as a whole, at what teachers of creative writing call a full narrative arc. That he now owned his own detached house having started life in a tied farm cottage was manifestly a source of great satisfaction. However, he did confess to a natural circumspection about spending money, which might not have served him well when he joined Arsenal. 'I remember Don Howe taking me out to Hadley Wood, where houses cost a million pounds even then. He said, "Get a house round here and get the biggest mortgage you can." Which was good advice at the time, but being ultra-cautious I went a few miles up the road to Brookmans Park, which wasn't as smart, and bought a house there for £180,000. Mind you, I could have sold it a few years later for £600,000, but my wife at the time didn't want to sell. Then there was the property crash and we ended up selling for £240,000.'

Wood's first wife had been a Blackpool girl, and together they had a daughter, Jane, who has given him two grandchildren. 'Unfortunately we got divorced, but I've been with Gail twenty-four years,' he said, just as Gail came into the room with a couple of mugs of coffee, and threw me a wry look as if to say, 'Is that all? It seems longer.' They have a son, James, of whom he is inordinately proud. 'He turned out dyslexic [dyxlectic], like myself, but he's good at sport. Cardiff Blues wanted to sign him.'

Wood settled in South Wales after finishing his playing career there. He had only stayed at Arsenal until 1983, the year that Pat Jennings, the man he was unable to dislodge from the Arsenal goal, rubbed it in by becoming the first player to make 1000 appearances in English football.

The Arsenal manager, Terry Neill, and his right-hand man, Howe, had earmarked Wood as big Pat's successor, but the amiable Ulsterman wasn't ready to go. He made rather a habit of that. At

Tottenham they thought he was coming to the end of his career in 1977, so they sold him to Arsenal where to the dismay of the White Hart Lane faithful he played in the first team for eight more years.

Moreover, it's an oft-forgotten postscript to Jennings's long and illustrious career that in 1986, at the age of forty, he signed for Everton, to provide cover for the injured Neville Southall and reserve keeper Bobby Mimms in the FA Cup final that I would end up following from an outhouse overlooking the Buffalo River in Tennessee. A few weeks later, Jennings made his 119th and final international appearance for Northern Ireland in the World Cup, against Brazil. It was his forty-first birthday, and he'd made his international debut aged eighteen, in 1964. They really don't make 'em quite like big Pat Jennings any more. They didn't make 'em much like him then, either. For sustained excellence, only the great Peter Shilton could stand comparison.

By the time Everton were back where they deserved to be, at the top of the league and at Wembley, Wood had joined Crystal Palace. He played for Palace 192 times, more than he did for any other club, before joining Cardiff City in 1987. In 1989 he was briefly loaned back to Blackpool, followed by a short spell at Hereford United, and then he joined mighty Merthyr Tydfil, just as his old teammate Bob Latchford had a few years earlier. At the other end of the football spectrum, the Premier League was starting up, and salaries were beginning the upward spiral that would eventually lead to men being paid hundreds of thousands of pounds a week to do what Wood had once hoped might, over the course of an entire career, pay off his mortgage.

From Merthyr he went to the splendidly named Inter Cardiff, not quite as grand as their Milan counterparts, but they did qualify through the newly formed League of Wales for the 1994-95 UEFA Cup. 'I remember playing the Polish team, Katowice, out there in Poland,' Wood recalled. 'We were 3-0 down at half-time and the manager turned to me and said, "C'mon, Woody, you're the senior player, what do you think I should do here?"

'I said, "To be fair, gaffer, you're the gaffer." But that was when I made my mind up that I was going to be a gaffer. I thought if he could do it, then I could. Because I'd always thought I'd play forever, but towards the end I realised that I was good at coaching. So I went on a goalkeeping course and did all my badges. And realised that the game becomes even better when you're a coach. The different shapes teams are, it's like a game of chess. So I became even more enthralled with football. I weaned myself off playing and became hooked on coaching.'

He duly took over as manager of Inter Cardiff. 'Aye, but the chairman didn't tell me that the club was almost bust. I was given £1000 a week to look after a squad of 18, and I was told that my assistant and I could split whatever was left. Which was nothing, in fact less than nothing. We had to dig into our own pockets. I went up to the Valleys to recruit players, because the lads are tougher up there. We signed eight boys from the Valleys, paid them £25 a game, and lost one game all season. We got into Europe again, and drew Celtic in the UEFA Cup.'

Wood chortled at the memory of it. 'The committee were all thinking, "How much money are we going to make?" I was thinking, "What's the record defeat in Europe?" Our team was literally the postman, the fireman, the milkman. We even had to get one lad out of jail to play. Before the first game, at our place, I got all the players to put their heads down and put their hands together. Then I started reciting the Lord's Prayer. They all burst out laughing and that relaxed them a wee bit. We only lost 2-0, and one of them was a penalty. In Glasgow we lost 4-0, and again, one was a penalty. Those games made the club £250,000.'

'After that, the chairman wanted to go mad, but I said, "No, we've got to look to the future." I started an under-18s, all the way down to an under-10s. But I'd had enough by then. I left, and as soon as I left, they took all the kiddies out of the club.' He shook his big head, still aggrieved at the memory.

After that he became a goalkeeping coach, working at Cardiff City, Hartlepool United, Swindon Town and Blackpool before fetching up at Palace under Ian Holloway, who'd worked with him at Blackpool and liked the cut of his jib. And no wonder, for his jib is as impressively cut as it's always been. But still, as he drove me back to the station at the end of more than two hours of cheerful nattering, I couldn't help reflecting on what he had been – a sporting idol to tens of thousands – and what he was now, a comparatively anonymous professional, coming and going on a white-collar housing estate on the edge of the Rhondda Valley, pretty much ready for a quiet retirement somewhere in the French countryside. He could just as easily have been a middle manager at the local steelworks.

I got out at the station and shook his hand. He told me that if ever I fancied tickets for a match at Selhurst Park, I should give him a call. He'd be only too happy, and all that. But I never have. This book would have been a non-starter if I had subscribed to the theory that you should never meet your childhood heroes, but it doesn't do to get too pally with them. Otherwise, you get to know them on entirely new terms, and the much purer relationship you had with them from a distance is gone forever.

As I sat on the train chugging back towards my home in Herefordshire, pondering a day that had started in Cumbria with the Prince of Wales, some more of the old Gwladys Street songs came into my head.

One of them had been a chant that went through the entire team – another that you never hear any more – to the tune of the venerable French-Canadian song about plucking the feathers off a lark, 'Alouette, Gentille Alouette'.

It started, invariably at Fozzie Bear's instigation: 'Everton, oh we love Everton … Everton, oh we love Everton. And we love our Georgie Wood. Oh, we love our Georgie Wood. Everton, oh we love Everton … Everton, oh we love Everton. And we love our Davey Jones, oh we love our Davey Jones. Davey Jones, Davey Jones. Georgie Wood, Georgie Wood …' And so on, until we got to the No. 11, Davey Thomas, and then back through the team, with, for scanning purposes, 'Big Bob Latch' rather than Bob Latchford, and 'Supermac' instead of Duncan McKenzie.

It's no wonder you don't hear that 'Alouette' song any more; so spectacularly polysyllabic are the names of many footballers playing in England today that it would last from the opening whistle almost to half-time. Back then, virtually all the names were Anglo-Saxon, or Celtic, and if perchance there was a foreign-sounding surname, like that of Everton's left back Mick Pejic, it was a pound to a penny that the player was the son of immigrants who'd settled here during or just after the Second World War.

At Everton, fortuitously, most of the names scanned: Georgie Wood, Andy King, Trevor Ross, Billy Wright and so on. But there were some that didn't. In terms of that particular song, the most problematic position was right back. Dave Jones played there quite a bit, and by making it Davey Jones, we had the three syllables we needed. But when Terry Darracott or Neil Robinson wore the No. 2 shirt – in those halcyon days when shirt number denoted position on the field – we had, even if nobody on the terraces expressed it quite like this, a scansion dilemma. 'And we love our Neil Robinson, oh we love our Neil Robinson. Neil Robinson, Neil Robinson …'

Paul Simon and Art Garfunkel might have done marvellous things with the name Robinson, but making it scan was entirely beyond the Gwladys Street faithful. It was frankly a relief when, in serenading the players, we got back to Georgie Wood.

Most of the 1977-78 players were easy enough to find when I set about researching this book, thanks not least to the estimable Philip Ross at the Everton Former Players' Foundation, and the ever-obliging Darren Griffiths in the club's media department. And that was certainly true of Neil Robinson. I was given his phone number, gave him a call, and we agreed to meet up the following week, in a hotel round the corner from Lime Street station. Simples, as those annoying TV meerkats say.

Robinson only played seventeen times for Everton, but I remembered him clearly, and recognised him instantly. It helped that, unlike some former players, he had not put on weight. Indeed, he was as lean and fit in his mid-fifties as he had been in his teens. And he was still a strict vegan. He would be the first to admit that he was a decent footballer without ever tearing up trees, but if he is remembered for anything by students of the game in the 1970s and 1980s, it is for being one of football's first vegetarians, and then the game's inaugural vegan, at a time when players were encouraged to eat as much chicken and beef as they could digest.

I once spent a hugely entertaining afternoon at the Wirral home of Ian St John (without ever confessing to being an Evertonian, especially when afternoon gave way to dusk and the malt whisky came out), who recalled the strict lifestyle guidelines laid down by Bill Shankly, in terms of what they should eat and even when they should, or shouldn't, have sex.

'He told us to wear boxing gloves in bed on Friday nights, and if that didn't work, to send the wife to her mother's. He was a big boxing fan, Shanks, and he'd read once that Joe Louis trained on steaks. So that was it. On Fridays, we'd have steak. Saturday lunch, steak. Saturday night on the way back from the match, steak. When you left Liverpool you went vegetarian.'

St John was joking about turning vegetarian. Footballers didn't, in the 1970s. But Robinson did. When he was thirteen, he had watched a television documentary about Amazonian tribes, and a sacrificial slaughter of a cow, in which tribesmen stamped on the animal's neck to force the blood out more quickly, so revolted him that he swore never to eat meat again. And then, ten years or so later, he went that step further, giving up eggs and milk as well.

I confess, as an enthusiastic carnivore, to being innately suspicious of vegans. Not, I think, because I disapprove of their lifestyle choice, but because I'm pretty sure they must disapprove of mine. I recall one of those magazine questionnaires in which two young people were sent on a blind date. He was a vegan, she wasn't, and when asked whether they had kissed, he said that they hadn't, because he didn't like meaty breath. It was the kind of sanctimonious response that I'm afraid I associate with vegans.

But Robinson wasn't like that at all. There are some people you meet in life with whom you feel an instant connection. I'd liked Latchford and Wood, but I hadn't felt that connection. With Robinson I did. He was a humble, quietly spoken man, and as we talked it became clear that life had dealt him more than a few set-backs since the end of his playing career. Somebody clever once said that every set-back is a set-up for a bounce-back, which may well be true, but you still need real strength of character for those bounce-backs. That's what I detected in Robinson. Of all the ex-players I interviewed for this book, there were two with whom I thought I could quite easily be friends. One was that thrilling left winger Dave Thomas. Robinson was the other.

We talked for ages. The starting point, of course, was his part in Everton's 6-0 destruction of Chelsea on that famous day in 1978, and like every Evertonian who is old enough, he remembered the game for the thrilling significance of a single goal.

But in his case, unlike that of every other Evertonian, it wasn't the sixth goal, Latchford's penalty, that reverberated in the memory. No, it was his own, the third. For the simple, unvarnished reason that it was his first and only goal for the club he had supported since he was old enough to walk, on the ground that loomed practically at the end of his road.

Robinson was born and grew up at 45 Spellow Lane, making him, then as now, almost certainly the Everton player born closest to Goodison Park. They say that a true Cockney has to be born within the sound of the Bow bells. By the same reckoning, Neil Robinson could hardly be a truer Evertonian. When 18-year-old Derek Temple scored for Everton against Manchester City, on 22 April 1957, the roar from Goodison Park would doubtless have reached the ears of the tiny infant destined to play for Everton himself.

It is entirely fitting that Neil Robinson's only Everton goal would come twenty-one years later in a 6-0 demolition of Chelsea, because he had been born forty-eight hours earlier on the day of another six-goal match between Everton and Chelsea, albeit at Stamford Bridge, and albeit a 5-1 defeat. That was 20 April 1957, so the 1978 game fell just over a week after his twenty-first birthday. And what a way to come of age; surging forward from right back and scoring his first goal for the club.

'I was ecstatic,' he told me, laughing. 'But no one congratulated me. No one. There's me tearing round the pitch, waving to my family and all that. I just kept on running – I virtually had to get a bus back into the ground – but eventually I turned round to see all the other players remonstrating with the ref to try and get a penalty instead, so that Bob could take it.'

He still can't believe that the TV cameras weren't there for Latchford's final assault on the summit. But they weren't, and so there is no visual record of his goal. 'I can't remember the build-up,' he said. 'All I can remember is that it was a low drive from outside the box, against Peter Bonetti of all people.'

Robinson had made his Everton debut just over two years

earlier, on 31 January 1976. He was eighteen. 'I can remember the date because it was the same date I got married, two years later.' He didn't say whether his wedding anniversary helps him remember the date of his Everton debut, at home against Burnley, or vice versa. Either way, it was a significant game for me, too, a 2-3 defeat plunging me into a gloom that intensified somewhat when my dad died suddenly four days later.

'It was a surprise when Billy Bingham told me I was playing,' Robinson added. 'I was nervous, but dead excited. Unfortunately, when I got to the ground I couldn't find my boots. And I never did find them. I had to borrow a pair, but that wasn't the same. It's like a snooker player with a cue. You don't feel right in someone else's boots, especially at that time of year, on a hard pitch. So that unnerved me a bit, but then I nearly scored a goal early on. Gerry Peyton tipped my shot round the post, and I still sometimes think to myself, "What if that had gone in?" As it was, I didn't play again that season, in fact not until the following January. I always felt that if I'd been given a run then things might have been different.'

I relished the detail about his boots going walkies. Everton in 1976 was by common consent one of the best-run clubs in English football, yet still it was possible for a player's boots to be pinched on the eve of his debut, forcing him to play in a hastily borrowed pair. And yet, the vanished boots, the disappointing scoreline and the 'what might have been' lament notwithstanding, he at least has the eternal satisfaction of having played for the club he had followed passionately from boyhood, and having thus delivered some joy to his chronically disabled Evertonian father.

Just to add to Robinson's Goodison Park pedigree, his father, Jim, had at one time run the Winslow Hotel, the Victorian pub just outside the ground on Goodison Road where hundreds of thousands of pre- and post-match pints were supped – not a few of them on the night of 29 April 1978 – before the place closed for business in 2012. Happily, it has since reopened.

Jim Robinson had been a decent footballer himself. In the 1920s he was offered terms by Bradford Park Avenue, but his mother wouldn't let him go and that was that. Then, in 1959, he was labouring at the local Kodak factory, working on a wooden derrick, when the rope holding it up suddenly snapped. He had told the crew an hour earlier that the rope was rotten and not to use it. They checked with the foreman. He told them to use it anyway. And as he and the derrick went crashing to the ground, Jim Robinson's neck was broken. His distraught family was told that he would be unlikely to survive for another twenty-four hours. In fact, such was his strength of character and irrepressible will to live that he survived for eighteen more years.

'I was only two years old at the time, and so I have no memory of my dad ever walking about,' the youngest of Jim and Ethel Robinson's seven children told me. 'The accident left him paraplegic, bordering on tetraplegic. He could just about move his arms and his head, but that was it. He spent the rest of his life either in bed or in a wheelchair, for which he was eventually awarded £18,500 in compensation. This was meant to cover his wages for the next twenty years, with a small amount on top "for his trouble". He'd worked all his life providing for his family, sacrificed everything for us, and had to work away from home a lot while my mum looked after us seven kids. And my next brother up, Ken, had been crippled by polio at the age of four. The industrial accident not only meant that my dad couldn't work any more, but that my mum, as well as looking after all of us, had to give him round-the-clock care. And £18,500 was all he got. That's what his life was worth. A nonsense, isn't it?'

Robinson recalled all this in a spirit of sadness rather than bitterness, and chuckled when explaining that the meagre payout was at least enough to help the family move from Spellow Lane to a bungalow across the Mersey, among fields just outside Widnes, with an acre and a half of land. 'God knows,' he said, 'we could have ended up like the Dead End Kids in Spellow Lane. Widnes offered a much better life for us. We were like the Clampetts moving to Beverly Hills.' He knew that, as a child of the 1960s, I would understand his reference to that American sitcom of blessed memory, *The Beverly Hillbillies*. 'An acre and a half of land! My brother John and me had our own small football pitch. It was unbelievable.'

His brother Ken, alas, could not join them. He had been put to bed one night in 1954 with a splitting headache and a fever, and when he woke up the next morning, he couldn't move; his legs were wasted. 'It was a polio epidemic, but he was the only one in the family who got it. It was before my dad's accident and he was heartbroken, because of all his sons, Ken was the one with big stocky legs who he hoped might become a footballer and play for Everton.'

So Jim Robinson changed tack, and began to encourage Ken, who could only walk with his legs in calipers, to make an effort at school. In those days, kids with disabilities had few prospects and were usually destined for menial jobs or remedial programmes. 'But my dad didn't want that for our Ken, especially after his own accident. He said, "Look son, you've got to focus on your education." It was education, education, education. And Ken pushed himself, and went to the grammar school, then on to university. It was down to Dad, that, driving him on all the time. He became a teacher, and then a professor, at Warwick University. And then he moved to America. And now he's Sir Ken Robinson, a global expert on education and creativity, and one of the funniest blokes I've ever met.'

We had taken something of a tangent from Neil Robinson's own career, but there was something so moving and inspiring about this image of a paralysed father driving a polio-stricken son onwards and upwards, that I wanted to know more. He told me that his brother has forged a reputation among educators as one of the world's most inspirational speakers, regularly sharing platforms with people of the stature of Bill Clinton and Bill Gates. He suggested that I should look on YouTube for these talks, which are delivered on behalf of an organisation called TED, established to bring together people from the worlds of technology, entertainment and design – hence the matey acronym.

And so I did, and was mesmerised. Sir Ken Robinson is indeed one of the finest orators I have ever heard: natural, funny and con-tagiously passionate on the subject of education. And there are just enough remnants of Spellow Lane in his accent to identify where he came from, and the upbringing that so improbably made him what he is now.

'Ken did a lot of swimming as a kid,' Neil Robinson also told me. 'In fact, he became a champion swimmer in disabled swimming cir-cles. He went to a swimming club in Garston where they had sessions for the disabled kids. And at hospital he'd become mates with another lad from Liverpool with polio, Bert Massie, who also went on to get a knighthood. Bert got his for campaigning for people with disabilities to get the same chances as everyone else. Isn't that amazing? These two working-class kids, both disabled, growing up in Liverpool in the 1960s when disability wasn't treated like it is now, both becoming knights of the realm.'

It is indeed amazing, an incredibly heartening affirmation of what can be achieved in life with positivity of spirit. Especially by Evertonians.

Chapter Eleven

One can only imagine what surges of pride passed through Jim Robinson's broken body as Ken powered forward in education, and young Neil made his debut for Everton.

Sadly, he did not live quite long enough to hear that his youngest son had got his name on the Everton scoresheet. 'He died at the time of the League Cup final, in 1977,' said Robinson. 'I was in the squad and we travelled down on the Friday. He took bad that day, and just before we left I phoned my mum. She said, "They've taken him into hospital, but he'll be fine, don't worry." She didn't want me to be distracted. But he died that weekend.'

Neil Robinson confirmed the truth of what I'd heard from his illustrious brother on *Desert Island Discs* in 2013, about the character and extraordinary forbearance of their mother, Ethel. 'She never lost heart, and she could talk for England. She and my dad were remarkable people, they really were. It's easy for a son to say that, but anyone who knew them knows that to be the truth. Never mind me telling my story, or even our Ken's story. Their story is worth telling.'

Nonetheless, I was there to hear his story, and he told me about the excitement he felt when Billy Bingham invited him to sign professional terms with Everton, at the age of seventeen. 'My first wage was twenty-seven quid a week, and I'd been getting eight quid a week as an apprentice, so that made me the richest man in the world, you know. The height of my ambition was to become a first-team regular and stay for ten years, but it didn't quite work out.'

One of the reasons for that, he thinks, was a crippling lack of self-belief. 'I was very shy when I first joined Everton, but I always felt confident on the training pitch. I was a great training-ground player, but that didn't always show in matches. I'd be good all week and then be pretty average on a Saturday, and I think that was all about self-confidence. Looking back, I think I started to lose confidence after that very first game against Burnley. I'd done OK, and I was interviewed by local radio after the game, and told them about the borrowed boots. Then Billy Bingham phoned me and I thought he was calling to say, "Well done, son". But it was to give me a ticking-off about the boots.'

Bingham probably didn't think twice about issuing that rebuke, but given how vividly Robinson still remembered it so many years later, it clearly undermined his already shaky self-esteem. Of course, Bingham left Everton long before he did, and he found Lee more congenial, but Terry Darracott or Dave Jones seemed to be Lee's preferred choices at right back. So in 1979 Robinson left Everton, and joined John Toshack's upwardly mobile revolution at Swansea.

'Bill Shankly put a word in for me with Tosh. Shanks lived just by Bellefield (the Everton training ground), and the story was that he wasn't welcome at Melwood (Liverpool's training ground). So he'd come in to Bellefield most days and get treatment from our physio, Jim McGregor. I used to love sitting in the treatment room with him, hearing all the stories. And because he saw me in training, he'd seen the best of me. So he recommended me to Tosh. Tosh was on the phone to Shanks all the time, you know.

'Anyway, I can still remember Gordon Lee calling me in on a Friday morning. He said, "John Toshack's just been on the phone. He wants you to have a chat with him." Well, by eight that evening I was down in Swansea with my wife. We couldn't see the area because it was dark, but the next day we had a walk around, and that was that. We'd only been living in our house in Huyton for six months, and she was expecting our first child. But football is full of those life-changing events. Within twenty-four hours you can be living in another part of the country.'

Robinson's first game in Swansea colours was for the reserves, against Bristol City. He lasted less than five minutes before his cartilage popped out, and with Toshack having taken a rather sudden mid-season sabbatical, his assistant and old Liverpool teammate Tommy Smith, authorised an operation.

When Toshack returned to work, he was furious that his new signing had been booked in for a cartilage operation practically before kicking a ball. Angry words were exchanged between him and Smith, and in the spirit of Evertonians getting one over Liverpudlians in any way we can, I can only celebrate the improbability of such a mild-mannered Everton man being the catalyst for a barney between two such famously forceful Anfield heroes. A serious barney too, by Smith's own account. In his autobiography, *Anfield Iron*, he cites 'the Neil Robinson incident' as the reason why he did not pursue management as a career option. 'I just didn't want the hassle that went with the job,' he wrote.

I later had a run-in of my own with Tommy Smith, by the way. In 1999 I went to interview him for the *Independent*, and he told me a remarkable story that he would later include in *Anfield Iron*, which went some way towards explaining his dislike, verging on proper loathing, for another old Liverpool teammate who in due course would end up reunited with Toshack at Swansea, Emlyn Hughes.

Smith's tale related to a match against Arsenal on the exciting final day of the 1971-72 season, when any one of three clubs – Liverpool, Leeds United or Brian Clough's Derby County – could still win the First Division title. Derby had already played all their matches and topped the table, but only by a single fragile point. Their season complete, Clough's right-hand man Peter Taylor had taken most of the Derby players to Majorca to relax while Liverpool and Leeds tried to overtake them. Clough, characteristically, had instead gone on holiday to the Scilly Isles with his children and his 'mam and dad'.

So if Liverpool won by two clear goals at Highbury and Leeds lost at Wolves, Derby would be displaced from the top and the title would go to Anfield. As Smith told it, Hughes sidled up to him in the dressing-room ninety minutes before the game and said that he'd been chatting to a couple of the Arsenal team, who were prepared to throw the match for £50 a man. Hughes apparently suggested that the rest of the Liverpool players would be more inclined to listen to such a proposition – each of them providing £50 from their own pockets – if it came from Smith.

Suitably disgusted, Smith related all this to Ian Callaghan, who ventured that perhaps Hughes had not spoken to the Arsenal players, but was merely trying to 'create trouble' for him. 'Over the years I have pondered this matter a lot,' Smith wrote in his book. He had reached the conclusion, he added, 'that in all probability Emlyn hadn't spoken to the Arsenal lads of this sordid proposal. I knew the Arsenal lads; I couldn't imagine them agreeing to such a thing.'

In the event, Liverpool drew 0-0 with Arsenal and Leeds lost 2-1 at Molineux (despite Revie's own attempt to fix the result, according to an allegation made by Clough in his autobiography). The title was Derby's.

As for Smith's accusation, I knew in 1999 that I couldn't possibly print it, as Emlyn Hughes was still alive and would almost certainly sue. However, Hughes had died by the time I wrote my memoir about growing up as a sports nut, so I did use it. It was too good a tale not to tell. But before the book was even published, I got a call from a guy I knew at the *Liverpool Echo*. They had been sent an advance copy for review purposes, had seen Smith's rather incendiary allegations, and had phoned him to ask about them. He in turn had told them in no uncertain terms that he wanted to speak to me. So, with some trepidation, I called him.

Confronting an angry Tommy Smith on the phone wasn't quite the same as having him bearing down on you on the football pitch, but I still felt almost physically intimidated as he harangued me furiously for relating a story that he flatly denied telling me in the first place. It wasn't my finest hour as a sports writer, because it turned out that without a tape-recording or any notes to refer to, and relying only on memory, I had got one important detail wrong. I wrote that Smith had told me that Hughes had wanted his own teammates to throw the game, not the Arsenal players.

An exchange of solicitors' letters followed, and the story was duly removed from the paperback version of my book. And yet the essence of what I'd written corresponded with Smith's own account, which, it later emerged, he was saving for his own book: namely that Hughes had indeed raised, or claimed to have raised, the possibility of bribes being offered and a First Division football match being thrown.

If nothing else, with allegations of match-fixing still a burning issue in football, this shows that nothing is new under the sporting sun.

But since the star of this chapter is meant to be the irreproachably decent and honest Neil Robinson, let me return to him. He had his cartilage op, got into the Swansea first team, and in due course was transformed into an efficient and effective midfield player, enjoying the best season of his football career in 1980-81, the year Swansea gained promotion to the First Division and signed my hero Latchford for their inaugural top-flight campaign.

In 1984, Robinson moved from Swansea to Grimsby Town, who of course had been responsible for one of the most wet and miserable evenings of my own life as a football fan, but gave Robinson four more playing years before he made the final move of his career, to Darlington. 'I retired there at thirty-three, under Brian Little. Funnily enough he was kind of my nemesis, really. I'd played in the second replay of the 1977 League Cup final against Aston Villa, which was only my fourth game in the Everton first team. It was a bit nerve-wracking, to be honest, and for one of the goals [in that heart-rending 3-2 defeat], I was a little bit in error. Brian nicked it off me and went and scored. Anyway, he offered me a job as the youth coach at Darlington, but I didn't feel ready to retire, so I turned it down. I said, "If you don't want me as a player, I'll go." So I went on the transfer list for a bit, but then I went back to him and said, "I don't want to go." He said, "No, I've made my mind up, you can go." So that was it really. And then I did my ankle, so I retired. And from retiring, I went on the dole for eighteen months.'

The dole. It's not a word that's used much in connection with modern-day footballers, even those who never quite make it in the Premier League but enjoy a respectable career in the lower divisions, like Robinson did. But in 1988 it was the only option open to him and other footballers who weren't qualified to do anything except kick a ball. Well, maybe not the only option. Plenty of them went into the pub trade. But the cliché of the ex-footballer running a pub is firmly entwined, alas, with the ex-footballer running a pub into the ground.

'We weren't destitute,' he added. 'We had three children by then but I had my PFA pension, and because I retired through injury I got about £10,000, which helped us through and gave us a bit of a cushion. We moved back to Widnes from Darlington, and I joined one of my brothers, who had a bit of a business in the fireplace game, but that didn't work out.

'I've always been keen on fitness, so over another twelve months I raised the funds to start a gym, and that opened in 1995, in Widnes. I ran that for four years, but I didn't have the money to keep it going, so after that I did a ten-week course to become a personal trainer. But I couldn't find any work as a personal trainer so I became a postman. That seemed like a dream job, in the sense that you post a few letters and then go home, but I hated it and the money was crap – 120 quid for six days a week.

'So then I did some office work with my brother. Not the fireplace one. Another brother, Keith. That was sales and marketing, spreadsheets and all that. Then I was on the dole again for another twelve months, racking my brains for things to do. As you know I was a vegan, in fact a low-fat vegan, a vegan de luxe, and I'd regularly go on walks with the family but have nothing nutritious to eat, and I remember saying one day that when I got home I was going to try making my own bars.

'So I thought of the ingredients I wanted and that's what I did. I made some bars, took them with me, and the family liked them too. It turned into a little cottage industry, you know, and then I emailed this guy to ask if he could recommend a bigger machine, and he emailed back and said cottage industries don't last long, but if I wanted he could put me in touch with a small manufacturer who makes vegan stuff.

'So that's what happened. The guy was in Cambridge so I went down there and he said he could do a short run for me. Then we got some investors, and a bit of momentum, and launched a company. The original bar was called Alikat, after my two daughters, Alison and Katherine. They're both vegans too, like. We called it the Bare Food Company, but then we changed that to the Frank Company. As in frank and honest, not because the bloke who'd put the most money in was called Frank. And we got them into some good shops in London, Planet Organic and all that. But I became an employee of the company and went without a wage for almost two years, living off an overdraft, while we were trying to get it up and running. I only recently started taking a salary.'

As with Robinson's stories about his father, and his brother Ken, all this seemed like a heart-warming affirmation of what is possible in life with a sufficiently resolute will. When I got home that night I went online and ordered a case of Frank chocolate bars, which actually went down well with my family too, even though none of us are vegans. They were properly delicious.

Then, a few months later, I emailed Robinson and asked how it was all going. He said that since we'd last talked the company had made him redundant, which seemed dreadfully sad and unfair, such had been his manifest passion for the enterprise. He felt pretty bitter, he said, and yet even his email radiated optimism. He was excited that, having never been during the 'dreary' Moyes era, he was about to attend his first Everton game for twelve years. 'Onwards and upwards,' he wrote, and while he was referring to his own life, it's a maxim that has sustained Evertonians for as long as I can remember.

Chapter Twelve

Dreary it may have been in certain respects, but the great achievement of David Moyes was in restoring Everton's status as a team more likely to finish nearer the top of the Premier League than the bottom. That feat never cut much ice with alumni of the School of Science, all those Evertonians raised in the golden age of the 'Golden Vision' Alex Young and, later, of Kendall, Ball and Harvey. Or, for that matter, with those who came of age in the mid-1980s. But for those of us who were too young to support the team properly in the halcyon 1960s, and by the glorious Reid, Bracewell, Sheedy years were already moulded as Evertonians, accustomed to the 1970s promise of great deeds but never the realisation, Moyes was a welcome presence at the tiller.

I've heard it said by some of those old enough to remember the late 1970s that he was Gordon Lee reincarnate. Reincarnated as a ginger Glaswegian, anyway. And certainly there's some substance to the theory. Moyes and Lee: two decent, highly principled football men, both with a decidedly dour public image that in fact was at odds with their private warmth and many kindnesses. Moyes was perhaps a more astute manager than Lee, cleverer in the transfer market, but it should never be forgotten (and it very often is) that it was Lee who introduced a young Scottish lad called Graeme Sharp to the Everton team, and also gave Kevin Ratcliffe his chance. Besides, very rarely did Moyes's teams produce football as entertaining as Everton did in the first couple of seasons under Lee, and they certainly weren't nearly as free-scoring.

On Saturday, 10 September 1977, the Blues went to Filbert Street and thrashed Leicester 5-1. After failing to score in his first three games that season, Latchford bagged the opener, setting him on the long and winding road to the *Daily Express* prize. Then, less than a month later, Everton visited Loftus Road and inflicted exactly the same scoreline on Queens Park Rangers. This time, Latchford scored four.

Regrettably, I didn't make it to either game. Instead, I sat in my bedroom, exultantly listening to the commentary on the radio. But on the morning after each of those 5-1 away wins I cycled to Holders newsagents at the bottom of Lynton Road and, dipping heavily into my meagre savings, bought all the Sunday newspapers. Every single one of them. In those days, Sunday papers weren't the massive and unwieldy bundles of sections and supplements they are now, but it was still something of a challenge to carry them all home. After that my task was easy. I carefully cut out each of the Everton reports and Sellotaped them around the top of my bedroom wall, creating a frieze of rhapsodic headlines that stayed there, peeling and yellowing, until my mother remarried five years later and the house was sold.

Sticking five past Leicester and QPR, even on their own grounds, was an example of what in cricket is called flat-track bullying. In other words, those teams weren't very good, and Everton's scoring fiestas that season did tend to come in matches against the weaker sides. Leicester would finish the season in twenty-second and bottom place, with a nightmarish goal difference of -44. To put that in perspective, Tottenham Hotspur – the once mighty Spurs! –

Bob Latchford scores the penalty against Chelsea that took him to 30 goals for the 1977-78 season, securing a £10,000 prize from the *Daily Express*. Somewhere above and to the left of the camera, I celebrated as though he'd just won the ten grand for me.

Bob Latchford in training, either waiting for the ball to descend, or watching a plane coming in to land at Speke Airport. The tight shorts and the unruly perm fix the era precisely. It could only be the late 1970s.

Latchford as he is now . . . still stuck on the Toffees. Even in his sixties he remains what my dear old mother would call 'a dish'.

George Wood in 1978, the year he really should have been Scotland's, Scotland's, number one. Not even the great Neville Southall had a relationship with the Gwladys Street faithful like Georgie Wood.

Wood in 2004, on the coaching staff at Cardiff City. He still lives in South Wales.

We all agreed, Duncan McKenzie was magic. Here he is at Old Trafford, in action against the Arthur Albiston-era Manchester United, in March 1978. Latchford scored both Everton goals that day, in a 2-1 win.

The lugubrious-looking miner's son from Staffordshire, Gordon Lee. He is still unfairly maligned by many Everton fans old enough to remember the 1970s.

Martin Dobson, the classiest of midfielders, with the dodgiest of perms.

Andy was our King. Here he celebrates his goal against Chelsea in November 1978. The Luton larrikin remains a devoted Evertonian. He claims to be a Scouser with a funny accent.

Mike Lyons and Aston Villa's Chris Nicholl stage a dress rehearsal of the 1977 League Cup final. Note the Subbuteo floodlights. You had to move them when you wanted to take a corner.

Dave Thomas, socks down, in his pomp. One of the great thrills of supporting Everton in those days was seeing him fly down the left wing, before landing a cross on whichever part of Bob Latchford's forehead the big man wanted it.

Stan Bowles, Thomas's former teammate at Queens Park Rangers, was always given bespoke taunting at Goodison Park. What a rascal, but what a player.

Mike Pejic, Gordon Lee's first signing for Everton. It was £150,000 well spent.

Pejic in 2009 . . . He confessed to me that he'd been so depressed when injury terminated his playing career that he considered suicide.

Andy King nutmegs Geoff Palmer of Wolves, in January 1978, in conditions less suited to Palmer and King than Torvill and Dean. John McAlle, George Berry and Bob Latchford look on.

Only these two managers finished ahead of Gordon Lee in 1977-78. Brian Clough and Bob Paisley both came from the north-east, were both the shrewdest of cookies, yet could hardly have been more different.

Another son of the north-east, in fact Don Revie and Brian Clough both hailed from Middlesbrough, yet they loathed each other. How different England's fortunes might have been if the irrepressible Clough had succeeded Revie as manager.

Ally MacLeod and his Scotland squad before setting off for the 1978 World Cup. Nothing went right for them that summer, not even this picture, in which Bruce Rioch and Kenny Burns are inexplicably gazing elsewhere.

My son Joseph was an Everton mascot at the Merseyside derby on his eighth birthday, 19 April 2003. Here he is with his proud dad on the hallowed Goodison turf before the game, which the Reds disobligingly won 2-1. For Joe it was an early lesson in how Liverpool always seem to manage to wreck an Everton party.

A young man destined for great things . . . and Wayne Rooney.

had come bottom the season before a mere 24 goals in arrears. As for QPR, they avoided relegation by just a point in 1977-78, and to nobody's great surprise took the plunge into the Second Division the following season.

I had a soft spot for QPR and still do. My affection for them began during their *annus mirabilis* of 1975-76 when they pushed Liverpool all the way to the title and indeed led by a point after finishing all their games. If Everton couldn't win the league, which that year they plainly couldn't, finishing a distant eleventh, then the next best thing was that other team I liked to root for, anyone-but-Liverpool FC.

The climax to that bizarre season in the mid-1970s is worth considering in light of the modern, and it has to be said, far more sensible convention of every team playing its last game of the season at the same time. It might have been cooked up for the delectation of a TV audience, but it still yields a much fairer climax than in the days when one or two teams could continue to push for the title when their nearest rivals had all finished their challenge. That was palpably unfair and, of course, ripe with opportunities for corruption, hence those allegations against Don Revie and Emlyn Hughes.

But even by the standards of the times, in the spring of 1976 the fixture list was in a mess. QPR finished their campaign with a 2-0 home win over Leeds on Saturday, 24 April. That was scheduled to be the final day of the season, and Rangers ended it top of the league. Unfortunately, Liverpool had a game still to play, and did not play it for another ten days.

The club had asked for a postponement of their final fixture against Wolves because Joey Jones and John Toshack had been called up by Wales for a European Championships qualifier in Yugoslavia. So not until the following Tuesday, 4 May, did Liverpool visit Molineux, and with the release of *Star Wars* still a year away, I don't suppose anyone cracked the pun, 'May the fourth be with you.' But it was. The poor QPR supporters had not only had to wait ten days to find out whether they'd won the First Division title for the first time, they then had to suffer the agony of getting within fifteen minutes of glory, before it was snatched away. Liverpool were 1-0 down to a Steve Kindon goal until Kevin Keegan equalised and John Toshack then Ray Kennedy added two more.

So I empathised with the QPR fans, since they too knew what it felt like to be denied by Liverpool. But there was more to it than that. I liked their quirky name, their blue-and-white hoops, and in particular I liked the buccaneering way they played. If ever a team was cast in the mould of the chairman, rather than the manager, it was Jim Gregory's QPR. A boyhood QPR fan who had apparently left school at fourteen barely able to read or write, Gregory had made a fortune from second-hand car dealerships. He was a charismatic man who wanted his players to show the same flamboyance, and unashamedly made favourites of those who did, such as Rodney Marsh and above all Stan Bowles.

Bowles was one of those players who wound up opposing fans simply because he scared the life out of them. When he came to Goodison Park, the Gwladys Street rocked to another anthem with Cole Porter-esque lyrics: 'Oh Stanley, Stanley . . . Stanley, Stanley, Stanley, Stanley shithouse Bowles.' Of course, those lyrics were eminently versatile, as long as the man turning out for the opposition conveniently had a two-syllable first name, followed by a one-syllable surname. I can remember similar refrains being aimed at Rodney Marsh, Charlie George and, with particularly heartfelt vehemence, at Liverpool's Jimmy Case.

But Bowles did have one chant that was all his own, and which surfaced shortly after newspaper reports that his wife had left him. Then it was an even more raucous: 'Stanley, Stanley, where's your wife? Stanley! Where's your wife?' Probably like most people on the Gwladys Street terraces, I wouldn't have dreamt of issuing such a cruel taunt in a one-on-one situation, but, of course, I joined in with gusto. It was and will ever be thus, being a football fan. Being in a mob confers bravado, if bravado is what it was, taunting Bowles about his errant missus.

It can't have surprised anyone that Mrs Bowles walked out, mind you. Her old man was a wonderful footballer, capable of doing things that very few of his contemporaries could, but he was also a compulsive gambler, and chronically unlucky, or perhaps just chronically rubbish. His very own mother once said that if he invested in a cemetery, people would stop dying.

In October 2005 I interviewed Bowles, meeting him in a shabby pub in Spitalfields, in the East End of London. I spent a fascinating hour with him, but a day or two later as I wrote up the piece for the *Independent* I mused that nostalgia, much as we all enjoy indulging in it, is fundamentally delusional. That's rather a strange admission to make in a book that is overwhelmingly nostalgic, but it is true, all the same.

At the time I met Bowles, England's footballers had just qualified for the 2006 World Cup. And yet there I was, waiting to meet a man who more than most footballers of his generation, symbolised a decade in which England failed to reach successive World Cups, a man who openly consorted with gangsters, who once accepted a bribe to throw a game, in fact who made some of the most poorly behaved players in the modern game look like paragons of virtue. Yet despite all that, to most football lovers of roughly my age, myself very much included, the name Stan Bowles evoked a golden era.

I have already touched on that paradox in these pages: the crowd violence of the 1970s, the muddy quagmires masquerading as pitches, and the sometimes sluggish nature of the game itself, with only two points for a win promoting negativity, and no laws against repeatedly passing back to the goalkeeper, are inadequate barriers to those of us who cleave to the belief that it was football's most romantic age.

I suppose this springs partly from our own age; I don't know any football fans who reached their teens sometime during the 1970s and don't feel that sense of romanticism. But it isn't just an illusion. For giant-killing exploits in the uniquely romantic FA Cup, up to and sometimes including the final, the 1970s unarguably remains the supreme decade. Moreover, it was a decade that somehow showcased the skills of those inordinately gifted players to whom I have already referred – magicians such as Alan Hudson, Tony Currie, Rodney Marsh, Frank Worthington, Everton's own Duncan McKenzie (is Magic), and, of course, Bowles. Maybe Bowles above all.

But what a rascal he was. I asked him whether, to fund his gambling habit, he was ever invited to conspire in fixing matches. After all, some of his closest boyhood friends were members of Manchester's Quality Street Gang, who didn't earn that name by having soft centres and were reputed to have been the inspiration for the Thin Lizzy song 'The Boys Are Back in Town'.

It is also said that when Ronnie and Reggie Kray took the train up to Manchester, having heard that there were rich pickings up north if they could expand their crime empire, they were met at Piccadilly Station by a few of the Quality Street boys, who none too politely suggested that they should take the next train back to Euston, which they did. The former gangster 'Mad' Frankie Fraser, whom I once memorably interviewed in the back of a limo while he showed me round the gangland sights of the East End, has questioned that tale. He said that the Krays never travelled by train and never felt the need to operate outside London. But still, why let Frankie Fraser get in the way of a good story?

Anyway, Bowles laughed when I asked him whether he'd been asked to help fix matches. 'It may have cropped up,' he said, rather coyly for him, then surprised me by taking a reflective puff on a cigarette and coming clean. 'The only time I done it was a five-a-side. Do you remember the national five-a-side tournament? I was playing for QPR and we reached the final against Leyton Orient. I had a good mate who was an Orient supporter – Jewish Dennis he was called, he's dead now – and he'd backed them to win the thing – £1000 at 8-1. He said to me, "If you go boss-eyed in the final, you've got a grand."

'Well, I only stood to get £200 if we won the final, so I said "Certainly". I scored a goal but we lost 6-1, and our manager, Gerry Francis, said to me afterwards: "You looked a bit tired in the second half."'

Bowles's nicotine-infused laughter rang round the pub. 'But it was only five-a-side,' he said. 'It didn't matter.'

Playing for England never mattered to him, either. 'I was happy playing for QPR, that was all,' he told me. 'I played five times for England, for three different managers. Some say I got them all the sack.'

I told him what Alan Hudson once plaintively said to me, that the trio of him, Bowles and the similarly blessed Frank Worthington did not collectively get as many England caps as Carlton Palmer. 'Yeah,' Bowles said, and lit up another Benson & Hedges, which he smoked in the time-honoured way of the sixty-a-day man, cupped in his hand with the tip all but brushing his palm. 'I even had less than Ralph fucking Coates.'

But if he didn't care about playing for England himself, why should it have bothered him so much who did? Maybe, in his own way, he cared too much. When the caretaker manager Joe Mercer withdrew him just after half-time in the home international against Northern Ireland on 15 May 1974, Bowles decided he'd had enough of the England set-up. 'I left the hotel the next day,' he told me, 'before the game against Scotland. Mick Channon was my room-mate, and he said: "You can't do this to England." I said, "Watch me. You see that car outside, that's the one I'm jumping in." I went to White City dogs that night, and there were loads of reporters following me around. Unfortunately one of them, a *Daily Mirror* reporter, got knocked out by one of my ... associates. He fell down the stairs and hit his head on the concrete. The next day it looked as if about eight people had beaten him up, but it wasn't like that.'

Whether or not it was like that, it's literally impossible to imagine such a narrative unfolding now. Just picture it: even the most mercurial of the current England squad getting stroppy about being substituted, walking out of the team hotel in a huff, spending the evening at a dog track with an entourage of hardmen, and then watching as one of them 'bumped into' a reporter and knocked him down a flight of stone steps. Think of the flap the media get into now when a footballer wears an inappropriate costume at a fancy-dress party, or is spotted holding a cigarette. Times have not so much changed as transmogrified beyond recognition.

So in that sense, if a single footballer might be held to represent the 1970s, it is Stanley Bowles. That is why I have devoted the best part of a chapter to him, but it is time to get back to Everton, and specifically to a player who made his England debut in the same match that Bowles did, against Portugal in Lisbon in April 1974, but for whom playing for the national team was a source of infinite pride. His name was Mike Pejic.

Chapter Thirteen

I met Mike Pejic in a hotel opposite the station in Stoke-on-Trent. Prior to this, and without the slightest clue as to what had become of him, I'd looked him up on Wikipedia. There it was rather alarmingly stated that his most recent football job had been at Ipswich Town, as a youth coach, until he was suspended following allegations of bullying. Could it be so?

The hotel was his suggestion, but I'd been there before, once buying myself lunch there while waiting for a delayed train. I amused myself that day by eavesdropping on a group of young people in their early twenties, seated at a neighbouring table. One of them was in full flow, telling the others about a film he'd seen, when suddenly he stopped, aghast, and gestured out of the window.

'Bloody hell,' he spluttered, almost apoplectic with indignation. 'Someone's put a traffic cone on Josiah Wedgwood's head!'

There was indeed a statue outside the station of the great 18th-century pottery-maker (who by the way was also the grandfather of Charles Darwin), and it had indeed been crowned with a traffic cone. But what amused me most about this young fellow's outrage was that he belonged to precisely the generation that might be expected, as a late-night drunken prank, to show such disrespect to one of Stoke's most famous sons. Coincidentally, I'd read only days earlier in my own local paper, the *Hereford Times*, about a bloke of twenty-five who claimed to be traumatised after riding through a wood on his mountain bike and coming across two pensioners having sex in a clearing. I heartily approved of that reversal of the natural order of things, and hoped very much that it had been a couple of codgers in their sixties who had picked up the cone and plonked it on poor Josiah, causing such affront to the twenty-somethings.

But it couldn't possibly have been sixty-something Mike Pejic. No, as a first-generation Englishman, whose father Milovan was a Serb who settled here at the end of the Second World War, Pejic would have had far too much respect for Britain's heritage to have cocked a snook at such a respected historical figure. In fact, it's a shame it wasn't Pejic rather than Mick Channon rooming with Stan Bowles prior to that Scotland game. He'd have clocked him.

As with many of the other old Everton players I interviewed for this book, I recognised Pejic instantly. Like Neil Robinson, he hadn't put on any weight, and helpfully he still had roughly the same haircut that he'd sported the last time I'd seen him, some thirty years earlier, which now made him look a little like an ageing roadie. He also still looked like a bloke who would as soon break your arm as shake your hand, and I remembered what Bob Latchford had said at the Cheshire Yeoman: 'I wouldn't want to argue with Pej.'

Contrary to appearances, however, he was softly spoken, almost shy, but engagingly keen to tell me about the twists and turns of his life. We started with the fascinating story of how his Serb father and English mother had met.

His father came from Vrgudinac, a small farming community in southern Serbia, and grew up fully expecting to work the land. But then came the war and the German invasion of Yugoslavia, which exacerbated tensions between Serbs and Croats. Milovan joined the anti-German partisans in the hills, who were led by Josip Tito, a Croat, although most of the fighters were Serbs. Towards the end of hostilities he ended up in a British military camp in Italy – Pejic wasn't sure how – and decided to chance his arm in England rather than return to his family. So Milovan moved first to Cambridgeshire, and then after a short while, to a hostel in Newcastle-under-Lyme. It was there that he met a young local girl, who gave birth to their first son when she was only sixteen.

'Can you imagine the impact of that back then,' said Pejic. 'I could have ended up in a children's home.'

Milovan became a miner, and spent the next thirty years working at Parkhouse Colliery as a coal cutter. He was by no means the only Serb to have wound up in Staffordshire, and he and his compatriots formed a Serbian football team, which played in the Newcastle league. Young Michael grew up watching his dad playing football, and having kickabouts himself in a field by the nearby gasworks.

'When I was fourteen my dad took me down to Stoke. They asked me to train Tuesday and Thursday evenings, and Frankie Mountford, who was also the first-team trainer, must have liked what he saw, because he asked me to continue, and then to sign associate schoolboy forms.'

It was 1964, and Stoke City were back in the First Division after a ten-year absence. They had secured promotion in the final home match of the previous season with a 2-0 home victory against Luton Town that was inspired by 48-year-old Stanley Matthews. The great man's final game for Stoke was on 11 February 1965. Stoke beat Fulham 3-1. Matthews was fifty years and five days old. Later, he decided he'd retired too early.

At the other end of the age spectrum, young Pejic left school and expected to be signed as an apprentice. But terms weren't offered. 'So I worked on the Corona pop wagon, delivering pop to shops. I did that for twelve months.'

The Corona pop wagon's gain was Stoke City's loss, but the following year, Stoke held a trial game and Pejic acquitted himself well enough to be offered a one-year apprenticeship. Then, in a match in Birmingham, he went to head the ball out while defending a corner-kick and was booted hard in the face, smashing his nose to bits and knocking him unconscious. He was in hospital for a week, but in his first game back, on a snow-covered pitch at the Victoria Ground, he played fearlessly. When he came off, he was invited to turn professional.

'I was a quiet lad but I knew my own mind,' he told me. 'I'd been a winger, but I played in a reserve game at full back, with Bill Bentley at centre back. We drew 0-0 and I didn't do badly, but Tony Waddington, the manager, dropped me. So I stopped him in a corridor and asked him why. I was all of sixteen. But that's what I'd been like at school if I thought I'd been hard done by. I remember a teacher bawling at me from the touchline during a school match on the Saturday, which I thought was unfair, so I told him to be quiet. On the Monday he gave me the stick.'

Whether or not Waddington was impressed with Pejic's effrontery in demanding to know why he'd been dropped, he plainly recognised the lad's talent. 'Towards the end of the 1968-69 season, just before the first team set out for an evening game away at West Ham, he told me to go home and get my stuff, said I'd be travelling with the squad. Then an hour before kick-off he said, "Get your shirt on, you're playing." West Ham in those days still had Bobby Moore, Geoff Hurst, Martin Peters. And Harry Redknapp was playing on my side. He was a flier, Harry, a roadrunner. But there was no time for nerves. And I did all right. We drew 0-0. But the next game, he dropped me. So I went to see him again. Early the following season

I made my home debut against Sunderland, which we won 4-2, and after it he dropped me again. So I went to see him again.'

Pejic chuckled at the memory. 'I had belief in myself and I was quite feisty. He brought me back in after that and I made the place my own, ahead of Bill Bentley. The following season we won the League Cup. I was on forty quid a week basic by then, but a lot of the older players were on ninety quid basic, so I went to see him about a rise. He offered me another ten quid a week so I told him to shove it up his arse.'

More laughter. 'That was the season I got into the England under-23s. Alf Ramsey was still the England manager and he took the under-23s as well. Frank Lampard Senior was the left back, but I managed to displace him, and then Alf gave me my senior debut against Portugal.'

Pejic's first game for England, in April 1974, would prove to be Ramsey's last. He was sacked just over a fortnight later. 'He was a great man, Alf. Brilliant. I was driving when the news came through on the radio that they'd sacked him, and I remember stopping the car outside my house and breaking down. Cried my eyes out. I don't for a second feel any embarrassment about that. I kept crying, even when I was inside the house.

'He'd been great with me, Alf, and he treated everybody the same, whether it was someone who'd played for England for years or a new lad. He treated me the same as Bobby Moore. Every time we met he'd give you something to work with, and of course he'd been a full back himself, like. Just before he was sacked he was on at me to get crosses in with the inside of my foot, whipping them in behind defenders. Great man.'

Ramsey was succeeded by Joe Mercer, of Ellesmere Port, and for that matter Goodison Park fame. But Mercer was no Ramsey, at least not as far as Pejic was concerned. 'I played in the Home Internationals in May that year, 1974, and although me and Colin

Todd scored an own goal each in a 2-0 defeat to Scotland, I put in some decent performances.

'But after one of the games, on the bus to the team hotel in Welwyn Garden City, Joe Mercer asked me to sit next to him. He told me he was calling Alec Lindsay [the Liverpool left back] into the squad. I said "All right". There were no other words. But I knew he was telling me I'd lost my place, and I knew Emlyn Hughes had instigated it. Emlyn Hughes had a lot of influence on Joe Mercer. When we went training the next day there was a fifty-fifty between me and him, and he chickened out. He knew I'd have killed him. Toddy was shouting out, "Stay away from Pej this morning."'

Pejic took a sip of tea and smiled ruefully. 'Emlyn Hughes. Never liked him. He was a squealer on the pitch, always on at referees, manipulating people. There was one meeting with Alf Ramsey, and he rang Alf to give some excuse for not being there, so Alf told us all he'd had Emlyn on the phone. Laughing at him, like. He couldn't manipulate Alf.'

As expected, Mercer dropped Pejic for the next game, a friendly against Argentina. 'From being in the England squad, getting in the team under Alf, my future had looked good. It all changed. There was an Eastern European tour coming up and Alf had picked me for the squad, but after he was sacked I thought I might not go, until my father talked me round.

'My relatives were coming to Belgrade to see me, that's why I went. But for the game in Belgrade I wasn't even sub. My dad's brother, his sister, her two daughters and his two lads, had come all the way on the train, and I wasn't even sub. It was quite sad, really. They came to the hotel, where I was sharing a room with David Mills, the lad from Middlesbrough. They'd brought a sheep with them. A whole cooked sheep, wrapped in polythene.

'David vacated the room for the afternoon and we sat there

eating the sheep, and drinking Sljivovica, which is plum brandy. I only had a few words of Serbo-Croat, but I'd been there before, as a fourteen-year-old. My dad drove us there, over the mountains, in a Vauxhall Cresta.'

It is an irresistible image: an England footballer spending all afternoon tucking into a whole sheep with his Serb relatives, unable to converse much with them but with the plum brandy doubtless breaking down the communication barriers, while a 2-2 draw between their country and his unfolded at the national stadium.

From an Everton perspective, that Eastern European tour was significant because it introduced another future Toffee, Martin Dobson, to the England midfield. Dobson had actually made his debut alongside Pejic and Bowles in the Portugal game, but on the four-match tour he was an ever-present, and looked for all the world as if he would be an England regular for years to come. In fact, he would finish with only one more cap than Pejic.

The England team that played Yugoslavia that day – 5 June 1974 – was: Clemence, Hughes, Lindsay, Todd, Watson, Dobson, Keegan, Channon, Worthington (winning the sixth of just eight caps), Bell and Brooking. The two goalscorers were Channon and Keegan, which was in itself an achievement because Kevin Keegan, in an extraordinary incident which one hopes could no more happen now than that a squad player could while away an afternoon eating a sheep and drinking plum brandy, had been beaten up a couple of days earlier by Yugoslavian customs officials.

It was an eventful year for Keegan, 1974. In May he scored two goals in the FA Cup final, helping Liverpool beat Newcastle 3-0. Then in August he was sent off during the Charity Shield game against Leeds United, for scrapping with Billy Bremner. Both men were banned for eleven games.

The most bizarre episode in his year, though, occurred between the high of the FA Cup final and the low of the Charity Shield, at Belgrade airport. Mercer's team arrived from Sofia, where they had beaten Bulgaria 1-0. Unfortunately, the FA's travel agent had rather ineptly overlooked the fact that Sofia was an hour ahead of Belgrade, which meant that the delegation of Yugoslav football officials had been given the wrong arrival time and were not there to greet their guests. In the meantime, a Bulgarian air stewardess had issued a complaint that one of the England players had goosed her during the flight. History, alas, does not record who had done the goosing, or for that matter, given what your typical Bulgarian air-hostess might have looked like in 1974, whether the alleged bottom-pinching was a case of wishful thinking.

Whatever, as the *Guardian*'s venerable football writer David Lacey recalled thirty-five years later, England did not look much like an international football team when they came through immigration. Most of them were wearing jeans and T-shirts, and several of them had a few days' worth of stubble. Alf Ramsey would certainly not have tolerated it, and nor in Ramsey's presence would one of the players – as it happens, Pejic's replacement Alec Lindsay – have started to 'fool around' on the baggage carousel.

Keegan, carrying two bags of souvenir pottery from Bulgaria, had done nothing more provocative than sit down on the edge of the carousel, but he was the one singled out by a 'scruffy little man in a brown suit', as another venerable football writer, Brian Glanville, would later record. This man tried to wrench Keegan's bags from him, which Keegan resisted, only for a 'huge policeman in peaked cap, grey uniform and jackboots' to march in and drag the player off to a back room. There he was forced, in his own later words, to 'kneel like a prisoner of war' while being punched, clubbed and kicked. He was then charged with the assault on the stewardess (of which he was certainly innocent, having slept through the flight), assaulting a security guard and disturbing the peace.

Again, one can only imagine what repercussions such an episode might have ignited now. As it was, a small posse of English officials, including Mercer and the FA secretary Ted Croker, managed to calm the situation by explaining to the guards exactly who it was they were attacking. Those were still the days when footballers of another nationality, even one as famous as Kevin Keegan, could be expected to pass through a foreign airport unrecognised. He was released, in tears, and the charges were dropped.

As Lacey remembered the incident, Croker hoped that the reporters travelling with the team might be persuaded not to write about what had happened. But the *Evening Standard*'s man Bernard Joy was having none of that. He phoned his office intending to dictate his report to a copytaker. Unfortunately, it wasn't a copytaker who answered the phone but a caretaker, who told him that, it being a Sunday, there was nobody else in the building.

Nonetheless, the incident did get some attention in the British press, but precious little from diplomats, who felt that an official protest might hinder their efforts to gain freedom for two British men jailed a few months earlier for that staple crime in totalitarian countries: photographing military aircraft. The Eastern European tour plodded on, and Pejic ate his sheep. But even for those who played in the matches, and even taking the roughing-up of Keegan out of the equation, the tour rather symbolised a distinctly unhappy year for England in international football terms.

Just five years earlier they had been champions of the world, and yet a week after the players got home from that summer tour, the 1974 World Cup began, very much without them, in West Germany. Rightly or wrongly, the blame for England's absence was heaped squarely on Ramsey, yet his sacking was a shabby business, forced through by the FA's autocratic vice-chairman, Professor Sir Harold Thompson. Outrageously, the man who had masterminded the World Cup win in 1966 was not, eight years later, even offered a chance to ease himself out of the managerial hot seat before he was ignominiously dragged.

Incidentally, is there a single body in British public life that has scored more own goals over the past fifty-odd years than the Football Association? I can't think of one. From the sacking of Ramsey to the bewildering contract extension and bountiful pay rise handed to Sven-Göran Eriksson, the FA seems to have lurched between sheer lack of class on the one hand, and pure folly on the other. But never was it led by a man as loathsome as Harold Thompson. He was a brilliant academic, a renowned chemist who as an Oxford don had tutored the young Margaret Thatcher, but as Leo McKinstry writes in his absorbing 2006 biography of Alf Ramsey, Thompson was also a figure of 'almost suffocating pomposity' who never referred to England's most successful manager, even to his face, as anything but 'Ramsey'.

According to McKinstry, Thompson was also something of a dirty old man, with a particular reputation for touching-up air stewardesses that once resulted in a formal complaint to the FA from British European Airways. So maybe it was him, rather than a player, doing the goosing on that flight from Bulgaria. Whatever, Ramsey couldn't bear him and the feeling was entirely mutual. As McKinstry also writes, during a trip to Prague for a friendly match against Czechoslovakia in 1973, Thompson sat at the breakfast table at the team hotel smoking a fat cigar. Ramsey asked him politely to put it out, as the cloud of cigar smoke was unpleasant for his players. Thompson did so, but grudgingly and resentfully. He had never been spoken to like that by a mere 'employee' before. 'Alf's fate may have been sealed in that Czechoslovakian breakfast room,' McKinstry concluded.

One of the sources used by Leo McKinstry to construct his engrossing portrait of Ramsey was Pejic, who told him: 'Alf somehow built up this rapport with you, this trust, this feeling for him.

When he was in charge, you didn't want a penny for playing for England. You would have paid him.'

England's next permanent manager, Don Revie, might have approved of that idea. Revie was appointed on 4 July 1974, and Pejic of Stoke, unlike Latchford of Everton, wasn't even invited to the gathering of eighty players, summoned by Revie to the Midland Hotel in Manchester to hear his plans for the future.

'I'd always had issues with Leeds,' Pejic told me. 'I either scored against them or was sent off, so I felt that Don Revie didn't like me very much. I became very disillusioned with football around that time, because it had always been one of my main goals to play for England. I bought a farm in the hills near Buxton, and ran away from football in a way. My form dipped, and then I broke my leg in a game against Wolves at the Victoria Ground. I spent six weeks in plaster, and I was at home one day when my daughter Clare, who was only three at the time, wanted to go to the local shop.

'So we got up to the Congleton-Buxton Road, in heavy sleet and snow, and when we came to a corner, my brakes locked. A Vauxhall Velox 2.3 estate, it was. And it rolled over and over, fell about 70 feet and ended up upside down on a bridle path. There are three things I can remember: my daughter going over me, thinking "hurry up and stop" as the car kept rolling, and coming round to hear my daughter crying. I pushed her out of a window and managed to climb out myself. Luckily, neither of us had been strapped in. If we had been, we'd definitely have been crushed. It was an amazing escape. The police came and they couldn't believe it. In fact the story was later printed in a magazine, in a feature about miraculous escapes.'

It was bad winter weather that nearly killed him that day, and it was bad winter weather that would determine the next phase of his career. In January 1976 the roof of the Victoria Ground's old Butler

Street Stand was ripped off by gale-force winds. It turned out that the club wasn't fully insured, and over the next twelve months or so the cost of repairs necessitated the sale of several of Stoke's best players, including Alan Hudson, Jimmy Greenhoff and Pejic.

'I needed a decent move, because I was still building the farm. I had 25 acres, twelve suckling cows and I wanted to purchase some more land. Also, I still thought I was good enough for England. I thought I was the best left back in the country. So I was happy when Everton came in for me.

'They'd tried to get me before, actually. Harry Catterick had made a bid for me when I was nineteen, and then Billy Bingham tried. Brian Clough wanted me for Derby, too. He offered £400,000 for me in 1973. He wanted Shilton, Nish, Todd, McFarland and me as his back line, which he also thought should be the England back line. But Tony Waddington turned him down. Then Gordon Lee came in for me. He'd been Port Vale manager and knew all about me, and with the stand blowing down, Waddo wasn't really in a position to say no. But he still only let me go there because Everton were below Stoke at the time.'

Pejic was twenty-seven years old and he cost £150,000. It was February 1977 and he was Lee's first signing as Everton manager. A new era was beginning for both these sons of Staffordshire, and, we on the terraces all profoundly hoped, for the club itself. We had all been moping in Liverpool's shadow for too long.

Chapter Fourteen

In August 1977 came the start of the first full season at Everton for both Pejic and Lee, and with it, a coach carrying the Nottingham Forest team. Jonathan Wilson, in his magisterial biography of Clough, *Nobody Ever Says Thank You*, writes that there were considerable pre-match nerves in the away dressing room. Liverpool's success might have cast a giant shadow across Stanley Park, but Everton were still regarded as serious title challengers, and Goodison Park was an even more intimidating place to visit then than it is now. Especially, for all their promise, by players just promoted from the Second Division.

Martin O'Neill told Wilson that as they waited for kick-off, he and his teammates 'felt about two-feet tall'. But then Peter Taylor came in, and for ten whole minutes basically performed a comedy routine, telling jokes and stories so funny that many of the players were still chuckling as they stepped on to the Goodison turf. It was a deliberate tactic, endorsed by Clough, who later wrote in one of his own books: 'I would far rather have my players rolling about the dressing room floor laughing than have them trying to fathom a list of instructions and tactics before they went out and played a match.'

That wasn't how it was across the corridor. Lee was by no means as dour as he looked, but he was no Les Dawson. Besides, he had no need to quell any nerves, with or without jokes. Even with Latchford suspended, Forest were surely there for the taking.

What followed, instead, was the taking of Everton 1-2-3. But the home team's frailties at the back were such that the *Guardian*'s correspondent, for one, felt that the game offered no great insight into Forest as an attacking force. 'Brian Clough is quite a subdued fellow these days,' went the report in Monday's paper. 'The Nottingham Forest manager did not get carried away by his team's demonstration of their abilities on their return to the First Division after five years, and neither should anyone else. One cannot go overboard yet ... they have the element of surprise at the moment. However, the skills of players such as Tony Woodcock and John Robertson are quickly going to be recognised by more competent defenders than those on display at Goodison Park. When that happens, Forest should be prepared for hard times.'

It was a singularly unprescient report, the predicted hard times amounting to a league title, followed by a European Cup, and then another European Cup. But it probably wasn't wide of the mark in implying Everton's incompetence in defence that day. Pejic, with that enviable talent many ex-footballers have for remembering the good performances and blotting out the bad, had no particular recollection of the game at all. But he certainly remembered having to deal with Forest's coltishly leggy, marauding right back, Viv Anderson.

The following year, two days before his twenty-second birthday, Anderson would become the first black footballer to play for England. Laurie Cunningham had turned out for the under-21s in April 1977, becoming the first black player to represent England at any level, but Anderson's was the real milestone: a starting berth against Czechoslovakia at Wembley and a full international cap.

It seems remarkable now that it should have caused any kind of fuss, but of course it did, and not only the right kind of fuss. 'Yellow, purple or black, if they're good enough, I'll pick them,' declared England manager Ron Greenwood before the game, and irreproachably well meaning as that comment was, it now sounds rather shocking. Roy Hodgson's ill-advised 'space monkey' joke about Andros Townsend, in October 2013, showed that England managers still have to be sensitive about matters of skin colour, but at least they don't have to defend their selections for the national team on the basis that it doesn't matter whether the players are 'yellow, purple or black'. As a society we've made progress since 1977.

In 2008, in an interview with the *Guardian*, Anderson recalled his England debut with pride, if also some embarrassment at having become a significant historical footnote. 'I had a hand in the goal and we won 1-0,' he said. 'I remember Bob Latchford telling me I'd remember it for ever and he was right. It was a very positive reaction from the terraces. To them, it was all about the football.'

If only that had always been so. I have to remind myself continually that history does not regard the late 1970s with quite as much unequivocal affection as I do, and the biggest blight on the era, bigger even than rampant hooliganism, was that other, even more entrenched -ism.

It is interesting now how we English tend to recoil in somewhat superior disgust at the spectacle of foreign fans serenading black players with monkey chants. And if there's the odd inflatable banana in the crowd, we positively erupt in righteous indignation. When the Croatian Football Federation was fined 80,000 euros after Croatia fans abused Mario Balotelli during Euro 2012, the consensus among football enthusiasts here was that the punishment was absurdly inadequate, as indeed it was. When in October 2013 Manchester City's Yaya Touré complained about monkey noises issued by CSKA Moscow fans during a Champions League game, there was another burst of disapproval, ignited by the unspoken conviction that here in Britain we are a great deal more civilised. But the moral high ground has only recently been scaled. In the 1970s – when a prime-time sitcom, *Love Thy Neighbour*, resounded to words such as 'sambo' and 'nig-nog' – we really had no claim on it at all.

To cite only Anderson's experience – and it's worth remembering that he was a defender, who didn't worry opposing fans like black strikers such as Cunningham and Cyrille Regis of West Bromwich Albion did – he described in his poignantly titled autobiography, *First Among Unequals*, the first time he was subjected to full-on racism. It was just his second game for Forest, a League Cup tie away at Newcastle United, and the 'really vicious' abuse began while he was warming up before the game. When in the course of the ninety minutes he was poleaxed in a challenge by the Newcastle striker John Tudor, there was a thunderous cheer from the best part – or should it be the worst part? – of 50,000 people. Anderson was eighteen years old.

A year later, while merely coming off the substitute's bench to warm up during a Second Division game away at Carlisle, he was pelted with bananas, apples and pears and retreated hastily to the dugout. 'I thought I told you to warm up,' said Clough.

'I have done, boss, but they're throwing fruit at me,' replied Anderson.

Clough looked him in the eye, 'Well, get your fucking arse back out there and fetch me two pears and a banana,' he said.

Clough wasn't just being funny. It was his entirely typical way of telling Anderson that he had to rise above it, and Anderson did. But in a strange way those racist chants were even harder for disapproving fans to rise above, because we were part of the crowd shouting them.

It is sometimes suggested that Goodison Park was among the

half-dozen worst grounds in terms of racist abuse of black players in the 1970s, and further claimed that Everton were rather late in fielding black players because of some kind of institutionalised racism.

I'm about as sure as I can be that there is no substance at all in this latter charge. It's true that Everton didn't have even one black player turning out regularly until the exciting Nigerian Daniel Amokachi signed in 1994, but it's ridiculous to suggest that an unofficial whites-only policy prevailed before then. After all, the two-goal hero of the 1966 FA Cup final, Mike Trebilcock, had mixed-race antecedents, and I've even heard it suggested that the great Dixie Dean did, too.

In terms of abuse from the terraces I prefer to think that Goodison Park was no worse than most other grounds when black players took the field in the unenlightened 1970s. Which, admittedly, doesn't add up to much of a defence. Besides, Cyrille Regis in his autobiography offered contrary evidence. 'The grounds that really stuck out were Leeds, West Ham, Birmingham, Everton, Tottenham and Chelsea,' he wrote. 'At Spurs they used to sing: "Who's that up a tree – big Cyrille, big Cyrille." Three black players in a team [him, Cunningham and Brendon Batson] was just too much for some supporters.'

At The Hawthorns, the office staff used to dread opening the post. 'Laurie copped it worse because he went out with a white lady,' Regis wrote. One of the letters contained a bullet, intended as a warning about what would happen if Cunningham became the first black footballer to win a full England cap.

I'd be lying if I claimed not to remember the vile monkey chants when West Brom in particular came to Goodison. But what I can write, hand on heart – or would write hand on heart if I didn't need both hands to type – is that I stood silently, listening to it around me and wishing it would stop.

Heaven knows I didn't have some sort of super-developed

conscience as a 16-year-old. I'd done my share of minor shoplifting, for example, at least until the day when, on the way home from school, I surreptitiously lifted a couple of Mars bars and a Twix in the course of legitimately buying a packet of salt-and-vinegar crisps and was halted in my tracks on the way out of the newsagents by a furious shout behind me. 'Hey, you,' bellowed the shopkeeper. I froze, and waited, aghast, for him to vault the counter, order me to turn out my pockets, call the police, and hold me in an armlock until I could be dragged off to the cells by a couple of hefty constables. But he didn't vault the counter. 'You've given me an Irish penny,' he thundered, brandishing it as if he was a referee and this was his red card. In the blissful rush of relief, mixed with the fleeting horror that I'd been rumbled, I resolved never to pinch anything ever again. But I can't pretend that it was an acute sense of right and wrong that stopped me.

When those 'ooh ooh ooh' cries started, however, I felt a definite stab of shame. I loved that brotherhood of Evertonians. It gave me a real feeling of togetherness, of belonging, at a time in my fatherless, sibling-free adolescence when I really needed it. But I knew even then, even if I couldn't have quite articulated it, that they were letting themselves down with those chants.

Some of my friends joined in with them, too, but I never rebuked them for it and now wish I had, although I would probably have got short shrift. I was almost as uncomfortable when shouts went up aimed at the police, as they often did in those days. Among the Gwladys Street faithful, the police were 'pigs' and fair game for loud collective abuse. But I couldn't bring myself to join in with that, either, and actually it amused me that a couple of my middle-class mates, from more affluent homes than mine, did so. In the case of one friend mouthing his rage one Saturday afternoon, I knew that these so-called pigs had just helped his parents recover their stolen Jag.

I hope that doesn't make me sound sanctimonious. As already chronicled, I was not averse to telling opposing fans that they were going home in a fucking ambulance, even if I preferred to despatch them in a combine harvester. And there was another song with which I joined in with unalloyed enthusiasm, an aggressive rallying cry ironically set to the tune of a 1968 hit by sweet, pretty Mary Hopkin:

> Those were the days, my friend,
> We took the Stretford End,
> We took the Shed,
> The North Bank, Highbury,
> We took the Geordies too,
> We fight for Everton,
> We are the Street ... of Everton FC

Well, I had never taken the Stretford End, the Shed at Stamford Bridge, or the North Bank, Highbury. Nor had I taken any Geordies anywhere, except the little daughter of my mother's cousin Caroline, who lived in Gateshead and whom I had once taken to the park. I had never fought for Everton, and never would. But I was emphatically part of the Gwladys Street End – 'the Street of Everton FC' – and if that meant bouncing up and down pretending to be some kind of warrior, then so be it.

Nor did I mind showing prejudice against Liverpool FC, and Liverpool fans – except for the many who were my friends. That was entirely fine and reasonable. Towards the end of the previous season, with Liverpool shortly to play Borussia Mönchengladbach in their first European Cup final, there was a brisk trade along Goodison Road in green, black and white Mönchengladbach scarves. I still had one pinned up above my bed.

But prejudice against black people was different, beyond the pale, even on the day Viv Anderson made a monkey of Mike Pejic, which didn't happen very often.

'What I remember about playing Forest at that time,' Pejic told me in the hotel opposite Stoke station, 'is that they would sit back really deep, inviting us on to them, and then attacking us on the counter. They defended really deep, which was more like the way the game was played on the continent, not in England.'

By the start of the 1977-78 season, Pejic already had the firm approval of the Goodison crowd. It wasn't as though there was a rapport with him like there was with Wood, Latchford or McKenzie, or with the captain, big Mick Lyons, or for that matter with the cheeky, pugnacious Scouser John Bailey, who would replace him at left back, but we knew we could rely on him putting in a really solid shift. He was terrific going forward, and very few wingers got the better of him. A Pejic tackle was like the crack of doom.

He laughed, mirthlessly, when I asked him what he thought when he saw modern-day footballers writhing around after making the most innocuous contact, or even no contact at all, with an opposition boot or elbow. 'I can't stand it,' he said. 'I remember my first match against Terry Paine, of Southampton. I tackled him on the halfway line, and as he rolled over he came down with both his boots on my back. I got up and twatted him, and we only got booked, the pair of us. No, when you went down you got straight back up. I remember knocking Tommy Smith to the ground. He got straight up and we went nose to nose. Not the two nicest noses in the game. But then we just smiled at each other and to this day we have a hug. You didn't roll around for half an hour because you didn't want them to see you were hurt. You'd just get up and bide your time until you could get them back. And if you didn't manage it that match, you'd wait until the next match against them, or even the one after that. You didn't forget. I never forgot.'

At Everton, the hardman in Pejic found some kindred spirits. 'Terry Darracott was ruthless,' he told me. 'He was frightening in the dressing room, absolutely frightening. So up for it you felt he was ready to kill somebody. And Micky Lyons, he was a great leader. Incredible Evertonian. Blue eyes, blue blood. Then there was Roger Kenyon, amazing character. He had stitches everywhere. He was a gangster. Trevor Ross was tough. But we had some real good players. Dave Thomas was fantastic, a great player. Latchford, McKenzie. Martin Dobson, so cultured, and Andy King, a free spirit, a fruit and nutcase.

'There was a good camaraderie once Gordon Lee sorted out the cliques. There were a few cliques when I got there. David Smallman, Mick Bernard, lads like that. But Gordon, he disbanded all that. I liked being at Everton. I'd been with Stoke since I was a kid, but at Goodison, I just couldn't believe the passion. That 6-0 against Chelsea, at the end there were little kids of three and four running on the pitch, and grandads in their eighties. I couldn't believe I was involved in that. I've never forgotten that.'

Pejic had played for Stoke City in the 1972 League Cup final, in which, as thorough underdogs, Stoke beat Chelsea 2-1. So he knew what it was like to help realise supporters' dreams, but at Goodison we dreamt bigger than they did at the Victoria Ground. And plenty of those dreams involved getting the better of Liverpool. Three months after becoming Lee's first signing, Pejic found himself in a Merseyside derby that was also an FA Cup semi-final, and like pretty much everyone in blue that day, his anger with Clive Thomas still runs deep.

'He was a prat. He wrongly gave offside [against Bryan Hamilton's goal], then changed his mind and gave handball. He definitely cheated us. If you watch it now you can see me running after him, shouting at him. And after the match he had the audacity to come into our dressing room. I told him to get lost. But he also refereed the replay, and he gave a penalty against me even though I'd won the ball, going up in the area with Dave Johnson. I'm certain that's because of what I'd said to him on the Saturday.'

Pejic eventually would get the better of Liverpool, and has vivid memories of the glorious 1-0 win at Goodison in October 1978, but that is a story for another chapter.

For now, let's skip forward to September 1979. Pejic was twenty-nine, notionally in his prime, but that summer Lee had bought 22-year-old Bailey from Blackburn Rovers, who had just been relegated to the Third Division. With Mick Mills becoming a fixture in the left back berth for England, he never had got another international cap. And now, after less than three years, his time with Everton was up, too.

'I thought Gordon started disbanding that team that finished third, then fourth, much too early,' Pejic told me. 'I thought we'd have good times ahead, and I didn't want to leave. But I went to Aston Villa and had some bad injury problems there.

'Even while I was at Everton, I remember playing against Leeds and Tony Currie, who wasn't the quickest, pushed the ball past me. As I turned I felt a click. After the game I drank a bottle of milk, then stood up to go for a shower and couldn't bloody walk. It went downhill from there, really. At the Villa I saw three different specialists and got three different diagnoses. It turned out to be a double hernia, but I didn't want an operation and it finished my career. The year after I retired, Villa won the league using just 14 players, and three of them played in my position. That finished me off, that did. I'd been after a championship medal my whole career.

'I'd sold the farm in Derbyshire by then – I couldn't keep it on when I was playing for Everton – and moved to north Wales, in the middle of nowhere. When I retired from football I spent two years in a black hole, emotionally. I had a breakdown, didn't know where to turn. I wasn't getting any help from anyone. Then one day the headmistress at the primary school my kids went to asked me if I'd take the kids for football. I turned up on the first day shaking like a leaf, but I did that for a year, and eventually put a school team together. I saw a farmer who gave us a field, and we turned it into a pitch. That got me back into football again. And then a friend of mine, a high-class fruiterer, asked me to help him in his business, so I wound up working Liverpool market three times a week. Ron Yeats, the old Liverpool player, used to turn up there too. That gave me another bit of purpose, with the football, and gradually I pieced my life back together. Luckily I had my PFA pension, and to this day that helps considerably. Without that, I would have gone.'

I asked him what he meant by that: would have gone where?

'Gone. Well, gone.'

Did he mean he would have harmed himself?

'Well, yeah. Gone.'

Killed himself?

'Yeah.'

Chapter Fifteen

A heavy silence hung between us for twenty seconds or so. Naturally, I was aware of other sportsmen (although no women, strangely) for whom retirement, especially retirement forced by injury, presaged bouts of sometimes quite serious depression. I'd met both Andrew Flintoff and Ricky Hatton a few times, two intelligent guys neither of whom coped well without an active sporting career to give them drive and focus. In fact, Flintoff briefly took up Hatton's game as a way of keeping his competitive juices flowing. At the time of writing, Hatton has yet to take up Flintoff's.

I'd also interviewed Paul Lake, the Manchester City starlet once tipped as a future England captain, who could identify the very moment all his sporting hopes and ambitions were shattered: the 65th minute of a match between City and Aston Villa, in September 1990. That was when his studs caught in the Maine Road turf, and he ruptured his anterior cruciate ligament, which today would not have to spell the beginning of the end for a young footballer, but for Lake it did.

He called time on his playing career in 1996, at the age of twenty-seven, after recognising that despite years of rehabilitation he would never again be the player he had once been. 'Aside of my eldest son being born, and seeing Oasis's second-ever gig, all of the 1990s, ten years of my life, was a complete washout,' he told me.

His marriage caved in under the strain and one night he found himself walking the streets at 3am, and stopping on a motorway bridge in Cheadle, contemplating the unthinkable. 'A police car stopped, asked if everything was OK,' he said. 'I never really believed I would commit suicide, but I was at the stage where I had no self-worth whatsoever. My confidence was shot to pieces because I wasn't defined by the fact that I had played 130 games and had been a success; I was just a walking knee-joint. I'd be mentioned in the paper as a crock, or as "injury-prone Lake", and that used to ruin my whole week. It sounds pathetic, doesn't it? But all anyone asked me was, "How's that knee of yours?" It was genuine concern, but it made me envious, bitter, self-centred. I lost contact with friends, family. It was a horrible place to be.'

At least Pejic had passed thirty by the time he had to give up, and had an England career behind him. But every generation of footballers has yielded men like him and Lake, and until the advent of the Premier League gave a small percentage of players a lifetime of financial security irrespective of when they might have to hang up their boots, the sudden loss of earning power could be catastrophic. But not for those who had managed their PFA pensions sensibly. As Pejic said, if retirement had meant a sudden loss of income as well as a sudden lack of football, his depression might well have tipped him over the edge.

'But the money I made from my move to Everton, then my move to Villa, went in the pension pot. All my bonuses too. So that kept me going. I moved back to Stoke, bought a shop, and for the next three years I did wet fish, fruit and veg. But I was getting the football bug again. Leek Town asked if I could do some coaching with them, then Northwich Victoria. I took my badges, and eventually I joined Port Vale as youth coach. I set up the youth system for them, and then they sacked the first-team coach, Alan Oakes, so the chairman asked if I'd take over from him.'

The third match with Pejic as coach, was a third-round FA Cup tie against non-league Macclesfield Town, which Port Vale won. In the next round Tottenham Hotspur, then managed by Terry Venables, came to town. If the 1970s was the supreme decade for FA Cup giant-killings, the 1980s weren't far behind. The 30th of January 1989 is a date still engraved in the heart of every Port Vale fan old enough to remember one of the great FA Cup shocks, which Port Vale led 2-0 after 25 minutes, and held on to win 2-1.

'It was a great day, and really the start of my coaching career proper,' said Pejic. 'I later got the sack from Vale, and sued them for wrongful dismissal, but after that I worked in Kuwait, then back at Stoke under Lou Macari. Walsall actually came in for me to be their manager at that time but Stoke held me to my contract, and then I got sacked by them as well after Alan Durban came in. So then I went to work in Malaysia, and Zimbabwe, where I coached the air force team. They had forty-two players and seven coaches, all arguing with each other. I had to sort out three teams for them. It was mad. And while I was there Mugabe put the price of petrol up by 200 per cent. Bloody chaos, it was.'

Pejic came home and worked for the FA, coaching the under-18s and scouting for the then-manager Kevin Keegan, compiling reports on other teams. But by then he had another sporting passion. 'I'd taken up taekwondo when I was in Kuwait in 1994, and ended up doing it six days a week and competing in their national Open. My first proper fight was against the Kuwaiti number one, who was in the army, and I enjoyed it so much that when I came back to the UK I joined a club in Stoke, and eventually became an instructor. In 2011 I competed in the English national championships – in my age group, like, the over-sixties – and won silver. Then I won gold in the Scottish Open so I became

Scottish champion, and got into the Great Britain team. I've got my own academy now.'

Pejic becoming a taekwondo expert would have come as no great surprise to the footballers who had riled him in the 1970s, and been left prostrate on the turf by one of his crushing challenges. But it was the footballing arts, not the martial arts, that still formed the basis of his living. Kevin Ratcliffe, who became Everton's captain in the halcyon mid-1980s but had made his debut in less garlanded times under Gordon Lee, once told me that Pejic, with whom he later worked at Chester City, was one of the finest coaches he had ever seen.

Under the auspices of the FA, Pejic had run a course training prospective coaches for their A-licences, and one of his students was Roy Keane, who later invited him to join his regime at Ipswich Town. It's fair to assume that the Irish wolfhound saw in the Staffordshire bull terrier something of his own football philosophy. A Stoke City supporter put it more crudely, commenting on a fanzine message-board: 'Fuck me, Keano and Pej at the same club ... don't suppose any of their players will be shirking tackles.'

In June 2010 Pejic started at Ipswich, coaching the under-18s, but was suspended five months later under a cloud of suspicion, following those allegations of bullying that he assured me were completely unfounded. 'It was one kid,' he said, 'and it wasn't nice to be accused. The club held their own internal inquiry and Roy Keane got involved on my side, but I left anyway. Since then I've been doing some radio work, I've got a column in the *Sentinel*, and I've been building up my academy.'

Life, after so nearly leaving him for dead, seemed to have treated him pretty well. After two divorces – 'the first one was probably down to me, the second one just didn't work out' – he now had a long-term partner, and two adult children (Clare, the toddler who'd nearly died with him in the car crash, was now in her forties). In and around the Potteries he also enjoyed plenty of respect and recognition. After all, Stoke City's League Cup win in 1972 remains the club's only major honour, so the twelve men who beat Chelsea in the final – including George Wood's role model Gordon Banks, and Mike Bernard, who would briefly overlap with Pejic at Everton – became enduring local heroes.

Among Evertonians, Pejic doesn't quite qualify for hero status. He only had two full seasons at Goodison. But it's probably no coincidence that they were two seasons in which Everton played such entertaining football, for a good deal of it unfolded up the left, where Pejic linked so well with Dobson and Thomas.

Unfortunately, the team could sometimes be as leaky in defence as it was buccaneering in attack. Everton finished the 1977-78 season with a goal difference of +31, exactly the same as Liverpool's just above them, but while we had scored 11 goals more, they had conceded 11 goals fewer. Lee's team had 45 in the goals-against column, more than one a game, which wasn't the way to win titles, even if 76 in the goals-for column very much was. It was more than Everton had scored to win the championship seven years earlier, and more too than Liverpool had scored in winning the title the season before.

If there was a single game that season that symbolised this imbalance then, even more than the Boxing Day humbling by Manchester United, it was another eight-goal affair, the 4-4 draw against Newcastle United two months earlier, the game at which Ally MacLeod sat in the directors' box to run the rule over Georgie Wood.

October was not yet out, but the Magpies were already in the middle of one of their periodic crises; rare have been the decades unblemished by at least one Newcastle United crisis. Not only were they bottom of the First Division, they had also only just brought to an end the worst run of form in the club's long and proud history, losing ten league matches in a row. Everton, by contrast, had powered up the table following defeat in those first two games, and the Saturday before had left Anfield with a point, and a clean sheet. Lee's team had also stuck five past Leicester and QPR, three past Sheffield United, Norwich and West Brom. So that Saturday afternoon my friends and I got off the bus and swaggered rather than walked to Goodison. Newcastle were cannon fodder. If we'd known we were about to see eight goals, the division of spoils could only be weighted one way. Eight-nil wouldn't have seemed a ridiculous forecast, nor 7-1 or at worst 6-2.

So when we went 1-0 up after just six minutes, it seemed pre-ordained, the prelude to a massacre. Oddly, it was Pejic who opened the scoring. Oddly, because he only scored two goals in his Everton career and this was the second of them, a low shot which took a lucky deflection off Aidan McCaffery's boot. But five minutes later, Tommy Craig equalised for Newcastle. That wasn't in the script. And then Alan Gowling had the effrontery to put them 2-1 up just before half-time.

Alan Gowling. There are some names that have an almost mystical power to sweep some of us back to an era of Esso FA Cup coins and Wonderful World of Soccer stickers, and his is one of them.

Gordon Lee was aware of the threat he posed because he'd been Newcastle's manager before coming to Everton, and, in characteristic fashion, had favoured the hard-working Gowling over the St James' Park hero Malcolm Macdonald. But on the terraces Gowling wasn't just known as a useful striker, who as a promising youngster had briefly played in the same Manchester United team as George Best and Bobby Charlton. No, thanks to *Shoot!* magazine and regular newspaper features with titles such as 'Soccer Eggheads', we also knew him as one of football's few university graduates. He had a degree in economics, just like those other brainboxes Steve Coppell and Steve Heighway, while Heighway's Liverpool colleague Brian Hall was a maths graduate.

It's remarkable what nuggets of information the brain retains decades later. I have never forgotten those 'Soccer Eggheads', or their degrees, or even, a little unnervingly, where they studied. Gowling had been at Manchester University, Coppell and Hall at Liverpool, Heighway at Warwick. Of course, a university degree was no big deal. I felt pretty sure at sixteen that I'd end up with one myself. But I knew I wouldn't play First Division football. To accomplish both seemed almost superhuman to me at the time, and it was a source of some considerable disappointment that two of these high-achievers wore Liverpool colours. Hall had scored the winner against Everton in the semi-final of the 1971 FA Cup, but I couldn't bring myself to hate him for it. He had been to university. He deserved some respect.

The same was so of Gowling, even though he ruined my half-time that day. As a teenager I hated it when we got to half-time at Goodison and were losing. Not quite as much as losing and getting to full-time, obviously, but not far short. Half-time was a cherished opportunity to go for a piss and a pie and soak up the optimism that the first 45 minutes had generated. I loved the banter with strangers in the queue for the urinals, and used to tailor my vowels to make myself sound less like a 'woolly-back'. That was the label slapped by pure-bred Scousers on those of us who had come from surrounding areas perceived as more upmarket, such as Southport and parts of the Wirral.

There are various etymological explanations of the term woolly-back, none of which remotely applied to me or my forebears. One was that the original woolly-backs were people who tried to get into medieval markets without paying an entrance fee, by carrying a sheep on their backs. Another was that coal-delivery men from

Lancashire used to turn up in Liverpool wearing sheep fleeces to protect their backs against the heavy sacks of coal.

Whatever the explanation, a woolly-back was something I knew I was and didn't particularly want to be. It wasn't that I spoke posh. I had cousins in London who derived great pleasure from the way I said 'bath', 'path', 'laugh', and even though my accent evolved in later life, to the extent that one day in my mid-twenties I realised I was saying barth, parth and larf, the humiliation I felt at being laughed/larfed at as a kid has left me with a lifelong chippiness about northern accents being mocked by southerners.

A chap I used to play tennis with, when I lived in north London in the 1990s, consequently got more than he bargained for when he poked fun at me one day for my pronunciation of the word 'one'. He'd done it before, making snide remarks about the way I pronounced this word or that, and I'd let it pass. But not this time. 'It's not "won", he said, exaggerating the O sound, "it's 'wun'." I smiled sweetly, then gave him an overhead volley of abuse. 'With the greatest respect, it's whatever way I fucking say it. And it's whatever way you say it ... I can't bear the arrogance of southerners thinking you're right and northerners are wrong. There is no right and wrong.'

He took the point, a little huffily, and never poked fun again. But while I'm at it, let me just add that I hate the way journalists from the south of England present the nation's favourite expletive, when uttered by a northerner, as 'fook' or 'fooking'. Just because northerners pronounce those words differently doesn't require a different spelling. And we're not from 'oop north', either. I wish they'd fooking stop it.

Now that I've got that off my chest, let me return to 3.45pm on Saturday, 29 October 1977. Gowling's goal had also taken the gloss off another of the joys of the half-time interval: finding out the scorelines from the other First Division games, and above all on that particular day the game at Maine Road between Manchester City and the league champions, Liverpool. One of the peculiar curses of supporting Everton, then as now, was that an Everton win only really felt like a gift from the gods when it coincided with a Liverpool defeat. There was even a song for the occasion, a version of an old Tommy Steele number one that admittedly also had a City/United, Arsenal/Spurs and even a Blackburn/Burnley variation: 'We'll never feel more like singing the Blues, than when Everton win and Liverpool lose.'

It wasn't often during Liverpool's 1970s pomp that Everton did win on a day that the Reds lost, and we didn't that day either, but after watching a 4-4 draw that was nothing if not exhilarating, we received the immensely pleasurable news that City had prevailed 3-1. Better still, the scoresheet featured an erstwhile Goodison hero, Joe Royle, who had bagged the third.

But all three City goals that day came in the second half. At half-time, the Goodison Park announcer relayed the unwelcome message that Liverpool were leading 1-0, which, of course, compounded the misery of Everton being one down.

There is a lovely item about the institution that was the half-time scores update in a quite splendidly entertaining book called *The Lost World of Football*, written by Gary Silke and Derek Hammond. One of them wrote that he was recently at a match checking other scores on LiveScore.com, on his iPhone. It was taking a little longer to download than usual, perhaps four-fifths of a second longer, and he kept poking the screen in exasperated fashion before recalling that there was once a time – 'which now appears technologically equidistant between the Saxons and Samsung' – when a chap hung up metal plates under a series of letters to denote the half-time scores at other grounds, and which you could only decode by turning to your programme to see which letters referred to which matches.

By 1977-78 Goodison Park had moved on from the complicated letter/number arrangement. The other half-time scores were read out by the stadium announcer, with much shushing when he reached the Liverpool score. But, as I recall, they were also posted on a flashy electronic scoreboard.

It was entirely in keeping for Goodison to be pushing at technology's cutting edge, for although it is easily forgotten now that the venerable ground has slid into slightly shaming decrepitude compared with 21st-century citadels like the Etihad and the Emirates, it was once one of the architectural glories of English football. It was England's first purpose-built football stadium, the first with a three-tier stand, the first with dugouts, the first with undersoil heating. During the 1966 World Cup, it was second only to Wembley as a venue, and indeed hosted the semi-final between two countries whose very names bespeak a different era, and for that matter a different world: West Germany and the USSR.

As for the slightly less significant Everton v Newcastle United game a little over eleven years later, the half-time interval passed, with Everton one-down and Liverpool one-up, in a fug of gloom. There was no banter with strangers in the queue for the urinals, just a mutual lament that we were losing to a team that had just lost ten on the trot.

Happily, attacking the Gwladys Street End in the second half, the ever-reliable Bob Latchford soon restored our spirits, scoring a 54th-minute header from a Dave Thomas corner – as powerful a combination for the Toffees as the left jab and overhand right had been for Muhammad Ali a month earlier to the very day, in the epic 15-rounder against hard-hitting Earnie Shavers in which Ali eventually prevailed (although arguably it was that punishing fight which first caused him permanent and irreparable damage).

Quite bizarrely, by the way, that same Earnie Shavers, born into poverty deep in the American Bible Belt in 1945, ended up more than half a century later as a bouncer at Yates's Wine Lodge in Queen Square, Liverpool. He had fallen in love with a woman in Birkenhead – 'She's like a house with every brick in just the right place' was his memorable summary of just how perfect she was, which as poetic declarations of love go, doesn't quite rival Cyrano de Bergerac – and he needed a job. I went to interview him once at a greasy spoon cafe on the Wirral, and wrote that it was like running into Bob Latchford in Buffalo Crotch, Arkansas. I didn't know then, of course, that Latchford would end up living in rural bliss near Nuremberg, which was very nearly as improbable.

But I mustn't get sidetracked. In his book *30*, Latchford described his first goal against Newcastle, Everton's second, and suggested that it almost certainly would not have stood today. These days, the goalkeeper would have gone down under the centre forward's robust challenge 'like a sack of spuds'. Far from scoring, he speculated, he would probably have been booked.

That is doubtless so. Football might have gained a great deal in the past four decades – Russian oligarchs, American tycoons, Bentleys in every car park – but it has lost plenty too, both on the field and off. I really don't want to come across as one of those whingers in rose-tinted glasses, for as already asserted, great leaps have been made too, also on as well as off the field. Three points for a win, the back-pass laws, these were manifest advances. Away from the pitch, racism, hooliganism, safety issues ... these too, with varying degrees of success, have been tackled.

But what about the tackle itself? While it is perfectly reasonable to want to protect modern-day footballers from nasty injuries, especially now that their boots weigh about the same as an average pair of slippers, the art of tackling has been emasculated. Challenges that in the 1970s would have been considered strong but fair, part of a defender's job, now get yellow cards. Challenges that in the 1970s would have been thought a trifle on the robust side now yield straight reds. I've lost count of the number of retired footballers who have told me, in disgust, that since their day the game has practically become 'a non-contact sport'. Among them were two rugged old-school defenders and bona fide 1970s legends of their respective clubs, West Ham and Ipswich.

There was nothing 'non-contact' about Billy Bonds and Kevin Beattie, who didn't know each other except as erstwhile opponents until I brought them together for a memorable lunch in the City of London in 2007, during which they reflected happily on the good old days and considered what had become of their beloved game. They both told me that they would rather watch rugby than football these days.

'At least when those boys get knocked down they get back up,' said Bonds.

'That's something,' said Beattie, 'when two old pros like us would rather watch rugby on a Saturday afternoon.'

The Saturday afternoons he remembered were different. At Goodison Park, nobody questioned the legitimacy of Latchford's goal for a second, least of all the referee, Keith Hackett. And yet, within two minutes, Newcastle led again, the Northern Irishman Tommy Cassidy taking full advantage of a mix-up between Georgie Wood and Andy King. That made the score 2-3. Then Latchford equalised for a second time: 3-3. Then Gowling put Newcastle ahead again: 3-4.

On the terraces it was almost too much to bear, and so it was appropriate that it was an Evertonian at least as blue-blooded as we all were who saved us from the humiliation of a home defeat by the division's basement club. With eight minutes to go, the Everton skipper Mike Lyons bundled the ball home, creating rapture on the terraces. If Latchford had struck again to make it 5-4, I might still be there now, bouncing up and down. We fully expected that he would.

But it was Lyons who spared our blushes. Lyons, the lifelong Evertonian who radiated such devotion for the club that in 1982, on the day he left to join Sheffield Wednesday, he wept buckets. He was driving from Sheffield back to his home in Maghull, on the outskirts of Liverpool, and 'I'll Find My Way Home', by Jon and Vangelis, came on the car radio. That started him off.

'I stopped off for a pint at a pub in Maghull called The Meadows,' he would later recall, 'and was sitting at the bar still with tears in my eyes remembering all the good times. Then this fella came in, an Everton fan, and recognised me. He said, "I've heard you've just signed for Sheffield Wednesday, is that true?" Through my tears I said it was. He said, "I'm glad you've gone. I always thought you were shite."'

Chapter Sixteen

Lyons told me that story down a crackly phone line from Perth, Western Australia. He had lived Down Under for years, although the Scouse accent was unadulterated by even a whisper of an Aussie twang. Lyons was coaching the University of Western Australia football team, and if he was developing them in his own image, then I pictured them being aimed at brick walls in their training sessions, and told to run through them. In the Everton dressing room in the 1970s, Lyons had a famous pre-match routine. He would jump up and head-butt the ceiling.

'Yeah, it was like a little superstition of mine,' he told me, when I asked him about it. 'The lads thought I was a loony, like. But I had to jump up and head it to prepare me for the game. I only did it at Goodison, though. The ceiling at Arsenal was too high, I remember that.'

I told Lyons that I didn't know much about his childhood, except that he was raised in a family that was as staunchly Catholic as it was Evertonian. 'Well, I'll tell you a funny thing,' he said. 'I was playing for England B in Lisbon, at the Stadium of Light, and Terry McDermott was in the squad too. I happened to see his passport and noticed that his date of birth was exactly the same as mine:

8 December 1951. I said, "That's my birthday too. Where were you born?" And he said "Mill Road Hospital". Which was where I was born too.'

Ten years earlier, in 1941, Mill Road Maternity Hospital had suffered a direct hit during the Luftwaffe's devastating attack on Liverpool. Scores of women and their babies had been killed. So it seemed somehow symbolic of the city's rebirth after the war that on the same day in the same hospital should arrive two babies who would go on to become the beating hearts of Everton and Liverpool. 'It was lucky you weren't accidentally switched,' I told Lyons. 'You might have ended up playing for the dark side.'

He laughed. 'I'd never have had a moustache like that,' he said.

His father, he told me, had been a power-station rigger, while his mother worked for a time at Littlewoods Pools. 'So we had the same boss, John Moores,' he said. The Littlewoods magnate had come up before and would come up again in this story of the 1978 Toffees, as a kind of paternalistic benefactor. Where are such men now, I wonder? Maybe the existence of men like John Moores represented the last flickering of Victorian or Edwardian England as a nation where the self-made local tycoon gave employment to the people, owned the football club, bequeathed millions to the university. It wasn't such a bad system.

Lyons went to De La Salle secondary school, as would an even more famous Evertonian, Wayne Rooney, whose mother was a dinner lady there. Lyons was eight years old when his father first took him to Goodison, and as his devotion to Everton grew, so did the notion that he would put life and limb on the line for his team, even on the terraces. At fourteen, in September 1965, he stood in the heart of the Kop for the season's first Merseyside derby, proudly wearing his Everton scarf. Regrettably, Liverpool won 5-0.

Earlier in the week Bill Shankly had said to his assistant Bob Paisley, within deliberate earshot of the players: 'Bob, where's the nearest bookies? Get everything you've got on us for Saturday. I've seen Everton training from my house. He's got them back training in the afternoons, running the legs off them, and Saturday they'll be knackered. So get your mortgage on us.'

It was Ian St John, a scorer that day, who told that story of how Shankly had prepared his team. 'It was only later when I went to his house that I realised he'd have needed to stand on the roof to see into the Everton training ground,' St John added.

Of course, little did Shankly know that a decade or so later he'd be more welcome at Bellefield than at Melwood. But that's just me, belatedly getting my own back. On the day, Shankly's psychological ruse helped his players rise to the occasion, and young Lyons looked on, aghast. 'The Kopites all laughed at me,' he later recalled.

The following year, he went with three Everton-mad school-mates to watch the Blues play away at Blackpool, whose brilliant little midfielder Alan Ball, it was rumoured, was coveted by Catterick. 'It was the day Harry Catterick got assaulted for dropping Alex Young, and Joe Royle made his debut,' Lyons remembered. 'Before the match we were walking down the beach and coming towards us was Alan Ball. We couldn't believe our luck when he stopped to talk and we tried our utmost to persuade him to come to Everton. I remember it as if it was last week, and I still like to think that in some tiny way we might have influenced his decision, because Alan Ball changed the course of Everton's history.'

No such claim can be made for Lyons himself, but he was on Everton's books from 1969 to 1982, and so embodies the topsy-turvy 1970s more than any other Everton player.

'My mum wrote to the club to get me a trial,' he told me, 'and

I did OK, so they signed me. My first-team debut was in 1971, the week before Everton played Liverpool in the semi-final of the FA Cup. Harry Catterick rested a couple of players and so I played, away at Nottingham Forest. I played up front, and I scored, though we got beat 3-1. The game was on *Match of the Day* and with us 3-0 down there was a newsflash, saying that somebody in Africa had been assassinated. Then they went back to the football and the commentator said, "Oh, and Lyons has scored for Everton." They never showed the goal. But it evened itself out because when I scored that famous own goal against Liverpool from about 40 yards, Granada were on strike, so they never showed that, either.'

His own goal at Anfield came on 20 October 1979. I was standing in the Anfield Road End with Briggy, Mozzer and Bean. Scarcely had the game started than Lyons, unaccountably, under no pressure, turned and hit a high looping back-pass to George Wood, which flew over his head into the top corner. It was less than a week before my eighteenth birthday, but I can remember my eyes filling up with tears, like a little boy denied an ice cream. Why did these things always happen against Liverpool?

Even by the tumultuous standard of Merseyside derbies, it was an incredible game. By the time it finished, 2-2, sending my mates and I home feeling fairly contented, there had been the bizarre Lyons own goal, a female streaker (who three days later tried to commit suicide by throwing herself into the Mersey, after telling a bystander that she had a lot on her mind), and two sendings off, McDermott and Everton's Gary Stanley. But nothing about that game was less forgettable than the opening goal. In a BBC book about the great Merseyside derbies, co-written by Brian Barwick and Gerald Sinstadt, Lyons recalled going out for a drink with his teammates that night, and an Evertonian telling him what a great player he was 'when obviously I was sick after scoring a 40-yard own goal at Anfield. Eventually, Andy King asked him to leave me alone because I was so down. And the lad said, "Oh no, I'm made up with him! He's won me forty quid. I had him in the sweep to score the first goal!"'

In the same book, Gordon Lee recalled the goal too. 'Mickey was a born Evertonian,' he said. 'If you cut him open, he'd bleed blue. But all the same, you couldn't help asking yourself why that couldn't have happened to Bob Paisley.'

It was true. Liverpool always seem to have had mountains of good luck against Everton, even if they have created some of it themselves, and, of course, been gifted some of it.

I asked Lyons about Lee. 'Oh, I liked Gordon Lee,' he said. 'Liverpool had Shankly, who I admired tremendously. But in some respects Gordon was similar. He had a one-track mind: football, football, football. I liked him a lot.'

In a fascinating collection of Everton interviews called *Still Talking Blue*, compiled by the sister of an old colleague of mine, Becky Tallentire, Lyons elaborated on Lee's obsession with football. 'When we went down to Norwich the drive home was the coach journey from hell, about five or six hours,' he said. 'We were all dying for a pint and stopped at a pub. I was sitting next to Gordon and before I'd even had a taste of my drink he was doing all the formations using our pint glasses as defenders. Every time I tried to take a sip he was off again, moving us about all over the table. He only ever thought about football.'

He certainly put some thought into his tactics before the Merseyside derby in October 1978, almost exactly a year before Lyons's spectacular own goal. And he had to, because the talismanic Lyons was injured. The club captain had never been on the winning side in a league game against Liverpool, indeed his inaugural derby, in March 1972, was a 4-0 defeat. And he never would be on the winning side, either. But that day he asked Lee if he could sit on the touchline. 'The lads liked that,' he told me. 'But I'll tell you something, I jumped up on my one good leg when Kingy scored, and I was wearing this watch that my mum had given me for my eighteenth birthday. But during that game it just disappeared off my wrist. I still don't know what happened to it. I suppose it must have flown into the crowd during all the celebrations.'

Lee had left by the time Lyons moved to Sheffield Wednesday. Kendall had arrived, and soon made it clear that the big centre half, devoted Blue or not, wasn't going to be part of his plans. But at Wednesday he enjoyed a new lease of life, before leaving to become Grimsby Town's player-manager. Then came the siren call of Everton again – he returned as a youth-team coach – before an intriguing offer to become national coach of Brunei.

'I enjoyed that,' he said. 'I used to take the Crown Prince, Prince Billah, for training. He was a goalkeeper and his favourite player was Peter Schmeichel, but I wasn't having that, so I got him Neville Southall's shirt. He had his own team, and because he was the Crown Prince, we used to train in the national stadium. He was a really nice lad, but he wasn't a natural goalkeeper. I used to tell the opposition that they mustn't shoot too hard.'

After Brunei, Lyons accepted a job in Australia, coaching Canberra Cosmos. But his wife Trish had stayed in England and the marriage couldn't take the strain of separation. 'So we ended up splitting up, which was a shame,' he said. 'We had two children together. Our Michael is over here, he works down the mines, and he has a little boy. And our Francesca has a little boy too. She's still in Liverpool. She works in a bank. She's with a Liverpudlian, in fact, a season-ticket holder. But my grandson will end up an Evertonian, I'm sure.'

Lyons had a partner in Australia, he told me, and assured me that he had found contentment in Perth – 'I take great delight in ringing home and saying, "What's the weather like?"' Andy King, however, would later tell me that life out there wasn't all sunshine and barbies for his old mate, and that if he could, 'Lyonsy' would love to come home.

Who knows? Either way, I hope the University of Western Australia know just what a diamond they have in their football coach.

Chapter Seventeen

At the start of 1978 there were twenty-seven senior players on Everton's books, and it's interesting to note now that only one of them, Dave Jones, went on to manage in the top division. Across the park, by way of comparison, Graeme Souness, Kenny Dalglish, Sammy Lee, Phil Neal, Phil Thompson and Ray Clemence would all go on to be managers, or assistant managers, at a high level. Maybe, loath as I am to admit it, they were more profoundly schooled in the managerial arts, having played for Bob Paisley and in some cases Bill Shankly too, and been immersed in the famous Boot Room philosophy.

But let's stick with Jones, one of the few 1978 Toffees who really needed no looking for. In 2002 he was managing Wolverhampton Wanderers, then in the Championship, and I went to Molineux to interview him.

Growing up in Toxteth, Jones was a passionate Evertonian, so desperate to look the part as a footballer that he once augmented his Everton kit with a couple of makeshift shinpads – a pair of his mother's sanitary towels, strapped round his shins with Sellotape. His father was an accountant with a company that ran coal yards, but that didn't confer middle-class status. His mother still had to get a job as a cleaner, to keep the wolf – or more accurately local debt-collectors – from the door.

The young Dave Jones played football for Woolton Boys Club, which had been set up with a donation from the munificent Everton chairman John Moores. But it was Liverpool who picked him up first, and he might have gone the way of Rush, Fowler, Owen and co. after him, had not an elderly Everton scout called Tommy Ferfowl approached him one day.

'Are you an Evertonian?' the old boy asked. Jones replied that he was. 'Then you're coming to Everton.' It was what passed, *circa* 1970, for tapping up.

So Jones started training at Bellefield, where one day Harry Catterick passed him and said, 'Good afternoon'. It was the first time the manager, who could be an aloof, authoritarian figure even with first-team players, had ever acknowledged him. 'Good afternoon,' he replied. Catterick stopped him, sternly told him in future to say 'Good afternoon, boss' and strode on.

But Catterick the boss was also an employee. On a Thursday in 1973 came the devastating news dreaded by every boy on the books of a big football club, when Everton's youth coaches informed 16-year-old Dave Jones that he was being released. Two days later, Catterick was sacked, together with his coaching staff. So the following Tuesday, the youngster decided to turn up for training as usual, hoping that nobody would know he'd been let go. Nobody did.

'After that my career suddenly took off,' he told me. 'It was as if somebody had dropped a confidence tablet in my water. Shortly afterwards I became England youth captain with the likes of Ray Wilkins in the team, Glenn Hoddle, Bryan Robson, Alan Curbishley. And at seventeen I made my first-team debut for Everton.'

It was a good survival story, but thirty years later I arrived at Molineux hoping to hear about a different kind of survival – how

Jones had coped with trumped-up allegations of child abuse that ended in a high-profile trial.

At the time he hadn't yet talked about it at any length in the media, and I wasn't sure whether he wanted to or not. So at first we sat in his office chatting about his plans for Wolves, but also about how his football career had developed once he made it at Everton.

He was a clever, versatile defender, although his versatility back-fired, because under Billy Bingham and especially Gordon Lee he was constantly shuffled around the back four. His full debut was at left back, on a freezing day against Leicester City at Filbert Street in December 1974. His job was to mark Keith Weller, famous in the 1970s for his penchant, unique in those days, for wearing tights under his shorts. Bingham's pre-match instructions to Jones were short and sweet. 'If that player comes off that pitch and his tights aren't laddered, you'll never play for me again.'

Jones loved the camaraderie at Everton and became part of the F Troop, the hardcore revellers led by Andy King, George Wood and Mick Lyons. Wood had been uncharacteristically coy about telling me any good F Troop yarns, though King would later give me a doubtless expurgated account of some high jinks on a Nile riverboat, during an end-of-season trip to Egypt. Even in censored form, they were clearly the kind of jinks that these days would make all the front pages, and in those days didn't even make the middle or back pages.

Jones was on the Egyptian trip, too, and tells a good story in his autobiography, not about the riverboat capers but about the sheer unworldliness of Gordon Lee. Again and again, Lee's old players kept telling me what a decent cove he was, and how much he differed, in private, from his gloomy public image. But they were similarly united in poking affectionate fun at his lack of soph-istication.

The trip was for a tournament in which Everton, strange as it now seems, played the national teams of Czechoslovakia, who were European champions, and Egypt. On arrival in Cairo, Lee was interviewed by a group of local, French-speaking reporters. Unsurprisingly, he didn't speak a word of French. But Duncan McKenzie, who had picked up the language during his time playing in Belgium with Anderlecht, offered to translate.

'Are you pleased to be in Africa?' the reporters asked.

McKenzie translated the question. Lee looked bewildered.

'We're not in Africa, we're in Egypt,' he said.

'The boss is very happy indeed to be here,' translated McKenzie.

'What do you know of the Czechoslovakia team?'

McKenzie put it to him.

'Nothing. Never seen 'em,' said Lee.

'He says they're a very good side,' McKenzie explained. 'It will be a good test for us.'

And so it went on. At the end of the interview, the reporters lauded the Everton manager's brilliant diplomatic skills. His players, in whom McKenzie had confided, were all in stitches.

'Gordon was something else,' wrote Jones in his book, and related how Lee once drove all the way to Newcastle, to watch a game, in his slippers. Not because he liked wearing slippers to drive, but because he'd forgotten to put his shoes on. Steve Burtenshaw, his assistant, pointed out the faux pas, but by then it was too late. 'He watched the game in full suit and slippers. That was Gordon all over,' wrote Jones.

Alas, he played Jones all over, too. All those years later, in his office at Molineux, Jones still wished that Lee, and Billy Bingham before him, had established him in one position. Instead, insistent that he wanted to play centre half, the role most likely to further his England career, he joined Coventry City for £275,000.

'But I hated it there,' he told me. 'And I picked up a bad knee injury.' Did he wish he had stayed at Everton? Just think; he might have featured in Howard Kendall's all-conquering teams of the mid-1980s. 'Which would have been brilliant. I was a good defender who could pass, and I look at Howard's teams ... Ratcliffe, Mountfield, good defensive teams. But then I might not be on the road I'm on now.'

After Coventry, Jones spent a lucrative eighteen months in Hong Kong playing for Seiko, the team owned by the watch manufacturer. 'We travelled all over Asia,' he recalls. 'Whenever anyone had a new Seiko scoreboard we had to go and open it.' And whenever the Seiko team was drawing at half-time, the chairman, a Mr Wong, would come in and offer the players bonuses if they could go on and win the game. 'The Chinese players soon got the hang of it. They'd say, "Keep score down till half-time. Then boss panic and more money."'

Jones enjoyed his time in the Far East, but his knee got steadily worse, so in 1984 he returned to England, and eked out a couple more seasons at Preston North End, where by then the manager was none other than his old slipper-clad boss, Gordon Lee.

'Then they went to Astroturf and that finished me. I basically retired at twenty-nine. But I joined Southport part-time and did a bit of coaching there. They had a pretty good team, the likes of Shaun Teale and Andy Mutch. In fact, I came down here with Mutchy when Wolves wanted him. The deal wasn't going through because he was looking for assurances and this and that. I said, "Mutchy, you're a carpet-fitter! Don't be looking for assurances. Just go!"'

His own career choices were less clear-cut. He wanted a full-time football job, but he had a young family and needed an income, so he applied for a job back on Merseyside, as a care worker at Clarence House near Formby, a school for children with educational and behavioural problems.

It was a job that came back to haunt him. But at the time it was just a job, and he needed the money. His wife Ann started working nights there too, also to make ends meet. Once again, it is a remarkable example of then and now. Jones hadn't been spendthrift with his wages as a professional footballer, and yet as soon as his playing career ended he needed an income sufficiently to take a job that was demanding, sometimes distressing, and didn't even pay all that well. It wasn't as if he felt a particular urge to help troubled children. He worked hard at it, but football was his vocation, not this. However, the school was conveniently near their home in Southport, he and Ann had three children of their own, and the Clarence House wages just about covered the domestic bills.

He stayed for three years, but kept an eye out for openings in football and in 1990 successfully applied to become Stockport County's youth-team coach. He was subsequently elevated to first-team coach, then manager, and in 1996-97 presided over Stockport's *annus mirabilis*, not only winning automatic promotion to Division One (now the Championship), but beating three Premier League sides: Blackburn, West Ham and Southampton, to reach the last four of the League Cup.

It turned out that beating Southampton, at the Dell, had consequences beyond reaching the semi-final. The Southampton chairman, Rupert Lowe, was looking for a new manager, and that summer offered the post to Jones. He was back in the big time.

In his first full season Southampton finished a hugely creditable eleventh. The following year, 1998-99, they avoided relegation only on the last day of the season, survival secured with a 2-0 win against ... Everton. But Lowe retained every faith in his manager's long-term plan to make Southampton a secure Premier League club.

Then Jones's world caved in. 'We were coming back off holiday.

My brother-in-law, who worked on the railways, had been hit by a train he didn't hear coming. We were on our way from Heathrow to Southampton to get gear for the funeral, and I phoned my secretary, Daphne, to see if there'd been any calls. She said a DC Curran had been on the line from Liverpool. I already knew there was an investigation [into alleged sexual abuse at the school] going on. I had signed a document saying I'd never seen or heard anything.

'Anyway, I went to the police station in Liverpool, the big one, in Wavertree Road, with my wife. I thought I'd only be there ten minutes. And then they told me I'd been accused. My exact words were: "Is this some kind of joke?" I expected Jeremy Beadle to jump out. I told them they were making a big mistake, but from there it just snowballed. The CPS [Crown Prosecution Service] lady thought she could earn herself a few stripes. And the police paraded me around the station as if I was a trophy. The desk sergeant was brilliant. I think he just felt embarrassed. But the others, I wouldn't piss on them if they were on fire.

'I'll never forgive them, or the CPS, because they took my children's innocence away. My youngster, Georgia, is only seven now, and knows nothing about it. But my son, and my two older girls, even I don't know half the things they had to endure. I would rather have been up for murder. If the police and the CPS were in football, they'd be Sunday league.

'It killed my father, too. I honestly believe that. He fell ill when the news broke. He was on holiday and he saw it on Sky News. The police promised me they'd keep it quiet, so I could at least tell my family, but when I walked out the door the press were all there. Someone in the police station must have made himself fifty quid. I couldn't even tell my son, who was working in a sports shop. He heard it on the radio.'

Jones was formally questioned on 15 June 1999. That November he was charged. 'Then, in January, once I'd actually been charged,

Rupert Lowe said he didn't think I could run the football club. I was go-karting with the players when he rang me. He said, "I need to see you, I want to put something to you." He said it wasn't bad news, that he was giving me twelve months to fight the case, and Glenn Hoddle would be coming in.

'I said if that was the good news I didn't want to hear the bad. I think he genuinely thought he was doing me a favour. But football was my sanity.'

Amid the trauma, there were moments of pure comedy. Jones was persuaded to see Ray Wyre, a distinguished sexual crime consultant who had worked extensively with the police. Wyre invited him to sit down and, with the assurance that it would be in absolute confidence, encouraged him to reveal his most private fantasies.

'I started going on about managing England, and living in a massive big mansion on the French Riviera. He stopped me after ten minutes. It turned out he was after my sexual fantasies. If he'd asked for them, I would have told him, but he just said fantasies.' Wyre knew that Jones was no sexual predator. He duly joined the defence team. But still the police and the CPS refused to drop the case.

Meanwhile, Jones was stuck on gardening leave. He was asked to scout for several Premiership clubs, but couldn't because he was still on the Southampton payroll. 'That August [2000] was the first time in my football life, as player, coach, manager, league and non-league, that I hadn't kicked off the season. And the first day of the season was my birthday, 17 August. My wife took me paintballing that day, and I shot everybody. I even shot my own team. My friend's wife ran up behind me and I turned round and shot her. She said, "But I'm in your team." And I shot her again. I must have gone through about 3000 of those paint bullets. I was like a man possessed.'

By this time, Jones, his secretary Dot and I were laughing

uproariously. The trauma continued, however. And on 1 December 2000, at Liverpool Crown Court, the case began. It was due to last three weeks. But four days later Jones was cleared. The case, said the judge, should never have been brought. 'If the football world hadn't believed me, it would have killed me. I would never have come back. But everyone was fantastic. After I'd been charged, I had to prepare Southampton for a game against Derby County, and that was quite scary.

'I didn't know what reaction I would get. But I got a standing ovation. That will live with me for the rest of my life. And at Old Trafford, with 60,000 Mancunians there, again it was unbelievable. There was only one club where I got a torrid time, and when the time comes I'll say who.' He paused. 'But there is one phrase I will never, ever use again. And that's "No smoke without fire".'

Six years later I met Jones again. By then he was manager at Cardiff City, whom he had led to the FA Cup final the season before. He had also just written his autobiography, which was aptly called *No Smoke, No Fire*. He told me that his wife Ann didn't know, until she read the book, that in the event of his being found guilty and sent to jail, he had decided he would not let her or their children visit him, to spare them the indignity. Such revelations reignited some of the emotions she had felt during the ordeal itself. She read them and screamed at him, he laughed at her for screaming, so she screamed louder. Ornaments were thrown. Maybe that is what is meant by catharsis.

I asked him why he had finally decided to write the book. 'I've had three publishers chasing me but I felt it wasn't the right time,' he said. 'I was worried about my children. But my youngest, Georgia, is old enough to read it now. Which she has.' He laughed. 'Although it wasn't the details of the trial that bothered her, it was things like my wife referring to a girl I'd gone out with as "Fish Lips". She was like, "Mum, you can't say that."'

Jones was pleased with the book, but wished he had been able to name his accusers, who it turned out were all in prison when they issued their claims that he had sexually abused them. One of them saw his photograph in a newspaper, and remembered him from Clarence House.

There was already an investigation into abuse at the school, called Operation Care. His accusers were told that they could expect compensation, should he be convicted. 'One of them was a would-be transsexual, who wanted the money to finish the operation. I would gladly have done it for him, with a knife.'

When the case was thrown out by the judge, who instructed the jury that the CPS's case had been completely discredited, he complimented the defendant on his dignity. But it was a silent dignity. Some of Jones's pent-up anger was later released in his interview with me and others. But it was the book that really enabled him to have his say, and to thank publicly those who stuck by him.

One of them was Sir Alex Ferguson. On 25 September 1999, when Southampton visited Old Trafford shortly after the charges had been made public, the newly knighted Ferguson told Jones he wanted to walk out of the tunnel 'shoulder to shoulder' with him, as a gesture of solidarity. The United fans echoed their support. Jones was overwhelmed.

Then the match started, an absolute classic cocktail of the sublime and the ridiculous, in which United looked rampant going forward and ridiculous at the back. It ended 3-3. Southampton scored first, after Marian Pahars deftly nutmegged Jaap Stam. Normally it would be easier to nutmeg a mermaid than the mighty Dutchman, but if Pahars made Stam look like a mug, it was nothing to the fool Matt Le Tissier made of the hapless United goalkeeper Massimo Taibi, whose fate it still is to be named in every list of Fergie's worst signings, alongside the likes of Ralph Milne and Eric Djemba-Djemba.

At 2-1 down, poor old Taibi made the blunder that continues to define his fleeting tenure as United's first-choice goalkeeper, allowing a tame and speculative 25-yarder from Le Tissier to pass through his legs. He later blamed the fact that he wasn't wearing the right studs, which made him even more of a laughing stock, for it was truly a shot that my mother could have saved – in her slippers. Anyway, United overcame their shock to restore the lead, only for Le Tissier to equalise again in the 73rd minute.

United stayed top, and would go on that season to win the title, for the sixth time in eight years, by fully 18 points. So in the scheme of the season, dropping two points to Southampton at home was hardly disastrous. But at the final whistle, Ferguson was none too pleased with his players. He put his arm round Jones's shoulder.

'You can fucking well walk back to the dressing room on your own,' he said.

Chapter Eighteen

Alas, not everyone in the game was as supportive as Fergie. The ground where Dave Jones was given a torrid time, not altogether surprisingly, was Anfield. 'That hurt me most because I come from Liverpool,' he said. 'And to be fair to [the then management team of] Gérard Houllier, Phil Thompson and Sammy Lee, they all told me they were disgusted by it.'

I wish I could declare that if the boot had been on the other foot, if an ex-Liverpool player had been accused of such vile crimes and returned to Goodison as the opposition manager, the home supporters would have been paragons of sympathy and understanding.

But that's not how football works, especially where city rivals are concerned. There is a paradox increasingly evident in the relationship between Everton and Liverpool fans, who rather enjoy their reputation as the most civilised of rivals, even while directing ever-more obscene chants at each other. Nor do the unofficial supporters' websites exude much in the way of brotherly love.

It used to be different, for sure. In the days when Liverpool and Everton fans hailed almost exclusively from in or around the city, there was a kind of Scouse (or woolly-back) fellowship that has been diluted by the increasing numbers of supporters from elsewhere in the country and, in Liverpool's case especially, elsewhere in the world. You're not likely to have an Evertonian brother, cousin or best friend if you're a Liverpool fan from Milton Keynes, or Oslo, or Phnom Penh.

Still, even now, not a Merseyside derby goes by without the TV cameras finding a diehard Blue and a devoted Red sitting cheerfully alongside each other in the crowd. And in January 2014 the illustrious *New York Times*, no less, published a long article exalting the forthcoming clash between the two clubs, at the time just a point apart in the Premier League, as 'the friendly derby'. The piece was datelined Liverpool, England, and began: 'European soccer rivalries have long been blamed for a variety of extreme circumstances, from deaths and vandalism to the lobbing of flares and the occasional appearance of a pig's severed head. Rarely, however, do they split a family at Sunday dinner. Except here.

'On Merseyside, as this region of north-west England is known, the rivalry between Liverpool and Everton has always been different. If the standard-issue European rivalry is something akin to street-gang warfare, the Liverpool-Everton relationship is more like two brothers who constantly bicker over who has the better car.'

The reporter had found a 58-year-old Evertonian, Fred Kennerly, whose oldest and youngest sons were Reds, but whose middle boy was firmly Blue. 'There's rivalry, absolutely, but there's no hatred,' Kennerly told the *New York Times*. 'It's not like Manchester, with United and City, where it's like straight down the middle. Here, there are a lot of families like mine.'

That is undoubtedly so. But I'm not sure about the absence of hatred. Of course, hatred is an emotive and perhaps melodramatic word to use in connection with football. But when Liverpool eviscerated Everton 4-0 in the very match that had prompted the *New York Times* article, something akin to hatred is what I felt.

Had one rival ever heaped so much disappointment on another? Here was a game at Anfield that Everton, playing lovely football under Roberto Martinez, might at long last be expected to win, or at least to compete in on level terms. At any rate, much was made before kick-off of the fact that Everton had not won at Anfield since 1999, and arguably had their best chance for fifteen years to do so. But that unexpected 4-0 drubbing joined what seemed to me like dozens of other similarly painful defeats down the years, including two FA Cup finals, and of course the 3-0 semi-final defeat courtesy of Clive Thomas. There comes a point at which it's hard to find anything in your heart but extreme distaste for an organisation that has caused you such prolonged misery.

It's not the losses to Liverpool that are at the root of my feelings for them, though. Rather, I cast myself, to paraphrase the *New York Times* article, not so much as a man who keeps bickering with his brother over who has the better car, but a man fully aware that his brother has not only the better car, but the bigger house, the more lucrative job, the swankier holidays and the sexier wife. A man who, every time he thinks he can claim a degree of one-upmanship over his brother, quickly gets batted back down.

One-nil up in the 1986 FA Cup final ... we lost 3-1. One-nil up in the 2012 FA Cup semi-final ... we lost 2-1. Having equalised with the last kick of normal time in the 1989 FA Cup final ... we lost 3-2. Ready to take on all-comers in the European Cup ... Heysel. Oh, and in his first nine years as Everton manager, David Moyes's net spend on players was £25.8 million; in his first nine months back as Liverpool manager, Kenny Dalglish's net spend was £110.7 million. Yet Dalglish never seemed content with the huge transfer funds handed to him, and Rafa Benitez and Gérard Houllier were even worse. I lost count of the number of times Houllier and later Benitez declared, having spent tens of millions in the transfer market, that they were just 'two or three players' short of having a team that could compete. As an Evertonian, that sort of talk gets right on your wick.

Perhaps most frustratingly of all in that elusive quest for bragging rights, when Everton beat Liverpool to fourth spot in the Premier League in 2004-05 (with a negative goal difference, astoundingly), we thought we had qualified for the following season's Champions League at their expense.

It was an exquisitely pleasurable feeling, duly compounded by the spectacle of Rafa Benitez's shell-shocked players practically staggering off the field at half-time in the Champions League final in Istanbul a week or two later, 3-0 down. When Everton's players trudged off the field 3-0 down after the first 45 minutes of that derby game on a wet Tuesday night in January 2014, they went on to lose 4-0. That's usually what happens when you're 3-0 down at half-time. But not in Istanbul. Liverpool stormed back, won on penalties, and our brief flurry of one-upmanship was over.

I must add that despite that dispiriting defeat at Anfield in January 2014, Everton had a marvellous first season under Martinez, finishing fifth. But Liverpool, as seemingly decreed by those malevolent football gods, had an even better season, being narrowly pipped to the title by Manchester City. That they just failed to win the league was of considerable comfort to Evertonians, who had turned up to Goodison for the game against City on 3 May with the peculiarly agonising knowledge that a home win might land the title for Liverpool. Which would, of course, have been absolutely bleeding typical.

I should perhaps interrupt my own rant here to state that, in precise accordance with the tone of that *New York Times* piece, several of my best mates are Liverpool fans. Some of them have been pals for forty years or more. I am proud to call the brilliant screen-writer Alan Bleasdale a friend, and he's a Red through and through. Ditto an actor pal, David Morrissey, who has furnished me with my favourite story about that Istanbul final. He would certainly have gone to Turkey to see it, but had signed to do a film, *Basic Instinct 2*, and was committed to being on set in LA that day. He duly missed watching Steven Gerrard inspire Liverpool's astonishing comeback for the very acceptable reason – maybe the only acceptable reason – that he was in bed from morning to night with Sharon Stone.

Nonetheless, the affection I feel for certain Liverpool fans in no way precludes me from feeling the way I do about the team they support. And for me, as for many Evertonians, it was in the 1970s that the persecution complex set in.

In the 1960s, the two clubs enjoyed comparable, almost copycat success. Everton won the league in 1963, Liverpool in 1964. Liverpool won the Cup in 1965, Everton in 1966. Bill Shankly was a great manager, but so was Harry Catterick. However, in the 1970s their respective fortunes began to diverge like in those sitcoms of the era – *Terry and June*, *George and Mildred*, you name it – in which a motorbike's sidecar gets unhitched and shoots off downhill while the bike itself accelerates uphill.

If there was a single season that showcased those diverging fortunes, it was 1976-77. Not that it was a bad season for Everton. Despite or maybe as a result of changing managers in January, we finished ninth in the First Division, and reached the League Cup final as well as the semi-final of the FA Cup. But we were firmly trumped by Liverpool, who went and won the League and the European Cup. True, they lost to Tommy Docherty's Manchester United in the FA Cup final, but any satisfaction we might have derived on our side of Stanley Park from their failure to turn a famous Double into an even more famous Treble, was of course torpedoed by the semi-final events at Maine Road. We knew it should have been us at Wembley.

I think that one of the reasons I have such fond memories of the following year, 1978, is that Liverpool didn't win the league. As winter gave way to spring it was clear that Clough's Forest team had confounded the ever-dwindling band of sceptics who reckoned they couldn't last the pace, although they almost certainly would not have done had Clough, rather than Ron Greenwood, succeeded Don Revie as England manager.

In December 1977, with Greenwood still in charge on a temporary basis, the FA had interviewed five candidates to take on the role permanently. Of the five: Greenwood, Clough, Lawrie McMenemy, Jack Charlton and Dave Sexton, only Clough had captured English football's most coveted prize, the league title. And, by December, it looked as though he had turned another unfashionable East Midlands club, just as Derby had been, into potential title-winners.

He was the popular choice for the England job, but the FA had other ideas. In fact our old friend Harold Thompson, Margaret Thatcher's former chemistry professor, serial groper, and by then the FA chairman, was reluctant even to grant him an interview. If Alf Ramsey had got up Thompson's supercilious nose, Clough got up it even further. Nor had he courted much by way of affection from Bert Millichip, who would succeed Thompson and was one of the FA's interviewing panel. Shortly before his interview, Clough publicly lambasted West Bromwich Albion for failing to offer their manager Ronnie Allen a contract. Millichip was the Albion chairman.

With the FA led by a man who seemed to take the same view of the general public as he did of successive England managers, namely that they were barely entitled to breathe the same air as him (though he could doubtless have given a fascinating lecture on the nitrogen, oxygen and argon of which air is mainly comprised), the popular clamour for Clough was never likely to exert much influence. Except, perhaps, of the negative variety.

Another of the men on the FA interviewing panel, the Manchester City chairman Peter Swales, later confirmed that of all the candidates, Clough had given the best, most dynamic interview. And Clough himself went back to Nottingham and told Peter Taylor that it had gone 'brilliantly'.

He added that, 'If it's straight, we've got it.' But it wasn't straight. Quite aside from Thompson's personal distaste for the outspoken Clough, the FA mandarins felt that he wasn't equipped with the diplomatic skills they needed from an England manager, especially in the wake of the Don Revie affair. They had a point. Clough had once told a gathering of Austrian journalists that it was a disgrace, the way their countrymen had 'lain down for Hitler'.

So Ron Greenwood was confirmed as the full-time England manager and Clough stayed with Forest, whose sequence of results in that month of December alone rather suggested that the FA, irrespective of the diplomacy issue, might have picked the wrong man. Forest played six games in December, winning five and drawing one. The draw came on Boxing Day, 1-1 against Liverpool, as Everton were being battered by United. Everton had started the month only a point behind Forest in second place. They finished it still in second place, but five points behind. Liverpool were a point further back, in third. Gordon Lee and his Liverpool counterpart Bob Paisley must have been no less sorry than the man in the street that Clough hadn't been handed the England job.

By the beginning of April 1978, Everton were still second in the table and only two points behind Forest, but crucially, had played three games more. We fans didn't think for a second that Clough and Taylor would allow such an advantage to evaporate, which is why we turned our attentions so passionately to Latchford's quest for 30 goals.

But what we weren't aware of, and it would have pained us terribly if we had been, was that Paisley was quietly building a

Liverpool team that, the following season, would put Forest back in their place – second – and dominate English football once again. A team, indeed, that would only really be dislodged from the summit of the domestic game by Howard Kendall's Everton. That detail, had we been aware of it, would have made up for the pain. And some.

In April 1977, Paisley had signed Alan Hansen, £100,000-worth of unrefined but hugely promising defensive talent from Partick Thistle. That August, a month after Kevin Keegan had left for Hamburg, he went back to Scotland for Kenny Dalglish. In January 1978 he bought another Scot, Graeme Souness, from Middlesbrough.

Souness's wasn't the only arrival that month for which Liverpudlians, even now, have cause to be grateful. A baby was born on 28 January 1978, and christened Jamie Lee Duncan Carragher. As we now know, Jamie Carragher would end up a stalwart of the Liverpool defence for more than a decade, yet there was no family more staunchly and proudly Evertonian than the Carraghers of Bootle, hence the choice of little Jamie's middle names.

The Duncan was in homage to Duncan McKenzie, new-dad Philly Carragher's hero, and the Lee a nod to Gordon Lee, although it was ironically meant, because on the day his boy was born, Philly was fuming that Lee had dropped McKenzie for an FA Cup tie away at Middlesbrough. Just over two years later, in the semi-final replay against West Ham, and with Everton 2-1 down, I watched from the Elland Road terraces as a man walked up to Lee in the dugout and harangued him furiously. It was Philly Carragher, and if I'd told him that his toddler son would end up being an Anfield legend, he'd have turned on me too.

More than thirty years later, I did get a taste of the Carragher temper. I was in Liverpool interviewing Jamie for the *Sunday Times*. He had just retired and was about to start work as a pundit for Sky

Sports. Aware that one of his new colleagues would be Graeme Souness, I rather hopefully asked him whether, like many Reds, he subscribed to the theory that the wheels started coming off Liverpool as a trophy-winning machine – oh joy! – during Souness's tenure as manager? 'What the fuck are you trying to get me to say?' he exploded, and the subject was swiftly changed. Of course, had Souness been half the manager for Liverpool that he was a player, they'd have even more silverware to polish.

In his 2009 memoir *44 Years With the Same Bird*, the *Daily Mirror* columnist and rabid Liverpool fan Brian Reade, recalled the purchase of Souness in January 1978 as 'another piece of Paisley genius'. And fair play, even from an Evertonian perspective, it was. Reade describes seeing Souness making his debut for Liverpool, at West Brom. 'With his first couple of touches you knew we'd signed someone who could stroke the ball around like an opening batsman,' he wrote. 'With his first couple of tackles you knew we also had someone who could hit an opponent like a world champion cruiserweight.' Lyrical stuff, but not untrue. A few months later, just before Souness helped Liverpool retain the European Cup that May, Bob Paisley told Stan Hey, a journalist who would later become a pal of mine: 'Most midfields are made up of a buzzer, a cruncher and a spreader. This boy is all three.'

So in retrospect it was portentous indeed when, with Everton having finished their league programme in the finest imaginable style with the 6-0 mauling of Chelsea and Latchford's 29th and 30th goals, Liverpool used their two games in hand to leapfrog us and finish in second place. Paisley knew by then that he had a team comfortably capable of winning back the title. Dalglish and then Souness had been like the two final rivets in a Rolls-Royce engine, and indeed it was from a Souness pass that Dalglish scored the only goal in the European Cup final against FC Bruges, at Wembley on 10 May.

A depressing pattern was unfolding. Latchford had won the

Daily Express prize and Liverpool had failed to win the league, two very good reasons for Evertonians to celebrate, only for Liverpool to go and become European champions for a second successive year. Meanwhile, with Paisley having bought Dalglish from Celtic the summer before, Lee swooped in the summer of 1978 for Mickey Walsh from Blackpool, celebrated for little more than having scored a single though brilliant goal – and more significantly still, a brilliant televised goal – in a Second Division match against Sunderland three years earlier.

It would be a little unfair on Lee to cite these two bits of transfer business as somehow symbolic of the difference between him and Paisley, and for that matter between Everton and Liverpool at the time, but their respective stats do tell a story of sorts. Both men were strikers, and both had cost a hefty amount. Yet Walsh would end up scoring only one goal in 21 appearances for Everton, before Lee cut his losses and swapped him for QPR's Peter Eastoe. He, at least, would muster 26 goals in 95 games. Dalglish, by dispiriting contrast, played 355 times for Liverpool, scored 118 goals, and created probably three times that number with his chicanery in and around the box.

Still, it's also worth adding that in September 1978, Lee paid Derby County £300,000 for Colin Todd. That was more like it. Todd might have been close to his thirtieth birthday but we all knew he was pure class, one of the finest defenders of his generation.

Moreover, by the time Todd arrived, Everton had started the 1978-79 season with a swagger. They won the opening three games – away at Chelsea, then at home to Derby and Arsenal. Then, in the second round of the League Cup on a Tuesday night at Goodison, they hammered Dario Gradi's Wimbledon 8-0. No matter that it was against Fourth Division opposition, it was exhibition stuff, the most ruthless attacking football I had yet seen at Goodison, including the defeat of Chelsea four months earlier to the day. Latchford scored five, Martin Dobson three, and on the Gwladys Street terrace Fozzie Bear kept us in good voice throughout.

The team's good run continued. We drew at Old Trafford, Villa Park and Loftus Road, but beat Middlesbrough, Wolves and Ipswich at home. In the UEFA Cup, we overwhelmed the Irish team Finn Harps 10-0 on aggregate. With the game against Liverpool inexorably heading towards us, like distant but approaching thunder, we remained unbeaten and had risen to second in the First Division.

Guess who was top? If we had started the season like a souped-up Ford Capri, Liverpool had started it like a bloody Ferrari. In their first five games they had scored 19 goals and conceded two. This included a 7-0 flattening of Tottenham, and the final goal that day, a thunderous Terry McDermott header at the end of a flowing move the length of the field, would later be voted the greatest ever scored by Liverpool at Anfield. Naturally, I have no intention of describing it in detail here. But I will quote Michael Charters, reporting for the *Liverpool Echo*. 'The current Liverpool team is playing better, more exciting, attacking football than any side I've seen since the war,' wrote Charters, ominously.

I remember that day. Everton were playing Manchester United and I had taken the decision not to go, not least because my late father had left me with a nagging worry about hooliganism. Old Trafford in those days was considered the most dangerous ground of all, and I was still congratulating myself for my good sense in not having gone to Stamford Bridge on the opening day of the season.

Whoever had overseen the fixtures programme for 1978-79 had dropped a right clanger. Everton had thumped Chelsea on the last day of the previous season, and for the Chelsea fans it had been a literal thumping; one-armed Babs and his crew had been given a bit of a hiding on their way back to Lime Street station, by all accounts. So naturally the fixtures picked out Everton as Chelsea's opening-day visitors, and just as naturally the Chelsea thugs had a send-off planned for after the game.

My acquaintance from the Cheshire Yeoman car park, Andy Nicholls, wasn't there but wrote about it in his book, *Scally*. The Battle of Kensington High Street is to football hooligans of the 1970s what the Tet Offensive is to veterans of the Vietnam War, if that's not giving nasty thuggery a status it hardly deserves. After the game, as a train carrying Everton fans arrived at High Street Kensington tube station, it was ambushed by a battalion of Chelsea skinheads. Fire extinguishers were used to jam the doors open, to keep the train at the platform. There were stabbings, bottlings, slashings. More than a few fans ended up in hospital. It was remarkable that nobody died.

'Everyone has their own favourite tale of the day and mine is that the Chelsea mob asked all the women and children in one carriage to leave the train before they attacked the Everton,' wrote Nicholls, adding that 'Chelsea have always had style'. Yes, very stylish.

Anyway, that was why I sat in my bedroom on that Saturday afternoon in early September, listening to Radio City's reports on Everton's fairly prosaic draw at Old Trafford along with annoyingly rhapsodic commentary from Anfield. Despite their thunderous start to the season, Liverpool hadn't been expected to make mincemeat of a Spurs team containing Glenn Hoddle and the exciting, newly arrived Argentinians Ossie Ardiles and Ricky Villa. Sitting on my bed, surrounded by the glorious frieze of newspaper cuttings celebrating Everton's goalscoring majesty from the season before, I was scarcely less horrified than Ardiles and Villa themselves.

Tottenham were still one of the so-called Big Five. And if Liverpool could hit them for seven, they could do it to anyone.

Chapter Nineteen

Before I can indulge myself and all Evertonian readers with an account of what did come to pass when Everton and Liverpool met the following month, however, I must take a step back.

Unlike the summer of 1977, when I followed every ball of an Ashes series and was able to put my passion for football on hold, the summer of 1978 was illuminated by a World Cup, the fifth of my lifetime but the first that I was able to watch on my own terms. I was sixteen, and although my mother had responded to my disastrous results in my O level mocks earlier that year by removing the television set that she considered a pernicious distraction, she had reluctantly had it reinstalled. So, as my real O levels approached, so did the mouth-watering prospect of watching Brazil, Italy, Holland and West Germany strut their stuff in Argentina. Not to mention the Argentinians themselves. And all in colour, too.

The first World Cup of which I'd been really conscious was the 1970 tournament, which I'd watched on our black-and-white telly. Only for the final, in which the Brazil of Pelé, Rivelino, Jairzinho and Carlos Alberto so stylishly disposed of Italy, did my dad take me to the home of our family friends 'Auntie' Sybil and 'Uncle'

Ronnie, whose capacious bungalow in Hartley Road was graced by a large colour set, and which I sat in front of, cross-legged, in utter thrall to the spectacle before me. Even by the 1974 tournament, we still hadn't joined the ranks of those with colour televisions. I can't think why, because my dad's overriding sporting passion was horse racing, and when he did finally succumb and rent a colour set from Rumbelows, he spent at least the next six months oohing and aahing at the verdant green of the turf, and the shimmering orange, red and blue vibrancy of the jockeys' silks.

Of course, my excitement about the 1978 World Cup was tarnished slightly by England's absence, but then they hadn't qualified four years earlier, either. For my generation, it was easier to come to terms with the disappointment than it was for those a few years older, who remembered the events of 1966 so vividly. So in 1978, as in 1974, I rooted wholeheartedly, without the slightest equivocation, for Scotland.

Adopting Scotland as my World Cup team made absolute sense to me. England weren't there, so naturally the Scots, managed by the irrepressibly optimistic, not to say downright hubristic Ally MacLeod, were the next best thing. Gradually I would come to realise that this pan-Britishness did not extend north of the border. It was a jolting shock to me to find football-loving Scots supporting 'anyone but England', in Andy Murray's joshing but infamous phrase, and I have always taken it rather personally, remembering just how far I jumped out of my chair when barrel-chested little Archie Gemmill finished his weaving run by scoring Scotland's third against Holland in Mendoza's San Martin stadium on 11 June 1978.

It was a goal that briefly but thrillingly reignited Scottish chances of making it into the knockout stages, giving Scotland a 3-1 lead in a game they needed to win by three clear goals to qualify. Alas, Johnny Rep then scored a howitzer from about 30 yards (nobody seems to know exactly how far it was, estimates varying from 28 yards to a mile and a half), to put Scotland's fate beyond doubt.

I suppose I might have been more sensitive as a 16-year-old to the antipathy some Scots felt for the English, or at least for England, which they regarded not so much as a place, more of a concept, a semi-mythical Tunbridge Wellsian land populated by snooty colonels who considered all Jocks, with the possible exception of Field Marshal Haig, Lord Reith and lovely Hannah Gordon, to be uncivilised ruffians.

It is perfectly true that several thousand Scottish football fans had done nothing to counter this perception by celebrating a 2-1 win in the Home International against England the previous May by running amok on the Wembley pitch, digging up the turf and swarming over the goalposts. One of them, a 21-year-old Glaswegian called Alex Torrance, was infamously credited with snapping one of the crossbars. As far as I can tell he did nothing else that was especially noteworthy in his fifty-four years, but when he died in 2010, after a long battle with alcoholism, some Scottish newspapers carried obituaries. One of the message board tributes, posted with no apparent irony, was: 'A legend of Scottish football, RIP Alex'.

That 1977 Wembley pitch invasion, complete with a swirling banner exhorting the fans to 'Remember Bannockburn 1314', was a fair indication of how quite a lot of Scots felt about the English, and as such it wasn't exactly an ideal curtain-raiser to the Queen's Silver Jubilee celebrations just three days later. Her Majesty, it seemed, reigned over a kingdom that was some way less than united.

Another indication was a line in a song written and recorded by a comedian called Andy Cameron, who actually went on to *Top of the Pops*, to the manifest bemusement not just of the teenagers shuffling around awkwardly in front of the stage but even presenter Tony Blackburn, to sing:

Hey, we're on the march wi' Ally's Army
We're going to the Argentine,
And we'll really shake them up
When we win the World Cup
'Cos Scotland are the greatest football team

According to Cameron, Ally's Army were representing Britain and were going to do or die, setting up the killer put-down: 'England cannae dae it, 'cos they didnae qualify'.

This was indubitably true. However, the song, which reached number six in the charts, would come back to haunt poor MacLeod almost as if he'd been the fellow draped in tartan on *Top of the Pops*. In fact, he might as well have been. For months before Scotland set out for Argentina, he repeatedly boasted, both in private and public, that Scotland would indeed return with the World Cup.

In fairness, MacLeod had Dalglish and Souness of Liverpool in his squad, as well as Robertson, Gemmill and Kenny Burns of Nottingham Forest. The long flight across the Atlantic on 26 May also carried Lou Macari, Willie Johnston, Bruce Rioch, Don Masson, Martin Buchan, Joe Jordan and Asa Hartford – who owed his unusual first name to a father who loved Al Jolson (born Asa Yoelson), was even more famous for having a hole in his heart and would early the following season join Everton.

They were all excellent players, and certainly the Scottish midfield, on paper, looked stronger than most. Not so the defence, which was missing a formidable duo in big Gordon McQueen and Celtic's classy full back Danny McGrain, both injured. MacLeod had asserted that Scotland would miss McGrain even more than the Dutch would miss the great Johan Cruyff. But not to the extent that it would prevent him making Scotland the world champions.

His repeated boast that Scotland would put all comers to the sword, or the claymore, was not quite as absurd as it would be today, even in the somewhat unlikely event now of Scotland actually managing to qualify for the World Cup. But it was pretty absurd.

And yet I lapped it up. Returning to school after the Easter holidays I could hardly wait for the tournament to get started, and read everything about it that I could get my hands on – which in those days, with only column inches about football rather than the column yards, furlongs and miles we get today, took proper dedication. All the same, if I'd been taking an O level on the 1978 World Cup, I'd have had a certain A in the bag. Regrettably, I wasn't. I was taking English, Maths, French, History, Latin, Geography, Chemistry, Physics and Biology.

From the beginning of May we were allowed to stay at home for revision purposes, which suited me nicely when Liverpool won the European Cup on Wednesday the 10th, since it meant not having to run the gamut of Koppite triumphalism on the number 15 bus to school, and relentlessly all day in the corridors.

My O levels were due to start on Tuesday, 6 June, four days after the opening game of the World Cup: West Germany v Poland. That seemed like an almost cosmically cruel clash of commitments. I was already disadvantaged by having to take exams in the summer because I suffered badly from hay fever, at a time when the only known remedy – or the only remedy known to my mum and me – was an anti-histamine called Piriton. It is still available for allergy sufferers, but with the crucial difference that it no longer causes drowsiness. In 1978 a single yellow Piriton tablet could have put a carthorse to sleep, meaning that I, and others similarly blighted, had to choose between sitting in the exam hall with streaming nose and eyes, or turning over the paper, just about digesting the instruction 'Answer ALL questions in Section A; answer FOUR questions in Section B; answer ONE question in section C' ... and then nodding off.

Nobody talked about double whammies in the 1970s, but if they had, hay fever and the World Cup was a hell of an example. And even on those blissful days when the allergy didn't strike, revising for my O levels seemed like an annoying distraction from the approaching fiesta of football. So I didn't, or at least, not very hard. What I did do was strain every creative sinew in the construction of revision timetables. They were little works of art, neatly and beautifully tabulated in primary colours, with hours allocated for different subjects, interspersed with four daily twenty-five-minute breaks for mealtimes, watching telly and kicking a ball against the garage wall.

Just as I'd have scored an easy A in an O level about World Cup teams, so I'd have bagged another if revision timetables had been handed in for assessment. And a whole load more if I'd spent as much time revising as I had drawing up the timetable in the first place. But as it turned out, it was the twenty-five-minute breaks that absorbed just about all my revision, and the hours in between that were spent eating, watching telly and playing one-twos with the reliably unselfish garage wall.

My first exam was maths, another cruel blow, since two years in the care of Etty Johnson had rendered me almost entirely incapable of estimating the radius of the base of a cone, let alone its perpendicular height, and certainly not the volume of water required to fill it. I just didn't see the point of maths, especially not on a day when Argentina were playing France.

By then, Scotland had played their disastrous opening game against Peru, which had awakened all my indignation at George Wood being overlooked. Don Masson missed a penalty to make it 2-1, but it was the first Cubillas strike past Alan Rough a few minutes later that really hurt.

'As Cubillas's shot sped towards him, Rough had hopped to his right, hovered on one leg and extended a hand loosely in the direction of the disappearing ball,' recalled Graham McColl in his engrossing and sporadically very funny book '78: How a Nation Lost the World Cup. McColl described the goalkeeper as looking like a man stepping off the kerb to make a token effort at hailing a speeding taxi ... 'something that Rough and some of his teammates may have felt like doing in the wake of that goal.'

By the time Scotland played out their dispiriting draw against Iran four days later – on the second day of my O levels – an even bigger disaster had engulfed the squad. Kenny Dalglish and the West Bromwich Albion winger Willie Johnston had been the two players chosen by FIFA to give urine samples after the Peru defeat, and a despondent MacLeod, desperately trying to lift his players, had cracked that 'at least that will turn out all right'.

It didnae. Johnston's sample contained traces of something called fencamfamine, contained in the over-the-counter medicine Reactivan, which he'd innocently taken without realising it contained a banned substance. Nevertheless, he became only the second player at a World Cup, after Ernst Jean-Joseph of Haiti four years earlier, to have failed a drugs test. He was sent home in disgrace, to be met in London by his manager at West Brom, Ron Atkinson, whose opening line was: 'Have you got any of those tablets left? I'm knackered.' Then he said that he did at least have some good news for Johnston. He'd negotiated a new contract for him ... with Boots.

Who knows whether Big Ron was as cheerful in receipt of gallows humour, when much later confronting his own crisis following accusations of racism, as he was in dishing it out? Still, I have a huge soft spot for him, partly because I've spent some time with him and he is still one of football's great characters, and secondly because his West Brom side of the late 1970s – with its unusually large complement of black players – was one of the most entertaining teams of that era. Laurie Cunningham, Cyrille Regis, Bryan Robson,

Derek Statham, Tony 'Bomber' Brown and co. were comfortably the equal on their day of Liverpool and Forest. Indeed, Atkinson has assured me that if, on taking the Manchester United job in 1981, he could have swapped the entire United squad for the entire West Brom squad, he would without hesitation have done so. Not a wish that a United manager would trouble a genie with now.

Returning to Argentina, Scotland's close brush with redemption, the match against the Dutch, took place in the Estadio Ciudad de Mendoza (which after the Falklands War four years later was point-edly renamed the Estadio Malvinas Argentinas) on the evening, UK time, of Sunday, 11 June. I had a history paper the following morning, for which my preparation had already suffered; earlier that day I had sat through Brazil v Austria in its entirety.

In Mendoza, such was Scotland's goal-difference deficit that like pretty much everyone else, I had entirely written off their chances of overturning it. Yet Gemmill's bit of wizardry made it 3-1, just one score shy of their target. Johnny Rep's subsequent piledriver punc-tured the balloon of optimism that Scotland might just sneak through, but at least their campaign ended with a certain nobility, and someone imaginative at the BBC put together a poignant montage of the team's high and lows, set to Julie Covington's beautiful singing on 'Don't Cry For Me, Argentina', a track which had briefly made it to number one the year before, even before *Evita*, the musical for which it was written, opened in the West End.

I can still clearly remember that montage – the hand containing two slightly melting yellow tablets of the kind that Willie Johnston had ill-advisedly taken, and, over the lyric 'the answer was here all the time', an image of Graeme Souness, who had been overlooked by MacLeod for the games against Peru and Iran, but was included against the Dutch, and ran the show in midfield. The 25-year-old's unwavering confidence in his own abilities wasn't appreciated by all his teammates – 'If he was a chocolate drop, he'd eat himself' quipped Archie Gemmill – but it could be that Julie Covington, even though she was singing about Eva Perón rather than Graeme Souness, was right. With Souness in the team from the start, maybe Ally's bedraggled army would've marched a little further into the tournament.

At least Gemmill gave them something to cheer about. If I had to rank the goals I have seen on TV over the years that have propelled me out of my seat and sent me running round the room in barely containable excitement, that one would probably make the top ten, along with Gary Lineker's equaliser in the 1990 World Cup semi-final . . . and eight Everton goals against Liverpool.

The one Everton goal against Liverpool that Blues of my generation remember more fondly than any other was still four months away as the rest of the World Cup passed in a surreal blur of exams and tickertape – Argentina's dubious gift to the football world rather as the Mexican wave would be Mexico's eight years later.

Happily, my O levels were over by the time Holland and Argentina contested the final on 25 June; I somehow escaped with six passes – two As, in English and History, two Bs, two Cs – but also a D, an E and, in Physics, an abject and humiliating U. Had it not been for the World Cup, there is no doubt that my grades would have been considerably better (though I might not have improved on that U). And I wasn't the only one to suffer. My football-mad (but, regrettably, Liverpool-supporting) mate Pete Venables had too. As we prepared to enter sixth form at the end of that summer, I can remember him pointing out that our A levels would coincide with the 1980 European Championships. It was really most unfair.

By the time I did become a sixth former that September, the World Cup in Argentina had already altered the landscape of English football. Literally so, in one sense, because the crazy tickertape celebrations that accompanied Argentina's victories had captured the imagination of supporters here, doubtless to the utter dismay of those whose job it was to clear the terracing of thousands of pieces of torn-up paper.

Everton began their home campaign, following the 1-0 win at Chelsea and the subsequent Battle of Kensington High Street, against Derby County on Tuesday, 22 August. And, as the players ran out on to the Goodison turf, everyone in the crowd threw fistfuls of paper into the air. Everyone but me, or so it seemed. I wasn't expecting it and, to my embarrassment then and embarrassment now, I ducked, covering my head.

It was the legacy of my dad again. There had been reports of batteries and other projectiles thrown at the Everton supporters at Stamford Bridge on the Saturday, so as soon as I caught sight of something in the air, I thought I was in mortal danger. Heaven knows how, because unless Fatima Whitbread had been among the small contingent of Derby fans at the other end of the stadium, there wasn't much chance of anything launched by them reaching me. Nevertheless, only slowly did I realise that it was about 100 small pieces of the *Daily Mirror* fluttering down over my head, not a barrage of Evereadys.

The other way in which the 1978 World Cup changed the landscape was rather more profound, and certainly longer lasting, since everyone got tired of the tickertape thing after a few weeks. A few days after Argentina's captain Daniel Passarella had lifted the World Cup, Keith Burkinshaw, the Barnsley-born manager of Tottenham Hotspur, was telephoned by his Sheffield United counterpart Harry Haslam. Actually, it was the *éminence grise* of White Hart Lane, Tottenham's Double-winning manager Bill Nicholson, who had popped into the office for a chat, who answered the phone. Haslam asked him if Burkinshaw might be interested in signing Osvaldo Ardiles, which to paraphrase a crack made a year or so earlier by

Brian Clough, was rather like the producer of *Coronation Street* being asked if he would like to sign Richard Burton or Robert Redford.

Spurs fans might take issue with the comparison, but their team had only just won promotion back into the First Division, and more to the point it was unimaginable, then, that a foreign player as excitingly glamorous as Ardiles, who had sparkled in the World Cup and featured in most people's team of the tournament, might want to ply his trade in England. An England, don't forget, about to slide into the Winter of Discontent. And never mind the Winter of Discontent, what about our regular winter, the winter of wind, sleet and rain? This fellow, with his classic Latin American looks, didn't look like someone who'd be happy running out at Burnden Park or Ashton Gate on a chilly February evening.

But Haslam knew, through one of his coaching staff, Oscar Arce, that Ardiles fancied playing in Europe. Not England, specifically, but Europe. Haslam couldn't afford him for Sheffield United, so was touting him around, and had already mentioned him to Terry Neill at Arsenal. That got Burkinshaw's attention. He flew to Buenos Aires a few days later and met Ardiles, who after consulting his wife said that, yes, he would sign. And by the way, did Mr Burkinshaw fancy signing his friend Ricky Villa too?

A friend and former colleague of mine, Nick Harris, has written a terrific history of foreign footballers in the English game, a book called *England, Their England*. We joked about it at the time of publication, because without knowing that he was doing it, I'd been half-heartedly working on a proposal for a history of foreign footballers in England, which I wanted to call *Who Ate All the Pasta?* Obviously, Harris's book strangled mine at birth, but it's a much more serious work of scholarship than mine would have been. And he acknowledges in his fascinating chapter on the arrival of Ardiles and Villa that dozens of foreigners arrived to play here before them, some of whom even came in pairs. But never from a country without

Commonwealth or colonial ties. And never a couple of freshly minted World Cup winners.

When the news broke on 10 July, it was described by more than one newspaper as 'sensational'. The following Sunday, Tottenham's new signings arrived, in a storm of publicity that even reached the news pages, jostling for prominence with a military coup in Mauritania, wherever that was. Then, a couple of days later, Haslam landed his own Argentinian, Alex Sabella, paying a record fee for Sheffield United of £160,000.

Had the United board been willing to shell out a little more, they could have had another player from Argentina, a promising 17-year-old weaving magic at Argentinos Juniors, by the name of Diego Maradona. With the well-connected Arce, Haslam had been on a scouting mission to South America and was so impressed with young Diego that he agreed to pay £200,000 for him. Alas, the Blades directors decided that was a bit too much for an unknown teenager with more vowels than consonants in his name, and so collectively joined the list topped by poor old Dick Rowe, the Decca executive who turned down The Beatles. Imagine how Maradona would have illuminated Bramall Lane.

Meanwhile, Manchester City confirmed their interest in the Polish player Kazimierz Deyna, and Birmingham in another Argentinian, Alberto Tarantini. At Southampton, Lawrie McMenemy announced that he had lined up the Yugoslav full back Ivan Golac. At Ipswich, Bobby Robson unveiled a classy Dutchman, Arnold Mühren, later followed by his compatriot Frans Thyssen.

Years later, Ron Atkinson told me what Gordon Lee, whom he'd known when they were both on Aston Villa's books in the 1950s, had said, entirely guilelessly, when he heard that Mühren had come from the Dutch club Twente Enschede: 'Bloody hell, is that all he is? Twenty yesterday?'

Foreign footballers weren't Gordon's cup of strong English

breakfast tea. So strong and so English was his tea, in fact, that he was probably related to the original Rosy Lee. And he wasn't the only Gordon discomfited by the new wave of arrivals. At the PFA, Gordon Taylor asserted with impressive prescience that, 'If a trickle of foreign players becomes a flow, it would be detrimental to our members. Whichever way you look at it, there could already be two English players out of a job at Tottenham because of the Argentinians.'

The England manager, however, begged to differ. 'They have acted as a stimulant on our soccer,' said Ron Greenwood, of the exotic newcomers. 'They have created a feeling of expectancy, excitement and glamour.'

More than thirty-five years later, exactly these same points of view continue to be aired – foreign players, good or bad thing? – albeit against a dramatically different backdrop. But it was those few weeks in 1978 when the scenery began to change.

In 1978 there was also a steady and increasing flow of British footballers to the North American Soccer League, some of them signing just for the English off-season. In fact, no fewer than 129 NASL players that summer came from England, more even than came from the United States. Even Trevor Francis, soon to become Britain's first million-pound player, spent the previous summer playing in America, arriving back at Birmingham City literally hours before the 1978-79 season kicked off. But the revolution that 26-year-old Ardiles quite unwittingly wrought changed the whole dynamic of English football. We were now importers as well as exporters.

Not, though, as we have discovered, at Goodison Park. Funny surnames with multiple vowels and Zs in them, that wasn't for Gordon Lee, the miner's son from Staffordshire. Players who couldn't even speak plain English? With strange dietary habits? No thanks.

It was entirely fitting, then, that the new hero of Goodison, following in Bob Latchford's bootsteps and crowned euphorically on 28 October, should be a man about as English as it was possible to be, born to Bill and Eileen, a hod-carrier and his wife, in the village of Markyate, Hertfordshire, which sits between Dunstable and St Albans on what was once known as Watling Street, now more prosaically the A5 – Andrew Edward King.

Chapter Twenty

Andy King wasn't a hard man to find when I researched this book, but he was a hard man to pin down for an interview. He was working at Northampton Town, first as assistant to Aidy Boothroyd, and then as caretaker manager following Boothroyd's dismissal in December 2013 in the wake of a 4-1 home defeat by Wycombe Wanderers that left Northampton bottom of Division Two and therefore ninety-second of ninety-two league clubs.

I phoned him several times, but he kept saying that he was too busy, that I'd have to leave it for a while. Eventually, in January 2014, we finally nailed a day and time for me to see him at Northampton's shiny Sixfields stadium.

First, though, let me turn the clock back to that unseasonably warm and sunny October afternoon in 1978. Liverpool were top, Everton were second. Both teams were unbeaten in the league. We had won six and drawn five of our first eleven games. But in doing so we had only scored 14 goals. They, in winning 10 of their first 11, had scored 35 goals. There had only been two blips in their season, although one of them was a hell of a blip, for their defence of the European Cup – a straightforward knockout competition then, as it really should be now – had fallen at the very first hurdle. And to make matters much worse, it was a hurdle in the irritating form of Brian Clough and Nottingham Forest.

Liverpool had also been knocked out of the League Cup by Harry Haslam's Second Division Sheffield United, without Maradona, but with Sabella. But in the league programme they took terrible revenge for these indignities.

We got an earlier-than-usual bus from Southport's Ribble bus station that day, my friends and me, the usual derby-day trepidation magnified by Liverpool's extraordinary goalscoring prowess in the season so far. I had turned seventeen just a few days earlier, and could hardly bring myself to hope for the most perfect birthday present of all: the first victory for Everton over Liverpool since shortly after I turned ten, and which I barely remembered.

Meanwhile, Dave Prentice, two years younger than me, was making his way from Formby on the train. 'It was a day of mixed fortunes for me,' he told me. 'I'd never seen Everton beat Liverpool, so obviously that was fantastic. But I was short of cash, so I bunked on the train with a used ticket. When we got to Bank Hall station, the British Transport Police were at the top of the steps, but there was a scrum of people, so I wasn't too worried. The fella took my ticket off me, but stupidly, rather than walking through, I asked for it back, because it was a return. That's when he looked more closely at it and nicked me. He took me to one side and asked for my name and address, and being young and naive I gave him the correct details. Walking to the ground and even during the game, it was on my mind the whole time. When Andy King scored that glorious goal down the Park End I celebrated wildly, of course, but it was still worrying me, that I'd been nicked by the British Transport Police and would get a right bollocking from my parents. It took the shine off my day a little bit.'

Nothing took the shine off mine. Rafe, Briggy, Mozzer, Mugsy, Bean and I arrived at Goodison to see a huge BBC truck outside, and while it wasn't exactly surprising to find the *Match of the Day* cameras at a game between the teams placed first and second in the league, and a Merseyside derby to boot, it was still an added thrill to know that we were going to be on the telly. Not that we knew just how much we would treasure the footage, and John Motson's immortal lines at the final whistle: 'That's it! Everton have beaten Liverpool, Andy King the scorer. Seven is his number, and seven years it is since this last happened … Liverpool's run of 23 league games unbeaten is over!'

At the opening whistle, the respective line-ups didn't seem to favour us. Lee's XI was: Wood, Todd, Pejic, Kenyon, Wright, Nulty, King, Dobson, Latchford, Walsh, Thomas. Bob Paisley's was: Clemence, Neal, Alan Kennedy, Thompson, Ray Kennedy, Hansen, Dalglish, Case, Heighway, Johnson, Souness. Alan Hansen would later tell me that of all the Liverpool teams he played in – including those spearheaded by Ian Rush, the ex-Evertonian who became a greater thorn in our side than anyone before or since, scoring an indecent number of goals against us as if to punish us for ever having stolen his heart – that was the pick of them.

In the Everton side, it seemed to me that there were a few weak links. Mickey Walsh already looked like a wholly inadequate replacement for the departed Duncan McKenzie, and Geoff Nulty never inspired much confidence in midfield, although he had rather unfairly become something of a whipping boy on the Gwladys Street. Especially for the little guy in front of me with the tight quilted anorak, who seemed to hate him with a passion that I thought should only be reserved for opposition players. 'Nulty, you're fucking crap,' he used to shout, with a rather troubling intensity. And that was during the warm-up.

Nulty was a huge favourite of Gordon Lee's – Dave Thomas would later tell me that he treated Nulty 'almost like a son'. Lee certainly rated him as a good team player. He had brought him to

Everton from his former club, Newcastle, and would take him to his next club, Preston. But Nulty went to Deepdale as a coach, not a player. His playing career ended abruptly during another Merseyside derby, at Goodison in 1980, when Jimmy Case somehow escaped a red card for a challenge that these days would ignite talk of assault charges. Dixie Dean died of a heart attack while attending that game, and I don't suppose it was Case's horrendous tackle that finished off the great man – he must have seen even worse in his own era. But it was a bad, bad day for Geoff Nulty, Dixie Dean and Everton, even taking the result – 2-1 to Liverpool – out of the equation.

Nulty later became a sub-postmaster, another job into which ex-footballers of that era sometimes fell. His job on that 1978 day of days, however, was to mark Ray Kennedy, twenty-seven years old and in his considerable prime. Nulty did it splendidly.

The match stayed goalless until the 58th minute, when Pejic clipped the ball to Dobson in the Liverpool penalty area, he headed it outside the area to King, who struck a sublime volley past Ray Clemence that Liverpool players, most ungraciously, dismissed as a miskick. 'And Goodison Park goes absolutely mad,' cried Motson, and it's perfectly true, we did.

So did the players. 'Everything we did went up a gear in those Merseyside derbies,' Martin Dobson later told me. 'Tackling, celebrating goals, everything. I was captain that day because Lyonsy was out, and it was my header that went to Kingy, and he's shinned it into the top corner.' He chuckled. 'No, he's caught it really well. And the noise was incredible. Just coming out of the tunnel at the start of those games was like hitting a wall of noise. I'd never come across anything like it, even in international games.'

In the crowd, if anything, the celebrations were even more hysterical than they had been six months earlier when Latchford scored his 30th. We had given full throttle that day to 'Bobby

Latchford walks on water', but for the remaining half-hour or so of the derby, the Goodison Park rafters positively shuddered to a rapturous chorus of 'Andy is our King, oh Andy is our king, oh Aaaandy is our King!' Fozzie Bear did well to hang on to his stanchion.

Also, unlike Latchford's goal, this one was captured for posterity by television. Moreover, the immediate aftermath of the game would become a staple of TV bloopers shows for years to come, an over-zealous police inspector having manhandled King and the BBC's reporter Richard Dukenfield off the pitch. 'My instructions are that at the end of the game there will be nobody on the pitch, and that means nobody,' he told Dukenfield, with impressive pomposity.

So, more than thirty-five years later I turned up at Northampton's Sixfields Stadium looking forward to shaking the hand of a man who, with a single swish of his right foot, had given me one of the greatest thrills of my teenage years.

I turned up at the appointed hour to find about forty people standing in the reception, varying in age from teenagers to pensioners, and none of them talking to each other, just looking around awkwardly or staring at their feet, or gazing at their mobile phones to save them staring at their feet. A couple of them looked at me and nodded, as if to welcome me into their circle. It was most disconcerting. I asked one of them if there was a receptionist about. She said she didn't think so. So I waited for a few minutes, trying to weigh up what on earth these people were there for. Were they all applying for a job? A vacant receptionist's job, perhaps? Eventually I asked a man in a duffel coat. 'Speed awareness course,' he said, glumly.

I phoned Andy King on his mobile and he told me to come through reception and meet him in the dining hall, where he and the players were about to have lunch. Unlike some of his old team-mates, he bore little resemblance to his 1970s self. The Andy King I remembered had a shock of curly blond hair, a bounce in his step, and a mischievous glint in his keen blue eyes. Now he was grey and mostly bald, and walked with a pronounced limp (the legacy, he told me, of a challenge by Brian Kidd on the Everton training ground decades before). But the glint was still there. He insisted that I get myself some lunch, so I walked with him to the kitchen where a chef lovingly plated up some overcooked fish and limp broccoli.

We sat down in an otherwise empty meeting room and he began to talk. And talk. On the phone, King had made sceptical noises when I said I'd need an hour of his time, but almost two hours had passed before I made my leave along the labyrinthine corridors, hoping not to turn into the speed awareness class.

He was as beguilingly entertaining company as I'd hoped he would be, and also piercingly candid about the gambling habit that had undermined his football career. But first we talked about the winning goal against Liverpool that elevated him from Goodison favourite to Goodison legend. 'Yeah, 15 games, seven years,' he said. He knew I knew what he meant. All Evertonians of my generation know how long it was since we'd last beaten our local rivals. 'You know, Mickey Lyons never won a derby game, and he was injured for that one.' I knew. 'So when I scored and ran over to the bench, everyone thought I was running to Gordon Lee. But it was Lyonsy I was running to. He was Everton Football Club, Lyonsy. I became an Evertonian, and still am. It's the only thing in football I love. But he was Everton born and bred. And we were close. He was the best man at my wedding. My first wedding, that is. I still speak to him in Australia. He phones me when he's pissed. If I could get him back, to coach with me, I would. I think he'd love to come back. I tell you, if I had three wishes, that would be one of them.'

King told me about his earliest steps in football. Ron Henry, who had played in Tottenham Hotspur's Double-winning side of 1960-61, lived in Markyate, and recommended him to the people running Tottenham's youth teams. 'I was in the same group as

Hoddle,' he said. 'But they released me at fifteen. Broke my heart that did. I wasn't a Tottenham fan – Luton was my team – but I was a Jimmy Greaves fanatic. Later, Bill Nicholson sent me a letter apologising, and saying he thought the coach who let me go had made a mistake. My mum's still got that letter. She keeps it in a case with all my other stuff.

'But mistake or not, I had to get on with my life. So at fifteen, I started work in a sheet metal factory called Skeltons, which I hated. I still played Sunday league football though, and one day my dad walks into the factory and says, "Luton want to sign you." So we called my Uncle Den, the only one in the family with a car, and he drove me over there.'

The Luton manager was Harry Haslam, later of Sheffield United and nearly-signed-Maradona fame. And while King was no Maradona, Haslam rated him highly enough to give him his debut – at a time when Luton were still in the First Division, although about to go down – aged seventeen, at Manchester City. The following season he became a regular, scoring ten goals from midfield. Everton were alerted, and Cardiff City.

'The thing in them days was that you only really knew the teams in your TV region,' King recalled. 'We was Anglia, so we knew Norwich, Ipswich. But the north of England we hardly got, so I hadn't seen much of Everton, and I'd never even heard of Cardiff. But I knew that Everton was a big club, so Harry took me up there, and Billy Bingham, the manager at the time, was clever. He took us up in a lift. I'd never been in a lift before. Amazing, it was.

'That was the beginning of the love affair. I signed for £37,500, which was a strange figure, but not when you know the circumstances. Luton needed £100,000 by five o'clock one night to save them from going bankrupt, so they sold a lad called Peter Anderson to Royal Antwerp for £62,500, and made the rest up by selling me. That's how they survived.'

To take a fleeting diversion, that same Peter Anderson went on to play for Tampa Bay Rowdies, settled in Florida and in 1997 formed a company called Bayshore Technologies, a highly successful computer systems integrator, whatever that means. In 2013 Anderson's company merged with another, and according to a trade paper, the merged company was projected to generate annual revenues of more than $140 million. It is nice to be reminded that some 1970s footballers fell on their feet.

King quickly found his feet at Everton. On Easter Monday 1976 he made his debut in a 3-1 home win against Middlesbrough, and two days later he scored two in a 3-1 win away at Derby. After a miserable run of results that had included five consecutive defeats, the last of them at Anfield, Everton won the final three games of the season, and King, not yet twenty, played in them all. It was quite clear that Everton's cheeky little Cockney, as he was generally perceived – leaving aside the minor detail that not even the Bionic Woman, Lindsay Wagner, could have heard the Bow bells from Markyate – could cut it in the First Division.

'We were told that if we won all of those last three games the club would take us to Marbella, which they did. I'd only ever been to Butlin's at Clacton. Marbella was another world.'

I invited him to elaborate on some of the F Troop stories that George Wood and Dave Jones had touched on. 'Oh, well. We were pretty wild, but not aggressive, not offensive. But yeah, we played in that end-of-season thing in Egypt, and we beat the Egyptian national side 1-0. I scored and Woody saved everything. So we were paraded around and that night we got back to our hotel, which was in the desert, to find a sign saying "Dancing Girls Tonight". That was Gordon's worst nightmare, that was.

'So we took these girls to a disco boat on the Nile, but there weren't enough of them to share. There were maybe four or five of them and ten or so of us, and George wasn't in the running, so he got a bit annoyed. It was harmless fun. "I'm having that bird" – "No you're not, it's my bird". That sort of thing. So there was a bit of pushing and shoving, and then George threw me over the side of the boat, so there I am, in the Nile, with fucking sharks and that.'

I roared with laughter, and pointed out that of all the dangers of being drunk and in the Nile late at night, a shark attack is almost certainly not one of them.

King didn't miss a beat. 'Yeah, well, I don't know that, do I? All I can tell you is that I couldn't swim, and I've never been in the sea since. Anyway, they threw the lifebelt thing for me and I get back in the boat, and there's a bit more rough-and-tumble, and a couple of ornaments get broken. The next day it turns out that the guy who owned the boat was a German who owned half of fucking Egypt. So we have our passports taken away and before we could get them back, F Troop had to pay for the damage. Not Latchy, Dobbo, Dave Thomas, the sensible ones. F Troop was me, Woody, Lyons, Mark Higgins, Billy Wright, Dave Jones, the younger lads.

'But I'll tell you a funny follow-up to all that. A couple of years ago I get invited down to Woody's sixtieth birthday party, in a hotel. I don't drink much any more, not since I had a heart attack five years ago, which I'll tell you about in a minute. But I did have a couple that night, and there's this geezer who keeps going on at me about what I earned. Turns out this fella has driven Woody and his missus mad over the years.

'Still, we have a good night. My missus goes to bed and I stay on downstairs, but the next morning I wake up and I've got this red mark on my forehead. No idea how it got there. So we go down for breakfast and I get this big round of applause. Turns out this fella had been banging on at me and Woody told me to stick the nut on him, so I did. He goes, "Kingy, you gave him the Kirkby kiss." So there you go. He's still getting me into fucking trouble. Even at a sixtieth birthday party.'

In 1978, King, unsurprisingly, was the team prankster. 'We used to go to the Atalaya Park Hotel near Marbella. Gordon loved it there. And one day Dave Thomas is running round the pool swearing his head off, which was highly unusual, because Dave never swore. He's going "Where's fucking Kingy?" He's brought this book with him, you see: 985 pages and he'd reached the end. But I'd torn the last page out. Which I thought was hilarious, but he didn't, for some reason.'

King chuckled. 'But you know, there was never any arrogance about that sort of stuff. We never flexed our muscles like they do now, some of them. And we knew the punters. Remember Eddie Cavanagh [the Everton fan sometimes billed as football's first hooligan, after running on the Wembley pitch and briefly leading the pursuing bobbies a merry dance after Mike Trebilcock made it 2-2 in the 1966 FA Cup final]? I was big mates with him.'

For a while after he arrived at Everton, King shared humble digs in Lauriston Road, just off Queens Drive. As a subsequent Goodison joke would have it, everyone in Liverpool knew where Queens Drive was, and also where to find King's drive – in the back of Clemence's net. But that was later.

'At Lauriston Road I shared a double-bunk with a lad called Drew Brand, even when I was in the first team. Then I got posh and moved to Kirkby, where I got to know Phil Thompson and Terry McDermott. And then I got married to my childhood sweetheart, which unfortunately was a mistake. I had a second wife, too. Love at first sight, so that didn't last long. I've been married to my third wife now for twenty-three years, so I got it right in the end. Mind you, my first wife, Sue, she give me a beautiful daughter, who's thirty-six now. If I'd stayed in Markyate and worked at Skeltons from 7am till 5pm every day, me and her would probably still be together. She was lovely, but football finished us.'

Uncharacteristically, King fell silent for a moment. 'You know,' he then said, 'I should be sitting here talking to you now with as many games for Everton as anyone, and England caps too. But I gambled, and that got the better of me. I gambled away my wages, and then I started borrowing against my wages. That's why I had to leave Everton. I should never have gone to QPR in a million years. But it wasn't just me. There were loads of us like that. Stan Bowles, Don Shanks, Kenny Sansom. Kerry Dixon was the worst. I'm in touch with a dozen football people who've had their lives ruined by gambling. And God bless my missus, Barbara. She's just what I needed, a strong woman. Because otherwise there lie I, but for the grace of God and all that. If it weren't for her, I'd be living in a one-bedroom flat now with Kerry Dixon. And I don't mean no disrespect to Kerry. We talk about it quite a bit. And before us, it got the better of a great man, Alan Ball. I was told he had to leave Everton because of gambling debts.

'No, it's my one great regret in life, all that. And if I catch a kid now, I'm hard on him. I sit him down and say, "I've met more women, drunk more pints and spent more money in the betting shop than you ever will, so don't think you can pull the wool over my eyes." But if you drink too much, you can put a bin-bag on and sweat it out. You go to the pub with £100 in your pocket and spend £40 and you're drunk. But you go into the bookies with £10,000 in your pocket and lose every penny, so for me, that's the worst of the drugs. Apart from actual drugs, maybe. Gambling's second worst. Drink affects your health, yes, but so does gambling, believe me.'

It was moving, getting this burst of heartfelt sincerity from a man whose default setting was gag-a-minute chirpiness. I asked him when he had finally managed to kick his corrosive gambling habit?

He regarded me solemnly across the table, with just the hint of a twinkle in those blue eyes.

'Last Wednesday,' he said.

Chapter Twenty-One

When I'd stopped laughing, I asked King to fill me in on what had happened to him after his playing career had ended. After four happy years at Everton, and less successful stints at QPR and West Brom, he had returned to Everton again in 1982, playing 44 more games and scoring 11 more goals. He then had spells in Holland and Sweden, followed by stints with Wolves, with Luton again, then Aldershot, Waterford United, Cobh Ramblers and finally, two appearances (and one goal) for my own home-town team, Southport. It was the CV of a man who manifestly loved playing football.

'Yeah, then I packed in and Brian Labone, God bless him, got me into insurance. After that I got into the hospitality business, but I had a little bit of luck ... I went back to Luton and the woman who ran the commercial department was going off pregnant, so I became Luton's commercial manager and that's how I got back into football. David Pleat was manager and I did some scouting for him. He thought I had it in me to be a manager, so he recommended me to Harry Haslam's son, Keith, who'd bought Mansfield. I never had a coaching badge or nothing, but I went to see Keith and I got the job that afternoon.

'I had a couple of good years at Mansfield. Colin Harvey had been sacked by Everton so I took him there as my assistant, and you can't get no better than that. We beat Leeds in the League Cup at Elland Road, and reached the play-offs, but Keith was a strange chairman, shall we say, and that summer he sold all my best players from under me, £1.8 million worth of players. So that didn't last, and I went to Grimsby for a while, then with Reidy to Sunderland. There's always been an Evertonian connection, funnily enough, because after that Colin Todd took me to Swindon, but he left after three months and the board give me the job. I stayed there for six years.'

After being sacked by Swindon, King became chief scout for Plymouth Argyle. But then came his heart attack. 'And that's when I had some good luck. I had a doctor's appointment because I was having my ankle operated on, and I mentioned that I had a peanut caught in my throat, which is what it felt like. The woman who ran the scanning machine thing was about to go home, but we caught her on the stairs, and they tested me and told me I'd had a heart attack. I was in Papworth Hospital the next day. But if she hadn't been there I'd have gone home and started smoking again, and who knows ... unlucky in gambling, lucky in life, that's me.'

The heart attack put an end to King's gambling as well as smoking. He used it to effect a complete change of lifestyle. 'I don't know if I like myself as much,' he said, 'but my wife says I'm a better human being.'

He still hasn't had the ankle operation. 'But I will. Everton were the first club to set up a players' foundation and it's still the best. Pat Labone, Brian's widow, is in charge, and I have her permission that when I can I'm going to have it done.

'Everton's just different, you know. There's nothing like that football club, in my opinion. I go to those old players' things, and the adulation you get is unbelievable. Whether you should live for that I don't know, but it's certainly a boost. I did one the other week with Latchy. He's in Germany, you know, with this young bird. Real gentleman, Latchy. But he lives off what he's got, and that isn't a lot. Kevin Campbell [who played for Everton from 1999 to 2005] was at the same do, and he looked a million dollars. He was wearing a Rolex that was worth me and Latchy put together. I said to Latchy, "We need to nick that, Latchy. You chin him and I'll nick it."'

We both laughed. King added that he didn't begrudge the modern players their fabulous wage packets. 'No, the way I look at it, there were greater players who came before me who didn't have what I had. Kendall, Ball and Harvey, all them. And before them, players who didn't have what they had. I went to Everton on £30 a week, and when I left I was on £450. Which people said was a lot, but my dad was getting £180 a week as a hod-carrier. He used to say, "You lucky bastard, more than double what I'm getting just for running round a football pitch." Double! That's a laugh, when you think what Rooney's dad earns compared with Rooney.

'But I've done all right. Lost loads to the bookies, but I own my house and I've got a little place in Spain. I'm better off than many. And I'm sitting here at fifty-eight, still working in the game. That can't be bad.'

I asked him if he could have predicted, in 1978, which of his teammates might prosper in life after football. 'Oh yeah. The sensible ones. That's probably what you've found, isn't it?'

I said that of all the ex-players I'd met in the course of writing this book, Martin Dobson and Dave Thomas seemed to be the most comfortable, seemed to have managed their affairs the best. 'There you go, that's what I said. Dave and Dobbo, the sensible ones. But lovely lads, both of them.'

He was right about that. I met Martin Dobson in the lobby of a Premier Inn near his house just outside Bolton, and he couldn't have been more accommodating. In fact he was more accommodating than the Premier Inn, which I'd tried to book the night before. Alas it was full, so I caught an early train and arrived five minutes early for our appointment. Dobson was already there, and the first thing he did was hand me a copy of Latchford's book, *30*, which was signed 'To Dobbo'.

'Here, keep this as long as you need it,' he said, his Lancashire accent as broad yet refined as an upmarket black pudding. 'I'm sure it will come in handy.' What a gent.

Like Latchford, Dobson came from a middle-class background. His father ran the family engineering works near Blackburn, which his brother took over in due course, and he went to Clitheroe Royal Grammar School, which was also the alma mater of a great Lancashire cricketer, Cyril Washbrook.

He stayed at school to do his A levels, but by then he'd played football for England grammar schools and agreed to join Bolton Wanderers, then in the Second Division. It was 1966 which, to paraphrase an old Nike ad featuring Eric Cantona, was a good year for English football: Dobbo turned pro. 'But the coaching at Bolton was from the dark ages,' he said. 'We just ran around the pitch. Their approach was that if you didn't have the ball on a Friday, you'd want it more on a Saturday. I thought, "I'm not learning anything here." And then at the end of the season I got a recorded delivery letter; thank you very much, goodbye. Nat Lofthouse was the reserve team manager, and he was a nice man, but he didn't even tell me to my face. So I showed my dad the letter and he could have told me to try something else, but instead he said, "I think you deserve another chance." He picked up the phone, dialled Burnley Football Club's number and said, "My name's Stanley Dobson, please could I speak to the manager?"'

Dobson chuckled. 'Can you imagine that now, Brian? And sure

enough, the manager, Harry Potts, came on the line. My dad said, "Mr Potts, I don't know if you remember my son, Martin Dobson? He's eighteen, and he's just been released by Bolton, but before that you showed a bit of interest in him." And Harry Potts said, "Tell Martin to come down on 1 July."

'Well, after the first day of training I thought, "If I don't make it here, I'll never make it anywhere." The balls were out every day, it was two-touch football, I loved it.' And they thought pretty highly of him. He was offered terms: £20 a week.

'I felt elated. I'd been on £14 at Bolton, and Burnley were a First Division club. We played a reserve team game at Burnden Park early the following season and the ball was bouncing at the edge of the box so I thought, "I'll just hit it." Well, I'm not saying I'm van Persie, Brian, or anything like that, but it just flew into the top corner. That felt sweet did that. I'd just been released by Bolton. It was a nice way to go back.'

Dobson laughed, heartily. He was sitting upright in his chair, and I was vividly reminded of the elegance with which he comported himself on the football field. Not only that, but he somehow exuded decency. A transparently good man. He kept using my name, too, which is a disarming habit, often used by politicians who want to ingratiate themselves with an interviewer, but sometimes, especially among Lancastrians, it is a natural expression of friendliness, of openness. And whatever it was that I saw, Jimmy Adamson, the former miner from Northumberland who'd captained Burnley in the 1962 FA Cup final, saw it years before me. He had succeeded Potts as manager, and one of his first acts was to make young Dobson his own captain.

'I said to Jimmy, "I just don't know if I can do it. How can I tell all these international players what to do?" And he said, "Leave all that. Just play. With experience you'll get more confidence and start dictating things, but until then, just play." Oh, it was brilliant.'

But one day in August 1974 Adamson's assistant called Dobson and told him to report to Turf Moor rather than the training ground at Gawthorpe. 'I got there and the receptionist said, "You're to go to the directors' room upstairs." Well, I'd been captain of the club for three years by then, but I'd never been there before. "Where's that?" I said. Anyway, I opened the door and there was nobody from Burnley even there, just Billy Bingham and Chris Hassall, the Everton secretary. I had absolutely no wind of it, Brian, didn't know they wanted to sell me, but it turned out they had a new stand to pay for. It was a bit of a shock and it stuck in my throat a little bit, but I signed within the hour.'

The transfer fee of £300,000 set a new English record. Latchford's value when he moved to Everton earlier in the same year had been set at £350,000, but was complicated by the player swap, so Dobson was for a while the most expensive player, in terms of straightforward cash deals, in the English game.

It is slightly heartbreaking for Evertonians now to know that the club set and then broke a transfer record in the same year, given how impoverished we currently are by comparison with the other members of the old Big Five, not to mention nouveau riche – and unspeakably vulgar – Chelsea and Manchester City. But who knows? Maybe Everton will get to flex their financial muscles again one day, if they can only acquire a set.

In the meantime, it's worth reflecting that the club was getting value for money in the form of the Burnley captain. A quick glance at the list of those who have broken the British transfer record shows that value has sometimes been elusive: Alan Ball, Trevor Francis and Bryan Robson might have been worth every penny, not so David Mills, Steve Daley and Stan Collymore.

But Dobson had already played five times for England. And five times, alas, is what it would remain. 'I played for three different managers, though,' he told me. 'Can you work out who they were?'

I thought for a while. 'Alf Ramsey, Don Revie ... and Joe Mercer,' I said.

'Bloody hell, Brian,' he said. 'Nobody gets that at the first attempt.'

While I was preening, he gave me his perspective on the East European tour, during Mercer's tenure as caretaker in 1974, that had so disappointed Mike Pejic. 'He made it very simple, did Joe. He'd say, "You're the best players in the country, so just play like you do for your teams." Before one game he said, "Toddy, you pick up Streich, and Dave Watson, you pick up Irmscher." Then Trevor Brooking piped up, "Er, boss, those are East German players. We played them on Saturday. This game's against Bulgaria." So Joe picked up his clipboard. He said, "Oh yeah. Well, just go and play like you did on Saturday, then."'

Dobson roared with laughter. 'It was bloody brilliant. But he was a lovely man, was Joe. And a shrewd old football man, too. After that game against East Germany he said, "Dobbo, come and sit here, next to me. Dobbo, you played very well today, but you know fuck all about the game." I wasn't offended. Tactically speaking, he was right. He talked to me about defensive responsibilities, how to get into position quickly. I never forgot that.'

Dobson didn't know then that it would be Everton, not Burnley, who would benefit from his new awareness. 'It turned out to be a terrific move for me, did that. Everton were a wonderful club. And it was more money: £170 a week basic against £120 at Burnley. I put £20 a week of it into my pension scheme. That's been very good, has that. And I bought a four-bedroom detached house in Palace Road in Southport for £23,000, with a mortgage of £300 a month.'

Everton also gave him a car. 'Yeah, now it's Ferraris and Bentleys that these boys drive, isn't it? Well, Duncan McKenzie got a sponsored Skoda, and I got a Lada. Straight up. I know all the jokes –

Why's a Lada got a heated rear window ... To keep your hands warm while you're pushing it.

'But it worked beautifully did this car. Although only for two weeks. Then, in Liverpool one day, the starter motor jammed. So I rang the garage up and I expected a mechanic to come out with a box of tricks. What did he bring? A hammer. He said, "I shouldn't really do this but it saves all the messing about." He said, "Watch what I do." And he smacks the side of the engine block. He said, "Try it now." So I did and it started. I said, "Are you telling me I need to carry a hammer around with me in case the car won't start?" He said, "That's right, pal, yes." So after that I had nothing in the boot except for this hammer, but the car was all right for a week or two.'

Dobson paused, to wipe away the tears of mirth that were starting to form. 'Well, then we played down at Arsenal one day and drew two-apiece. I scored the second goal. So we get back late into Lime Street and then go to Bellefield where the lads' cars are. By now it's really late and I get into my car and it won't start. So I get out, and you remember that episode of *Fawlty Towers* where he starts talking to his car? Well, that's me. I say, "Listen you, I'm going to smack your engine block, and if that doesn't work, this hammer's going through your headlights, and I'm going to slash your tyres as well!" So I give it a bit of a smack, and George Telfer's in the driver's seat and turns the key in the ignition. And the engine starts. So George gets out and we're doing high fives in the car park because we've got my Lada going.'

He wiped his eyes again. 'Oh, bloody hell, Brian. It was a different era.'

Happily, the team's engine was more reliable. 'I felt we had a very good side,' he said. 'Gordon got a bit of stick but he was a very honest manager, maybe not the best technical coach but he wanted us to play attractive football. And we did, certainly for a couple of seasons. We had some very good players. Dave Thomas was vital for us. And Pej, he was a bit naughty. He'd batter them. He'd say, "Dobbo, leave him to me." But he was creative too. And Latchy, it was a privilege to play with him. He was a wonderful pro, was Latchy. Very quiet off the field, a family man, but he loved playing, and loved the club. Have you seen him yet? He looks better now than when he was playing.

'He had a telepathy thing going with Dave. I'd played with Dave at Burnley too. He could have gone to any club in the country at sixteen, he was that good, but he came to Burnley because Harry Potts looked after his mum and dad. It was a pleasure to play with him again at Everton. He'd whip it in to the near post and Latchy would be on the end of it. Or he'd stand it up on the far stick and Latchy would be there too. It was wonderful to be a part of that. And we all contributed as well. Andy King loved to score goals. Trevor Ross could hit it from outside the box ...'

He paused, and sighed. 'The problem we had, Brian, was Liverpool, who were the best team not just in England, but in Europe. But we were closing the gap, and with another couple of players we could have done it. In 1978 we were in touching distance, we really were.'

He was right. And we knew it on the terraces, too. In fact, those six months between the blitzing of Chelsea and the pipping of Liverpool are still probably the happiest I have ever had as a football fan, encompassing a World Cup and an 18-game Everton record that read W13 D5 L0. Those were title-winning stats, and had it not been for Paisley's Liverpool and Clough's Nottingham Forest, I might have been spared the exquisite irony of having to wait until the mid-1980s for success, watching from afar as Howard Kendall's team swept all before them.

Chapter Twenty-Two

Instead of adding the couple of players Everton could have done with, Lee began to get rid of players Everton could hardly do without, presaging the two disappointing seasons that would end with him being sacked. In 1979 Dobson himself returned to Burnley.

'Gordon had offered me another contract, actually, but my heart ruled my head. Harry Potts, the man who'd signed me at nineteen, was back at Burnley, who were then in the Second Division. He came and talked to me at my house in Palace Road, told me I was the man to get them back into the First. He'd been an Evertonian as a lad, had Harry, so he knew how great the club was. But he made it very difficult for me to say no. The sad thing was that I realised after a few training sessions back at Burnley that I'd made a mistake. It wasn't the club I'd left, and the sad thing then, Brian, was that Harry soon lost his job and Brian Miller took over. Which was a double whammy. I should have stayed at Everton. I could have played at the back, at centre half. Maybe that would have been my position.'

In the 1984-85 season, an *annus mirabilis* for his old club Everton, Dobson joined Bury, as player-manager. He brought in a golden oldie, Sammy McIlroy, and a promising youngster, Lee Dixon, on a free transfer from Chester City. He also signed Mark Higgins, his old Goodison teammate and arguably the man, had he not been blighted by injury, who would have captained Howard Kendall's wonderful team rather than Kevin Ratcliffe. It was a potent mix and they got Bury promoted from the Fourth Division. But after almost five years there he left Gigg Lane for the United States – who wouldn't? – where he coached in Massachusetts and Indiana. Then he came back, did some scouting for Ipswich Town, then landed a job at Bolton, as academy manager under his old team-mate Colin Todd. 'But Sam Allardyce came in and wanted his own man, so I left, and actually, I worked for the Office of National Statistics for a while, which was good, Brian, because it taught me how to work a computer. Then Burnley came in for me again and I went back there for three years, as head of youth. After that fin-ished, Everton asked me to do some match-day hosting in the Dixie Dean lounge, which is great, and I also do match reports for Leicester City, looking at their next opponents, set pieces, strengths and weaknesses, all that stuff, which I do on a computer programme called Scout Seven. To be honest, Brian, it's nice to sit there and not be in the dugout. People ask me if I miss the cama-raderie and that. But I played 700-odd games, until I was thirty-seven. I don't miss it at all. You move on.'

Dobson, it seemed to me, had moved on as successfully as anyone. He radiated contentment. The only thing troubling him was his knee. 'But Harry Ross at the Everton Former Players' Foundation says, "Just get a letter of referral, Dobbo. We'll sort it out."' He smiled. 'I'm not loaded, Brian,' he added. 'My wife says, "You've got to keep working, Dobbo, we've still got three years on the mortgage."' I loved the fact that even his wife called him Dobbo, and made a mental note to stop calling him Martin.

'The wages are obscene now, aren't they?' he continued. 'Good players earning £250,000 a week, lesser players getting £50,000, and lesser than them getting £15,000 a week. Fifteen grand a week, and we're all expected to think of it as not very much! But I feel no grief about it at all. Why would I? I played for two great clubs and I've got a lot of wonderful memories.'

He and his wife lived in a detached bungalow, he told me. 'It's near here in Horwich,' he said, 'but the family, children and grand-children, are over in Burnley. We put the house on the market, but it didn't sell so we stayed and built an extension. I love it round here. And I'm learning the saxophone, although I've got to wait for my wife to go out. I've been at it for three years and I'm just get-ting to the level where I'm not absolutely crap. I wrote a book too. There was an initiative a few years ago, trying to get kids reading more, so I had a go. It's only fiction, about two lads trying to make it in the game.'

I said I'd like to read it sometime, though I wasn't sure I wanted to hear him playing the sax. He laughed, and we shook hands. We'd been talking for the best part of three hours. Dobbo asked me who I was planning to see next, and I said that I hoped to drive up to the north-east to visit Dave Thomas. 'Oh, you'll like Dave,' he said. 'He's a lovely lad, is Dave.'

After we'd parted it occurred to me that of all the ex-players I'd met, none of them had had a bad word to say about any of the others. The livelier lot, the F Troop brigade, clearly remembered the quieter, more responsible ones with great affection, and vice versa. I supposed that it was partly a reflection of the era in which they played, but also, I liked to think, it was something to do with a spirit of togetherness fostered by Everton. And also, perhaps, the fact that they all spoke the same language and were managed by the most English Englishman of them all. Andy King had told me that, during a pre-season trip to Jersey, Gordon Lee had actually sat in a deckchair on the promenade with a handkerchief on his head.

I looked forward to concluding my search for the 1978 Toffees by meeting up with Lee himself.

But first, I had Dave Thomas to visit, an exciting prospect for an Evertonian who came of age when I did, because he had thrilled me more than anyone. That's not to say that he filled me with more pleasure than Latchford banging in a header, or George Wood acrobatically saving a penalty, because nothing could. But there was no more thrilling spectacle than Thomas jinking almost to the corner-flag before delivering a cross that might have been guided by computer technology, if only we'd known about that stuff then.

Every other player in that Everton team has an equivalent today. Barnstorming centre forwards still abound. So do elegant midfielders, adventurous full backs, athletic goalies and uncompromising centre halves. There are still, in Bob Paisley's memorable phrase about Graeme Souness, buzzers, crunchers and spreaders. But the old-fashioned winger with chalk on his boots, who would beat the full back on the outside and not regard his job as done until he reached the by-line and fired in a cross, he is an extinct breed. Thomas was that winger, in excelsis. How he only won eight England caps is a mystery.

We had spoken a few times on the phone before I pointed my car towards a grand estate just outside Barnard Castle where Thomas and his wife Brenda live in what used to be the potting shed. That makes it sound decidedly humble; in fact it is anything but. It's a lovely, low, stone-built building, which has been extended, but must still have been a hell of a potting shed. It also has a spectacular garden, in which Thomas has built himself a golf hole, with both a men's tee and a ladies' tee, and a vegetable patch that hardly deserves the word 'patch'. Alan Titchmarsh or Monty Don would be proud of it. 'It's just heaven,' he said, walking me around, and I couldn't disagree. 'I've always been a country lad, me,' he added. 'I like my peace and quiet.'

It was a warm day and he was wearing shorts, which made it even easier to associate the lithe, slightly bandy-legged man alongside me with the quicksilver winger of yore. The distinctive cheekbones were the same, too, although I couldn't see his eyes. I had heard that Thomas was 'nearly blind', which wasn't true at all, but he was wearing dark glasses and always does, indoors as well as out. 'It's severe glaucoma,' he explained. 'I have very little peripheral vision, and it's been nine or ten years since they took my driving licence away. I suppose some people would have said, "That's my life finished". But for me, it was, "Right, I'll take that on the chin and move on."'

I had told him on the phone what I was striving for with this book, and he greeted me with engaging enthusiasm, wanting to know who I'd met. 'Have you managed to get hold of George Wood?' he asked. I said I had, and that Wood was now the goalkeeping coach at Crystal Palace. 'Is he? Get away. A good lad, Woody. He's into the birds in a big way, isn't he?'

I remembered Andy King's story about the floating disco on the Nile. 'Aye, he was always a keen ornithologist, Woody,' Thomas added, before I could say anything. 'What about Bob Latchford, have you seen him? And Gordon Lee? He's still around, I think.'

No, I said. I hadn't yet met Lee, still hadn't tracked him down. 'I liked Gordon Lee,' Thomas said. 'I don't like flash people, and he was my kind of person. What you saw was what you got with Gordon. I'll tell you a story about Gordon that sums him up to a tee. We were knocked out of the FA Cup one time so we all went away to Majorca for a few days, and stayed in this posh hotel in Palma. Posh as hell it was. Gordon would have been happier going down to Weymouth in a caravan. He wasn't into all that. Anyway, he comes down for dinner one night, and Jim McGregor, the physio, is sitting there with John Moores and Philip Carter, the chairman. Gordon looks at what Jim was eating, and he says, "What's that?"

Jim says, "It's Welsh rarebit". And Gordon says, "Is it? Fucking hell, it looks more like cheese on toast to me."'

Thomas roared with laughter. 'He meant it, too. Oh, it brought the house down, that. But that was Gordon. He had no time for Duncan [McKenzie], did he? Duncan was more of a Welsh rarebit player. I liked him, but if we got beat 3-2 and he'd scored two, he'd be happy. That wasn't Gordon's cup of tea. So he moved him on and brought in Mickey Walsh, didn't he? But poor old Walshy was terrible.'

Like Dobson, Thomas left Everton prematurely, when he still had plenty to offer. 'I had a bit of a contract dispute with them, thought I should be getting more, and the person who gave me advice was Bill Shankly. He used to come in to the training ground every day, you know, and one day I said, "Bill, could you give me some advice?" He said, "Aye, son. Come round to my house." So I did, and he made me very welcome. I told him what I was on, and he said, "Davey boy, that's absolute peanuts you're on, peanuts."

'I went back to Gordon, and to Philip Carter, who was a super chap, a gentleman, but he wouldn't budge. So I asked for a move. Latch put in for a move at the same time as me and the pair of us went down to Wolves to meet John Barnwell. I verbally agreed to go, shook Barnwell's hand, but Latch didn't. He went to Swansea instead. Anyway, later that same night, Man United came in for me. Jim Greenwood, the Everton secretary, rang me to tell me. He said, "The choice is yours, Dave." Well, I'd shaken Barnwell's hand so I went to Wolves. Biggest mistake of my life, that was. Turning Man United down? Absolutely disastrous.'

So why did he? 'Well, Wolves looked like a decent proposition. They were second or third in the league, they'd just signed Andy Gray. But I never wore shinpads. My socks were always down around my ankles, and I always wore rubber studs. Never wore boots. Well, Wolves had a coach, Richie Barker, who told me to put shinpads on and change my footwear. I wouldn't budge, so he made me train with the kids. Made my life hell.

'I was awkward, mind, but there was still no excuse for it. I played ten games for the first team, that's all. I absolutely hated it there. I was still living with Brenda and the kids near Parbold, travelling down the M6 every morning, and there was one day when they made me travel down to Wolverhampton to catch the reserve team bus to go back to Liverpool. But I was determined that they wouldn't break me, and they didn't. I stuck it for eighteen months, and then went to Vancouver Whitecaps. It was a shame, really, because my career nosedived. I came back from Canada, went to Middlesbrough for a couple of months, and then joined Portsmouth.'

Thomas hung up his boots, or at any rate his rubbers, at Portsmouth, and then became reserve team coach, but his coaching career, and indeed his love for football, was undermined by Alan Ball. That's a difficult sentence for an Everton supporter to write, the more so as it had been Ball, via my childhood friends Jez and Chris Sykes, who had made me an Evertonian in the first place.

'What happened,' said Thomas, 'was that Bally came in as manager, and although he knew me, because I'd played with him for England, we were total opposites in character, in lifestyle. The chairman had appointed me reserve team coach, and Bally agreed to it when he arrived, but then he got Graham Paddon in, who was his big buddy. The chairman called me up one day and said he wasn't going to offer me a new contract, because they were making financial cutbacks and Paddon would be taking over my duties.

'Well, I wasn't happy, but that's life. I left Portsmouth. And then, two weeks later, a local reporter told me that Peter Osgood had come in and taken my old job. Bally had gone behind my back. I was disgusted by that. A week after that, Bruce Rioch called me and asked if I fancied joining him at Middlesbrough. I said that I wouldn't go even if he offered me a million pounds. If that was football, what had happened to me, I wanted no part of it. So I went to teach PE at a secondary school in Chichester, Bishop Luffa, and I was there twenty years. I loved it. In teaching I was surrounded by people I could trust.'

I winced; saddened to hear that such a fine footballer had fallen out of love with the game. But I don't think he had, not really. Even as a PE teacher he had continued coaching Bognor Town, and taken them on a couple of decent runs in the FA Cup.

Moreover, we talked for ages about the game these days, and it was clear that he still watched plenty of it on TV, and thought about it deeply. 'People say football had changed,' he said. 'It hasn't. It's the same as it was when it was invented, 11 v 11. But certain things have changed. You see all these modern coaches writing things down, and it does my head in, it really does. You know why they're doing it? Because it looks good, doesn't it? It winds me up, big time. A sub coming on for two minutes, and the coach is showing him his notes. Don't tell me any of that is registering.

'No, Dave Sexton, who I played for at QPR, he was years ahead of this lot. He played out from the back. But now, you don't see full backs taking the ball from the keeper. They run upfield. They don't want the ball. They're going, "I don't want it, I'm only on £70,000 a week."'

Thomas chuckled. As with Dobson, there was no bitterness in his reference to silly modern-day wages, just faint, good-humoured disbelief at the way it had all gone. But football had treated him well, too. He and Brenda owned their lovely house outright, and he still enjoyed a decent income from his PFA pension. 'I always lived off my basic,' he told me. 'All my bonuses, all my transfers, that went straight into my pension. I'd say to the lads, "What are you taking your bonus for? Stick it in your pension."'

I said I could imagine how that went down with Andy King, on his way to spend his afternoon with William Hill, and Thomas laughed. 'Yeah, well. Each to his own. But I've no complaints. And I was lucky to play for Burnley, QPR and Everton. Wolves can go by the board.'

Chapter Twenty-Three

At that point we were interrupted by Brenda, bringing us a tray of tea and her own home-made scones with cream and jam. I had heard how life had unfolded for Dave Thomas since he left Everton, and I could see for myself that in more ways than one, and his failing eyesight notwithstanding, it contained plenty of jam and cream. But I wanted to know about his life before. It turned out to be a fascinating tale.

'My grandfather was the captain of West Auckland, the working-men's team that won the World Cup in 1909,' he said.

Actually it was the Sir Thomas Lipton World Football Trophy, provided by the tea magnate, but it was undoubtedly the forerunner of both the World Cup and the European Cup. Unlike the other European football associations, our own FA – obviously as pompous then as they would be for decades to come – declined to enter one of their country's top clubs, and so for some reason, the County Durham team of pitmen was entered. And went to Turin and won the thing, led by David Rhys Thomas, a tough wing half known as 'Ticer'. It was a nickname also given to his grandson.

'I took the grandchildren to his grave yesterday, as it happens,' said Thomas. 'He originated from the Stoke area, came here to work down the mines, and became pit secretary. My dad, who's ninety-seven now, went down the pit too, for a while. My grandad was eighty-nine when he died, and I was thirteen. He taught me to play football, in the back field behind my dad's big, long vegetable garden. I idolised him.'

The old man's coaching paid off. Through both Harry Potts and Jimmy Adamson, Burnley had strong connections and a good scouting network in the north-east. Thomas signed schoolboy terms. But then other suitors started wooing him.

'I played for England Schoolboys, and then they all come after you. My dad had a motorcycle and sidecar like Wallace and Gromit, and after we got home from a county match one day, I was sent out to buy a loaf of bread. Anyway, so there's this car kerb-crawling alongside me, and it's obviously followed the motorcycle and side-car home, because it's Don Revie and his chief scout, from Leeds United.

'He says, "I've been watching yer, and I'd like a word", and I said, "Oh aye? I've got to get a loaf of bread for me mother or she'll tell me off." So they went in to see Mam and Dad. This was 1965, and I was due to go to Burnley in the July. Revie said, "Mr Thomas, I've been watching your David play and I'd like him to sign for Leeds." My dad said, "Oh, he cannae do that, he's agreed terms with Burnley." So Don Revie says, "Mr Thomas, I think he'll progress better with Leeds. Look, how about I come back in forty-eight hours, see if I can get the chairman to come with." And my dad says, "You can bring who you like."'

'Well, bugger me; he was true to his word. Two days later a Rolls-Royce turns up in our little terraced street: Don Revie and Manny Cussins. Everyone in the street is outside looking at it. None of them has ever seen a Roller before. So they come in but my dad says again that no matter what they say, I'm off to Burnley. So Manny Cussins says, "Mr Thomas, how much have Burnley offered your David?" He says, "He's getting £4 a week, and they're paying his digs on top. I think that's a good deal." Now, bear in mind that my dad by then was a welder with British Rail, working night shifts, which he did for forty-two years. So Manny Cussins goes, "I see, £4 a week, eh? Well, look. What if we pay him £30 a week, and pay his digs? Will that tempt him?"

'That was a lot more than my dad was earning, and I was fifteen years old. Then, on top of that, they produce two grand in five-pound notes, in a black case. It would've bought the whole street. But my dad looked at it, and said, "I'm sorry, but I've given my word to Burnley that David will play for them." He was emphatic. And as he was leaving, Manny Cussins turned round and said, "I respect you for that, Mr Thomas. Not many people would have done that."'

It is an amazing story, and for all that so much of this book underlines the contrasts between football then and football now, the past is not always such a bewilderingly foreign country. There's not so much difference, in principle, between Cussins offering the Thomas family two grand in fivers, and FC Barcelona sticking £35 million into Neymar's parents' bank account.

The difference is that Thomas Senior wouldn't take it. But that's not to say that he wasn't suddenly more aware than he had been of his son's worth. 'After that, me dad asked for a meeting with Bob Lord, the Burnley chairman, and I went with him. I was sitting there in Bob Lord's office, absolutely shitting myself. He was a multi-millionaire butcher, like a bulldog he was, with bloody great bags under his eyes. "What do you want?" he said. And me dad said, "Mr Lord, seeing as our David's played for England Schoolboys, which is a credit to himself but also good for the football club, I think he deserves a bit of a signing-on fee." So Bob Lord looks him straight in the eye and says, "How much does he want?" And my dad says, "Would £500 be all right?" Bob Lord didn't bat a bloody eyelid. He said "No problem". And me and me dad came out of his office shaking.'

Lord's investment paid off. Thomas had six happy years at Burnley, but as a midfield player, not on the wing, before joining QPR in 1972. 'Terry Venables was in that team and I loved Venners. I always knew he'd become a coach, because he was always trying to improve your game. I was struggling there and Venners said he'd have a word with Gordon Jago, which he did. He said, "Why don't we try Dave on the wing?"'

I told Thomas about my soft spot for QPR that dated from the 1975-76 season in which he had himself been one of the pivotal figures in that memorable bid for the league title. I also told him about my encounter years later with Stan Bowles. He laughed. 'Oh, he was incredible, Stan. Did you ever meet his mate, Don Shanks? The two of them were summut else. The chairman, Jim Gregory, who was a vagabond if ever there was one, he loved Bowlesy. There'd be a brown envelope for him after every game, and Bowlesy had so much power. We had a coach there called Jack Mansell, and no one liked him. He sat all the senior players down once – Venables, Gerry Francis, Don Givens, Dave Webb – and he said, "Right, you southern softies, you need knocking into shape ..."

'So a few days later, on a Saturday afternoon, Stan comes down from the players' lounge like he always did at ten to three. He's been up there watching the gee gees, and there's no warm-up, no nothing, he just went out and played. He walks out past Jack Mansell and says, "Still here, Jack?" Jack Mansell says, "What do you mean?" He says, "You'll find out after the match." Only Stan could say that. He'd spoken to the chairman in the week and got him the sack.'

More laughter. 'You know the famous one about Stan, don't you? Him wearing two different boots when he played for England, one Gola, one Adidas, so he could get sponsorship fees off both companies. That was true. He'd do owt for money. No, I grew up so quick there. Venables, McLintock, Johnny Hollins, Phil Parkes ... magic, it was.

'But things changed. Dave Sexton left for Man U, and he was the best. There were two great football men in my life, Harry Potts and Dave Sexton. Did you ever meet Dave? Oh, the best. He'd been a boxer, and when he had Osgood at Chelsea, he offered him out, you know, and Osgood wouldn't go. He was a hard man, but a great man. So honest, he was, and full of ideas. He'd sometimes go straight from the match on a Saturday afternoon to Heathrow, paying his own fare, to watch continental sides on the Sunday. He liked to see how they played the ball from the back.

'He took us to a training camp in Germany once, pre-season, and we watched a Second Division side train. Normally, at free-kicks, the lads in the wall would cover their bollocks. But this team had cardboard figures, and if you hit them they'd bounce back up. Dave liked that, so he bought them from the club and got us to carry one each through customs, these 6ft high figures. Can you see that happening today?'

Thomas had signed a four-year contract to stay at Loftus Road, but when Sexton left he decided to agitate for a move – 'Even in those days contracts didn't mean anything,' he said. And so began the partnership that went together like a horse and carriage, indeed had Sammy Cahn written his famous song 25 years later, he would surely have included Thomas and Latchford as an example of things that fit like love and marriage.

'It was just my job, as a winger, to get the crosses in,' said Thomas, modestly, 'but Bob had this knack. He was strong and brave, and he'd knock 'em in off his backside, off his shoulder, off his knee. He just got in the way. Stan Bowles was more of a Jimmy Greaves-type finisher. He was clinical, Bowlesy. Latch didn't have that ability, but half a chance ... in!'

'We had a strong side. Dobbo, I'd played with at Burnley. He was Mr Elegant, class, absolute class. And Pej too, on the left. But more than that, it was the whole club. I couldn't believe how well organised it was. When I first came up, Brenda and the children were still living in Wokingham, so they put me in the Holiday Inn. Kenny Dalglish was staying there too, funnily enough. He'd signed a month before me. But then Brenda started coming up to look for houses, and Everton would always look after her, make sure there was a surveyor to go with her, get the club solicitor on the case. That's how good they were. QPR were hopeless at stuff like that, but Everton were the best and still are. The Foundation has paid for some of my medical bills; Harry Ross has said, "Any problems with the eyes, just let us know." The way they look after former players, it's unique.'

I was delighted to hear it, but then I knew it to be so because I'd heard it again and again. On the day I met Neil Robinson I'd had lunch with George Telfer, who'd played up front alongside Latchford in the celebrated Chelsea game. He told me that the Foundation had paid for him to have two hip replacements. 'And they paid for Gordon West to have both his knees done,' Telfer told me. 'I know that some of the ex-players have fallen on hard times, but the Foundation are always there paying bills and things. I was told at thirty-two that I had the hips of a 70-year-old. It was because I had one leg slightly shorter than the other. Everyone used to say I ran funny, and that was why. But they wouldn't do hip operations in those days, so I had to wait. Mine was one of the first and it cost about £10,000. The Foundation covered it all. I can't thank them enough. They're absolutely brilliant, and you know, they treat everyone the same, whether you were just an apprentice at Everton or played 500 games.'

Telfer still lived in Liverpool, although he owned a static cara-van in Scotland. He was a slow-talking, amiable cove, another boyhood Evertonian, whose father had been a Scotsman who moved to Liverpool just after the Second World War. 'He was a policeman, who met my mother in the police canteen, but then he left and got a security job with Littlewoods Pools. There was a big security operation there, because of all the postal orders and cash and that. My mother used to work there too and her job was to search the girls every night. But then they got the opportunity to run John Moores's estate in Scotland, so they went up there. My dad became a gamekeeper and my mum looked after the Moores family. But that wasn't really the life for her, so they came back to Liverpool.'

Telfer signed schoolboy forms with Everton in 1970 and made his debut, against Arsenal, three years later. He got married at twenty-one to Pamela and they were still together after thirty-six years. It had been rather reassuring, in my search for the Toffees, to find that a good few of them – Thomas, Dobson, Robinson, Telfer – had stuck with their original wives. Or their wives had stuck with them.

Like so many players of his generation, Telfer left English football for the North American Soccer League (where he played against both Johan Cruyff and George Best). The money he made at Everton had enabled him to put a decent deposit down on a house in Widnes, where he still lives and which is now paid for. But, unlike Dave Thomas, he couldn't be described as comfortable. His footballing pension amounted to about £4000 a year, he told me.

After his short stint with the San Diego Sockers, he returned to England and played for Scunthorpe United, where, for twelve memorable games, his partner up front was Ian Botham. 'He never scored, but he could drink. Oh my God, he was revolting. You'd go for a quick drink after a game and he wouldn't let you go home.'

I asked Telfer how he had coped with retirement, having called it a day, on account of persistent injuries, in 1983. 'I found it really difficult,' he said. 'I went to college and studied leisure management, and went to work in the voluntary sector for years. I managed playing fields, youth clubs. But I was made redundant last year. So now I just look after my grandchildren and do voluntary work at my local church. I read Bible stories to the children.'

Telfer proudly showed me photographs of his four grandchildren. He didn't seem unhappy with his lot, but he was still some way short of sixty and it seemed rather dispiriting that his main occupation should be reading Bible stories. I wondered whether there was a parable summing up his situation. Perhaps he was Jonah, and the whale was life. Or something. Whatever, he told me that he had applied two weeks earlier for a job running a new sports complex in Toxteth. 'I really fancied it,' he said brightly, and then added, a little sadly, 'but I didn't get it. They gave it to a woman.'

I had now talked to most of the Everton players who contested those unforgettable games against Chelsea in April 1978 and Liverpool six months later, and not surprisingly, their lives had taken very different directions. I left my lunch with Telfer feeling as faintly downcast as I had felt upbeat when driving away from Dave Thomas's house, replete with Brenda's delicious scones. But then, football, and Everton, had been their only common denominator. I could have tracked down eleven of my old classmates from King George V School in Southport and found a similar divergence of fortunes.

Of all the players on Everton's books in 1978, the two most extreme examples of fortune, both good and ill, concerned two men who had eluded me. One of them was Mick Buckley, the battling Mancunian midfielder, who in the 72nd minute of the match against Chelsea had provided the cross from which Latchford scored his 29th goal of the season.

When I started my quest, I was told that Buckley was in poor shape. He had descended into alcoholism, to such an alarming extent that he sometimes slept rough. That didn't stop me trying to see him through one or two people at the club who sometimes knew his whereabouts. But then another devastating message came back. To add to all his travails, Mick was now suffering from cancer. In October 2013, also not yet sixty, he passed away.

At the other end of the pendulum of fortune was Terry Darracott, whose wife, I was told, had enjoyed a sizeable, seven-figure National Lottery win. I did arrange to meet up with Darracott but then he cancelled; he was doing some scouting work for Hull City and had been asked to go to a match that afternoon. Clearly, a lottery win wasn't going to tear him away from football. I left several messages after that but he didn't return my calls. Which was a shame, because I was keen to meet him, remembering him as the absolute embodiment of a certain type of 1970s footballer: the honest grafter, who would rather run naked around the Pier Head than shirk a tackle.

Never mind. There was still one other man I wanted to meet above all, the man who I felt would put a silk bow on my search for the Everton team of 1978. The object of that festive-season chant from the Gwladys Street, to the tune of 'Silent Night'. Although, from everything I'd heard, I felt that Gordon Lee wouldn't strike me as a man who had ever inspired the reworking of a Christmas carol, even though I knew that he had, and had sung it as lustily as anyone. But I wasn't wrong.

Chapter Twenty-Four

Iknew that he was still alive. Darren Griffiths in the Everton media department had given me his phone number. But a cursory Wikipedia check revealed that he was now 79 years old. I had no idea what state of health he was in. It turned out in the course of two or three phone conversations that he had certainly become slightly deaf in his old age. I asked if we could meet, and he suggested Fairhaven Golf Club in Lytham, close to his home, as a suitable place.

'Shall we meet in the bar?' I asked.

'Yes, OK, in the car,' he said, and hung up before I could emphasise that I'd said 'bar'.

So it was that I found myself loitering, one chilly winter lunchtime late in 2013, in the car park of Fairhaven Golf Club. I had arrived in Lytham by train and walked a mile or so from the station to the golf club. Not wanting to miss him, I was forced to stay outside. By the time a large, newish Mercedes arrived and slowly did a circuit of the car park, I had lost the sensation in both my hands and feet.

It was more than thirty years since I had seen Gordon Lee, but there was no mistaking the long, lugubrious face behind the steering wheel, now grown old. I flagged him down, and he got out. He looked skinny and frail, with a decidedly grey pallor, and indeed told me that he had been to the doctor and diagnosed with shingles that very morning, poor chap. Still, insofar as one can make a snap judgment about a man based on the car he drives, life didn't seem to have treated him too badly.

We repaired, finally, to the bar, where the ladies of Fairhaven GC were engaged in a lively prize-giving ceremony. Lee and I took a table at the far end of the room, and ordered a pot of tea. Later, I wished that I'd offered him a Welsh rarebit.

I repeated what I'd said on the phone, which I'm not sure had entirely registered; that I had come of age as an Everton fan during his managerial tenure, and wanted to write about that time, and about the players of that era, and what had become of them.

Keen to travel further back in time than I had been able to do with the players, I asked him about his childhood. He was the youngest of ten children, he said, from a mining village just outside Cannock in Staffordshire. The flat Staffordshire vowels – like Stan Collymore, but without the animation – were still firmly in place.

His father had been a miner, as were several of his brothers, but he had been saved from the pit by a combination of National Service and a talent for sport. With nine siblings, he said, there was always someone to play football with.

'At Everton,' he then recalled, taking what seemed like a tangent from his Staffordshire childhood, 'possibly the best signing I made was a boy named Graeme Sharp.' He said this as if Graeme Sharp was someone of whom I might not have heard.

'I think I paid £120,00 for him,' he added, 'and he was sold ten or eleven years later for £500,000 or something like that, after scoring a lot of goals. But before I signed him there was one thing in the back of my mind. I met his parents, who were lovely people, from Scotland, but I think he was the only one, an only child, and in my mind that was a question mark. Because an only child often finds it difficult to make progress, you know, especially in football.'

I digested this revelation and thought of my own upbringing. If only I'd been raised with siblings, I thought, perhaps I'd have made it as a footballer. 'Anyway, he became an excellent player,' said Lee.

Over and over in the course of researching this book Gordon Lee had been described to me by his old players as an honest man, dead straight, and so I wondered whether he would have told me this story had he decided that £120,000 was too much to pay for an only child, and watched Sharp score 150 goals for someone else. I decided that he probably would.

A burst of applause interrupted my very fleeting reverie. Doris Shufflebottom, or possibly Mavis Sidebottom, was being handed the trophy for the best Stableford score of the day. Above the hum of excitement from the Fairhaven ladies, and repeated applause, Lee and I had to shout to make ourselves heard. But then Mavis, or Doris, came over and said, if we didn't mind, they were trying to have a prize giving and could we stop shouting.

'Oh, I beg your pardon,' said Lee, looking mortified. 'I beg your pardon. I beg your pardon.'

She turned tail, and although I didn't actually see her adjust her bosom as she went, I like to think that she did. After all, I recalled from a previous visit to Fairhaven that the great Les Dawson had been a member. He and Roy Barraclough, as Cissie and Ada, would have fitted right in.

I asked Lee how old his parents had been when he was born, given that he was the youngest of ten. 'Oh, that's a good question,' he said. 'I don't know. But I think my father died about 1955. I'll tell you what I clearly remember. Sitting with him, as he lay in bed, and him saying "Take me, Lord, take me".'

His own first steps in football were with an amateur team called Hednesford Town, who were managed by an old Aston Villa player called Jack Martin. It was Martin who recommended him to Aston Villa, who duly signed him, and where he stayed for eleven years, from 1955 to 1966. 'I played full back, wing half, inside forward, all over, and that was wonderful preparation for being a manager. I played against Stanley Matthews in pouring rain at Stoke, but the best player I played against was Bobby Charlton. Oh, he was wonderful.'

He had looked like an old, rather infirm man when we sat down, but as he talked about football a distinct light came into his rheumy blue eyes. I remembered what Bob Latchford and Mike Lyons had told me, that he was obsessed with football to the exclusion of almost everything else. I was delighted to find that the passing of the decades didn't seem to have changed that.

At least until football's egregious maximum wage was abolished in 1961, he was never paid more than £20 a week, 'with a £2 bonus if we won. But money didn't enter into it. When I was manager at Newcastle, I recall talking to Jackie Milburn, who'd been a Newcastle legend, you know. He'd been in the mines, and he told me he earned more down the pit than he did from football. Changed now, hasn't it?'

He gave a short, humourless laugh. More of a harrumph really. After he left Villa, he told me, he went to Shrewsbury Town as player-coach, thence to Port Vale, where Stanley Matthews was general manager. But Port Vale were mired in scandal, after it emerged that the club had given illegal gifts to so-called amateur players, including, horror of horrors, a tea service. They were expelled from the Fourth Division, so it was a non-league side that Lee took over in May 1968.

He spent six years at Port Vale, then moved to Blackburn and steered them to the Third Division championship. That got him a shot at the big time, with Newcastle United. But just as many Everton fans, among them Jamie Carragher's dad Philly, would not forgive him for selling Duncan McKenzie, so is he remembered on Tyneside as the manager who got rid of Malcolm Macdonald.

'There were lots of reasons,' he told me, with a flash of defiance, when I asked why he'd sold Supermac. 'From a football point of view, I thought he was a good player in a bad team. Before I got there, he'd always scored plenty of goals. He'd get 20 goals a season, but that helped them to stay up. I wanted him getting 20 goals to win the title. But as we became a good side, he wasn't able to score as many. In a bad side, as teams put pressure on them, he'd stand up top in plenty of space. As we became a good side, and started to knock it about, he had nowhere to run.'

In 1976, Macdonald was sold to Arsenal for the strange sum of £333,333. And 34p. Many fans were distraught. 'But most of the directors wanted him out of the door,' Lee assured me, defensive on the subject even now. 'I'd told them to get rid, and I guaranteed them two things. One: that we'd do 100 per cent better without him. And we did. We qualified for Europe. And two: that he wouldn't last two years at Arsenal. He didn't. He lasted eighteen months.'

Lee was embroidering history just a little, making it sound as though Supermac was a flop at Arsenal. In fact he scored 42 goals in 84 league games over two full seasons, before being clobbered by a knee injury. Even the most honest old managers, I suppose, like to justify themselves. Anyway, despite Newcastle's progression, he didn't have much hesitation in accepting the Everton job. Not least for domestic reasons, as the family had moved to Lytham while he was at Blackburn and only the youngest of his three children had gone with him and his wife to Newcastle; the two older ones were settled at schools in the north-west.

So with no rules in those days about a manager leaving one club for another halfway through the season, he succeeded Billy Bingham in January 1977, and thus was able to claim the credit for

Everton reaching both the League Cup final, against his old club Villa, and of course the FA Cup semi-final against Liverpool.

'That game,' he said, 'was the most disappointing thing that ever happened to me in football, or probably in life. I will never, ever forget that. I'll take it with me to my grave. Because I can remember when Bryan Hamilton scored, looking across at Bob Paisley and Ronnie Moran on the Liverpool bench, and they had their heads down. So did their players. They all thought it was a goal. If they hadn't, they would've objected. But none of them did. I still believe that Clive Thomas thought that football spectators had come to see him referee. I really believe that. And it had a big effect on Everton Football Club, that goal being disallowed. It was a catastrophe, really, when you think what might have been.'

I was taken aback by his enduring gloom. A catastrophe? Even I wouldn't have gone that far. It was only a semi-final, after all. But then he started waxing lyrical about the players he had at Everton, and the football he got them playing, and I could see that, for him, perhaps it did seem catastrophic. On the very big assumption that he would have masterminded a win over Docherty's Manchester United at Wembley, perhaps a prestigious trophy so early in his Goodison career would have propelled the club to greater things.

'Big Latchy,' he said, looking into the middle distance. 'When he was on his game, oh, he was terrific. Andy King was quick, sharp, a little bit naughty off the field, a loveable rogue if you like, but a good lad. And we had that triangle of Michael Pejic, Martin Dobson and David Thomas.' I noticed that light re-entering his eyes. 'Everyone knew what we were going to do but nobody could stop us. They were good players, and a good bunch of lads.'

I told him that I'd met up with most of them, and they all spoke highly of him too.

'Pardon,' he said.

'Those old Everton players. They all speak highly of you.'

Across the gaunt features there flickered the tiniest hint of pleasure.

'Ah, well, I did my best for them,' he said. Miners' sons from Staffordshire, I realised, are not given to self-congratulation. He took a celebratory sip of tea.

Of course, I hadn't met up with Duncan McKenzie, who perhaps might not have spoken so highly of him. I asked Lee whether, as often speculated, there had been some sort of personality clash between them? 'With Duncan? No, he was a good lad, a bright lad. The thing with him, well, it was the opposite to Malcolm Macdonald ... he was a bad player in a bad side, and a good player in a good side. He was sharp when the team was winning, but you wouldn't expect him to chase lost causes, run after hopeful balls. And that was no good to me. So Danny Blanchflower took him to Chelsea, and the way Danny later described it to me was right. Duncan was the cream on the cake, but if you hadn't yet got the cake, that was no good.'

This was insightful stuff, and I thought back to Lee being roundly harangued by the Goodison faithful when McKenzie returned with Chelsea and scored. Nobody withdrew the abuse when Everton went on to win the game.

'As a football manager,' he added, 'you knew that if you had a good team, then you could pick a team on Friday and be sure how nine of your players would perform. There might be two you weren't sure about. But if it wasn't such a good side, there'd be half a dozen you weren't sure about. Duncan was always one of those. Unpredictable. His unpredictability could be a plus, sometimes, but it could be a minus too. With Martin Dobson, you always knew what you were going to get. Wonderful player. Martin had a great ability to drag defenders out of position. And when the ball went to him, the other players knew he'd keep it, which gave them time to adjust. John Robertson did the same for Nottingham Forest.'

Speaking of Forest, what did Lee recall of his dealings with Clough? I didn't say so but I could hardly think of two football men more different than the irrepressible Clough, the José Mourinho of his day, and the seemingly taciturn Lee.

'Ah well, I do remember being asked in the middle of the season once if we wanted to take part in a tournament in Japan, a Minnie Mouse thing. I thought it would interfere with our preparation for an FA Cup tie the following Saturday, so we didn't go. But Cloughie took his team, and they got back on the Friday night, the night before the FA Cup ties. I can still remember the half-time scores coming over the Tannoy: Forest were 1-0 down at home, I think to Bristol Rovers. And I thought to myself, that's what comes of taking your team halfway round the world, that is.

'Well, we won 4-0, but Forest also won, 2-1. They got the winner in injury time. It's the old thing in football: if you win, you're right. I don't think Cloughie was right on that occasion, but they won, so it didn't matter. Mind you, for him not to become England manager that year was an absolute disgrace. The FA let England down badly there. Because he'd won the championship with what I call Group B clubs, by which I mean Forest, Derby, Norwich, Ipswich, those types of clubs. And then the European Cup. Remarkable, that was.'

Between them, Forest and Liverpool won four successive European Cups in the time Lee was at Everton. Liverpool's rampant success must have made life difficult for him, I ventured. 'Oh, it did. Bob Paisley was a wonderful man, unfortunately for me. He was straight, honest, friendly, a smashing fella. He never did anything stupid, never signed stupid players, always did the right thing, wasn't a big mouth. So he never gave me any ammunition.'

After two decent seasons, Lee's Everton project began to unravel. I asked him if he recalled the circumstances of his sacking. 'Well, I remember the game that did for me. It was an FA Cup quarter-final replay at Manchester City, and I remember Ray Varadi had an easy chance.' That was Imre Varadi, who, as my friends and I hardly ever tired of telling people, was married to a woman called Olive. I had once mentioned this to the comedian Frank Skinner, and being the quick-witted fellow that he is, he got the Oliver Hardy joke immediately, then countered with a better one, about Whoopi Goldberg marrying Peter Cushing. Should I run the Olive line past Lee? Sensibly, I decided against it. I might have still been there now, trying to explain it. Besides, he was still remembering the Varadi miss and the subsequent defeat. 'Our league position wasn't very good either, and that was me finished.'

So, as we know, Gordon Lee left, and Howard Kendall arrived, inheriting the youngsters that Lee had blooded, such as Sharp and Kevin Ratcliffe.

'Do you think that Howard built on your foundations?' I asked.

'To an extent. I hadn't been able to sign anyone for a while, and he was able to buy, and of course he bought very well.'

Seven months after being sacked by Everton, Lee joined Preston North End. He was there for two years, then got a job in Iceland, with the unpronounceable Knattspyrnufélag Reykjavíkur. Then he came back to England and worked at Leicester City as assistant manager to David Pleat, briefly taking over as caretaker manager when Pleat was fired in January 1991. His final managerial achievement was to keep Leicester in the Second Division on the last day of the 1990-91 season, avoiding relegation by beating Oxford United 1-0 at Filbert Street. After that, he did some scouting here and there, but a long football career was effectively over.

'Has football been good to you?' I asked him.

He considered the question. 'I think so. I have no complaints. If I did make a mistake it was probably going to Preston. I'd been offered the job at Wolverhampton Wanderers, too, and I should probably have taken that. But I did OK. I worked hard. I was generally successful. We're in the same house where we've lived for many years. And I had some experiences, I'll tell you that. I remember going to Libya on an end-of-season trip with Everton, and we played the national team. Well, Colonel Gaddafi was there, in a big camel coat, and he became an Evertonian that night. Said he would always be an Evertonian.'

It occurred to me that I had come a long way on this quest to find the Toffees of 1978, from Bob Latchford in the car park of the Cheshire Yeoman, to an image of Colonel Gaddafi in a camel coat, proclaiming undying allegiance to Everton.

As we left Fairhaven Golf Club, after talking for almost two hours, Lee offered me a lift to Lytham station. And as I got out he said, 'What was your name? I never caught your name.' It was precisely the opposite of my experience with dear old Dobbo, who barely uttered a sentence without uttering my name. But Gordon Lee was pushing eighty. He was entitled. I liked him, and I could understand, all those years on, why his players had liked him too.

On the long train journey home, via Preston and Crewe, I leafed through Jamie Carragher's autobiography, and found this passage, in which he talked about his childhood as a fanatical Everton fan, going to games with his old man. 'He was certainly more used to seeing Everton lose than I was,' wrote Carragher. 'He'd suffered the Gordon Lee era.'

That wasn't fair. It was perhaps, to conclude on everyone's favourite football cliché, an era of two halves. But for me football has never been so alive, so meaningful, as it was during the so-called Gordon Lee era. An era that yielded the two greatest wins of my life as an Evertonian. I will always feel indebted to him for that.

Epilogue

In February 2014, I entertained Ron Atkinson to an early dinner, or rather he entertained me. Later that evening we were due to share a stage at the Rankin Club, a social club in the small Herefordshire town of Leominster, five miles down the road from my house, where they had been hosting monthly sports evenings since 1981.

The list of speakers they'd managed to attract to such remote parts was astounding, amounting practically to a Who's Who of British sport. And coincidentally it had all kicked off with Joe Mercer, the Everton great from Ellesmere Port, where twenty-four chapters ago this book also began.

In recent years I have been able to use my contacts to find speakers, and one of them was Big Ron. Over dinner I asked him what he could tell me about Gordon Lee, whose Everton team were among Atkinson's main rivals when he was building his thrilling West Brom side of the late 1970s. He told me that as a teenager he had been on the books at Aston Villa when Lee was playing in the first team. 'Some unlikely people become managers,' he said, 'but I can't think of any less likely than Gordon Lee. I thought he might become a trainer. But a whippet trainer.'

Another of my Rankin Club speakers, the month after Big Ron, was Kevin Ratcliffe, who was given his debut by Lee. Indeed, his second-ever game in the first team was that FA Cup semi-final replay against West Ham at Elland Road, where a famous Frank Lampard song was inspired and from which my friends and I had such a disconsolate journey home.

I asked Ratcliffe about Lee. 'He was a nice bloke and I liked him,' he said, 'but he was an oddball. Whenever you went in to see him, you'd come out ten minutes later forgetting why you'd gone in, because he'd change the subject. He'd suddenly say, "How many brothers and sisters have you got? How old are they?" And then he'd go, "So your brother's eighteen. I see. So he was seventeen last year, was he?"'

I was able to share with Ratcliffe Lee's theory that siblings are important in the development of a young footballer, which shone somewhat belated light on some of their exchanges. He then told me what it had been like for a young lad on Everton's books at that time. 'It was a really intimidating dressing room, full of hard men like Roger Kenyon and Terry Darracott. I looked after the boots of the first-team players, and if you didn't knock on the dressing-room door before you went in, your life wasn't worth living. I thought my name was Towel for three years. Because they'd just look at me and go "Towel!"'

Nobody in that dressing room could possibly have suspected that Ratcliffe was destined to become the most successful Everton captain of all time, a linchpin of the great side of the mid-1980s. But if they had, would it have changed the way they treated him? Of course not. In fact, one could argue that it was because of the tough apprenticeship that Ratcliffe served, that he became the player and leader he did. A generation later, those uncompromising, boot-cleaning, towel-fetching apprenticeships that turned boys into men had all but fallen by the wayside.

On 19 April 2003, I went to Goodison Park for a Merseyside derby, as I had numerous times before, but this one was different. This time I was there with my son, Joseph, whose eighth birthday it was that day, and who was to be one of Everton's three mascots.

As a mascot, Joseph was allowed to visit the Everton dressing room just 45 minutes before kick-off, and better still, he was permitted to take his dad. Despite the significance of the impending match, Everton's captain at the time, David Weir, could not have been friendlier. He shook Joseph's little hand, and said to him, with a broad smile, 'Who's going to win the game today?'

I knew, and he knew, that he just wanted the bullish answer 'Everton!' and then he could move on to focusing on the match. Unfortunately, Joe had never met a man with a broad Falkirk accent before. To him, Weir might as well have been talking Flemish. 'Pardon?' he said, politely.

Weir smiled. 'Who's going to win the game today?' he asked again.

Joe looked at him blankly. 'Pardon?' he said again.

Weir's smile faded slightly. 'Who's going to win the game today?' he said, for a third time. This time I translated. 'Joseph, Mr Weir is asking who's going to win today's game,' I said.

'Oh,' said Joe, and thought for a moment. Weir towered over him, waiting, by now a tad impatient, for the answer.

'I don't know,' concluded Joe.

It was a short but memorable exchange, a meeting between the irresistible force of a footballer's banter, and the immoveable object of a child's logic. If Weir had asked him who he hoped would win the game, obviously that was Everton. But who would win it? Just as obviously with kick-off still some distance away, he didn't have a clue.

Anyway, my main reason here for bringing up that visit to the Everton dressing room was that there was another boy in there, somewhat older than Joe but still unarguably a boy. He was 17, and when I asked him if I could please take a photograph of my lad with him, he was scarcely less bashful and tongue-tied than Joe had been with Davie Weir. Yet he was already a star, already widely acknowledged as the brightest prospect in the English game since the young Paul Gascoigne.

I was moved almost to tears that day by the sight of my boy walking out on to the sacred Goodison turf – though naturally Liverpool did their best to ruin our day, winning 1-2, the miserable spoilsports. If I could feel that way about an eight-year-old mascot, what must it have been like for Mr and Mrs Rooney, whose son was making his first start in a Merseyside derby? And, before them, for the parents of every boy raised an Evertonian, who went on to wear the famous shirt? Some things in football never change, and parental pride is one of them.

But many other things do, and as I reach added time in this book, I want to reflect on just how different were the everyday lives of footballers in 1978, compared with now.

At Everton in 1978, the broad equivalent of Rooney twenty-five years later, in the sense that he was a prodigiously gifted youngster tipped for a glittering future, was a 19-year-old Irish boy called Martin Murray. If Rooney would end up being hailed as the new Gazza, similarly extravagant predictions were made in the late 1970s about Murray.

Murray was given menial jobs just like Kevin Ratcliffe, and lived in the same Lauriston Road digs as Andy King, spending his afternoons with King in betting shops. 'He was meant to be the new George Best but he never made it,' said King, when I rang him to ask a few more questions about what day-to-day living was like back then, once the players had finished training.

'How did we fill our time in them days? We'd go in the Hermitage pub opposite our digs. And other pubs sometimes, after training. In the famous words of John Bailey, we'd stop for a shandy on the way home. Only he always forgot to ask for the lemonade. Other than that, I'd play a bit of social snooker, though I didn't like snooker much. I didn't know about golf, didn't pick up a club until I'd finished playing. I didn't know any footballers who played golf in the 1970s. But I didn't spend much time in my digs, either, during the day. It wasn't like you could even watch telly. There wasn't anything on telly until six o'clock in them days.'

Starved of anything to fill those long afternoons, King, and many other footballers, drifted in and out of betting shops blowing £50 in an hour just as players now might blow £10,000. But the reason some Premier League footballers now develop such corrosive gambling habits – some of them so alarming that I have heard tell of men earning more than £100,000 a week yet struggling to pay their bookmakers – has more to do with their gargantuan salaries than the free time they have. After all, there are infinitely more ways now for a young man to fill his afternoons than there were then. But how does a young man spend £5 million a year?

Of course, there were perfectly wholesome ways for footballers to spend their free time then, just as there are now. 'I did a lot of fly-fishing,' George Wood told me. 'And I was a keen ornithologist, though not so much a twitcher, counting how many species I'd seen. I was more interested in studying resident birds; in fact I qualified as a bird-ringer. My job was to catch them and ring them, to find out whether the willow warbler, which left in the autumn, would come back to the same area in the spring, that sort of thing.'

Even now, he added, he liked nothing more in his free time than to sit on the banks of the River Taff, eating Welsh cakes made for him – he told me this as if it wasn't even a slightly bizarre detail – by Tom Jones's sister. He then recalled the day he took Brian Kidd, an entirely urban Mancunian, to a friend's farm to learn how to use a shotgun. 'I gave Kiddo the gun and it went off, blowing a hole in the ground about three inches from my foot.' Three inches the other way and that might have required a difficult phone call to Gordon Lee.

Meanwhile, other players were investing their spare time more pragmatically. 'I was looking to my future,' Martin Dobson told me. 'Because my family had an engineering business in Blackburn, I had an opportunity to go into it, so even while I was at Everton, living in Southport, I went to the factory in the afternoons to learn how the lathes worked and all that, and to Blackburn Technical College in the evenings. I didn't go into the family business, as it turned out, because I decided it wasn't for me. But at least I'd tried it.'

The 1970s was really the last full decade in which pretty much all footballers spent the twilight of their careers having to think about what they might do next. In 1972, Hunter Davies wrote his seminal book *The Glory Game*, documenting the season he had spent behind the scenes at Tottenham Hotspur, which included conversations with the players about what they wanted, materially, from the game. 'All I hope is that I'll end up with enough money to start a little business,' said 27-year-old goalkeeper Pat Jennings, the same Pat Jennings who a decade later was still keeping Georgie Wood out of the Arsenal team. Six years later, nothing had changed. Footballers earned decent but not extravagant money, and had to plan for their futures.

For Dave Thomas, one of the great advantages of being a footballer was the time it gave him with his young family. 'I saw my children grow up,' he told me, 'and I felt very fortunate. It seemed like the best life in the world, playing football for a living, and also being around to see your kids before they went to school. I know the money's changed beyond recognition but it's the same now, really. There are the family orientated footballers, the gamblers, the ones with a wandering eye. That's not football; it's people. The only thing that has changed is that there aren't the drinkers now that there were when I played.'

Like Dobson, Thomas was given a sponsored Lada by the club. 'Dobbo and I had blue ones, and a couple of lads from Liverpool had red ones.' I told him Dobbo's story about needing to travel around with a hammer, to bash the starter motor. He laughed. 'Mine wasn't any more reliable than Dobbo's. I remember the gear-stick coming off in my hand.'

I don't suppose anyone in the 1970s thought to take a photo-graph of the car parks at First Division training grounds, but if they had, it would yield a telling comparison between then and now. Even at lower-division clubs now, the car parks are full of BMWs and Mercs. Yet the players' parking berths at Bellefield in 1978 sported at least two Ladas, one with a hammer in the boot and the other with Sellotape around the gearstick, not to mention Andy King's yellow Vauxhall Viva.

I asked both King and Wood, the only two Toffees I had found who are still involved in the game on a day-to-day basis, how train-ing had evolved since 1978. 'The facilities are a hundred times better now,' said King. 'And there's so much done on the analyti-cal side, on the diet side, though whether any of that makes you better with a football is debatable. It's still 11 v 11 on the same size pitch, but you look at the footwear now, the balls . . . and that's the same in other sports too. Golfers are driving the ball 150 yards fur-ther than Jack Nicklaus did. But that doesn't make them better players than he was.

'No, players are spoilt now. It's ridiculous. Even at Milton Keynes there are four physios. At Everton back then we had one, and he treated everyone from the kids to the first team, and if there was something he didn't know about, we had to wait for the doc to come in on a Thursday.'

Training followed a schedule that was as rigid as a Swiss railway timetable, he recalled. 'Mondays was light training, and Tuesday was what we called bin day, when we put on bin bags and sweated as much as we could. Wednesday was a day off. On Thursday we'd work on our shape for Saturday's game. On Friday we'd be allowed on the little patch of grass at the back of the gym we called Wembley, and play six-a-side. That was where Brian Kidd nobbled me, and left me with this limp. After that I had to play with cortisone injections. Players now might be out for five weeks with injuries that we would have played with on a Saturday with a cortisone shot. But that's why so many players from them days are crippled now.'

I asked him what Gordon Lee had been like as a coach. 'He didn't do much coaching. I don't even know if Gordon played football.' I told him that Lee had made over 100 appearances for Aston Villa. 'Did he? I never knew that. I knew that Eric Harrison, the coach who went on to Man United and brought through Beckham, Scholes, Giggs and all them, had played in the lower leagues, because he would throw it at us as a weapon. "You superstars, you're pampered tarts," he'd say. "You should have played at my level." Pampered! That's a laugh when you think of players now.'

This was echoed by George Wood. 'It's incredible now,' he said. 'I'm a goalkeeping coach at Palace but the first goalkeeping coach I had was Bob Wilson at Arsenal. Never had one at Everton. You'd get 100 shots off the players and that was it. I'll tell you what, though. We took responsibility for ourselves in the 1970s, and that wasn't a bad thing. We thought for ourselves on the pitch, whereas now you keep seeing them looking towards the bench. Managers and coaches have taken the responsibility away from players.'

It was indubitably true. If I had learnt anything from writing this book it was that football's many leaps and bounds forward since the

1970s had been countered by plenty of steps backward. Is it a better game to watch now than it was then? Probably. But is it more fun to be a fan now than it used to be? Probably not.

I had also emerged from writing this book with one or two friendships that I could hardly have anticipated when I was pushing my way to my place behind Fozzie Bear's stanchion on the Gwladys Street terraces. Dave Thomas, bless him, sometimes calls just for a chat, which gives me more pleasure than he can possibly know.

Happily, for all the problems with his eyes, he is not one of those 1970s footballers who carries a debilitating physical legacy of his playing days. And he is generous-hearted enough not to begrudge modern players the billiard-table surfaces on which they play. 'Not a word of a lie, Brian,' he told me, 'but the pitch at QPR was so terrible that the groundsman had a nervous breakdown and Jim Gregory hired a helicopter to dry it out. It just hovered over the pitch. The idea was that it would dry the pitch with its rotor blades. Can you believe that? And the training ground at QPR ... you've never seen a bigger muckheap in your life. Bellefield was fantastic by comparison. Years ahead of its time. And I'm told that Finch Farm, the training ground now, is incredible. In another thirty or forty years, it will all be better still. You can't imagine it, but it will.'

That seems like an appropriate note on which to end a book that has mostly dwelt thirty or forty years in the past. But let me add one final personal reflection. In truth, my son Joe was a mascot at Goodison Park that day in 2003 not for his delectation but for mine. I made the arrangements, and the sentimental tears during the pre-match warm-up as he toe-poked unchallenging penalties at the Everton goalie Richard Wright were mine, not his. He supported Everton because I did, but he'd never lived anywhere near Merseyside. He wasn't what you'd call passionate.

Over the next few years, I persevered with Joe and his younger brother Jake, taking them to games, telling them tales of the days when Bobby Latchford walked on water, and indeed of the unforgettable mid-1980s, when at various times Everton boasted three of the greatest goalscorers ever to grace English football, in Graeme Sharp, Andy Gray and Gary Lineker. Slowly but surely they got the message, that for all the disappointments, all the false dawns, they were truly blessed to be Evertonians.

In April 2014 I got an email from Joe. He was eighteen and spending several months travelling through South America. He had found himself in Quito, Ecuador, on the day that Everton hosted Arsenal in the Premier League. It was a game they won thrillingly 3-0, not only putting Champions League qualification in their own hands, but also suggesting that perhaps they really were ready to rejoin the elite of English football.

'Set my alarm for 7.30am,' wrote Joe, 'then scoffed some cereal, got two metros and ran four blocks before asking puffily in four different sports bars before eventually finding the game on TV … caught the second half and it was utter bliss, out in the early morning sunshine with Steven Naismith running rings around Vermaelen. What a win!'

It was always lovely to hear from Joe during his travels, and so I immediately forwarded his email to my wife, Jane, who was away for the weekend. 'Aaah, isn't that just great,' she replied. 'What an ardent fan you've made there. A true Toffee xxxxx'

Jane was right. And should Joe and Jake have children of their own, I am confident that they will become true Toffees too, and perhaps even read this book, and picture the days when their doddery old grandad was a boy of sixteen, and embarking on the most enduring love affair of his life.

Acknowledgements

Writing this book was a pleasure rather than a chore, but it would have been a lot harder without the help and encouragement of plenty of people, starting, of course, with all those former Everton players who so generously shared their time and memories with me.

So, my thanks first and foremost to Bob Latchford, George Wood, Neil Robinson, Mike Pejic, Mike Lyons, Dave Jones, Andy King, Martin Dobson, George Telfer, Dave Thomas and Kevin Ratcliffe. And to the man who managed them, Gordon Lee. If I have made any factual errors in transcribing the many hours of taped conversations I had with them all, I apologise.

At the Everton Former Players' Foundation, one of the finest organisations of its kind anywhere in the game, Philip Ross and Pat Labone, widow of the great Brian, were most supportive. And I'd never have got started without the assistance of Darren Griffiths in the club's media department. Cheers, pal!

A former colleague of mine, Paul Newman, put me in touch with Terry Byfield who put me in touch with George Wood. Thanks to them both.

Dave Prentice at the *Liverpool Echo* was immensely helpful. And I'm grateful, too, to Rob Sawyer, Andrew Weir, Charles Mills, Colin Pinchen and John Keith, all of whom helped with contacts or reminiscences or both. Many contributors to the website Toffeeweb responded to my plea for recollections of the 1970s, and I hope they won't mind if I thank them collectively rather than individually, although I should single out Eugene Ruane for particular thanks.

My old friends Jez Sykes, Chris Barry and Jeff Brignall obligingly stepped back in time with me. I hope that my memories tally with theirs. A more recent friend, Martin Davies, was also a great help. So too were my friends Mark Johnson and Alan Preece, respectively a West Ham and a Wolves supporter, who remember the 1970s as fondly as I do.

I have plundered the work of others, too, and have tried to credit my fellow authors and their books in the text. If ever I neglected to do so, my apologies. Excellent books by Duncan Hamilton, Becky Tallentire, James Corbett and my former colleague at the *Independent*, Nick Harris, were of particular use.

At Simon & Schuster, my editor Ian Marshall – a lifelong Manchester United fan who admits to a soft spot for the Toffees – not only initiated this project, but has backed it with good humour and sound advice. My thanks also to Jo Whitford and Helen Mockridge at S&S, to Clare Hubbard for proofreading and to Julian Flanders, who did a marvellous job of copy-editing, and says that this book might inspire him to write his own, about following Chelsea in the 1970s. I hope it does. Chelsea fans need reminding of life before Roman Abramovich.

As for my own books, if I am the goal-scoring centre-forward in their creation, my agent Andrew Gordon is definitely the midfield playmaker, the Dobbo to my Latchford. As ever, I am grateful to him for his infallibly wise counsel.

Lastly, but never least, I must thank my wife and three children: Jane, Elly, Joe and Jake. Whenever I'm in danger of rising too early at the far post, metaphorically speaking, they keep my feet on the ground. My daughter has no time for football, saving her from a lifetime of frustration and pain, but it is a source of great pride to me, and not a little relief, that even though they grew up many miles from Goodison Park, I have managed to raise my two sons in the Evertonian faith. And as we all know, once a Blue, always a Blue.

Brian Viner
Herefordshire

April 2014

Picture Credits